The Worlds of James Buchanan and Thaddeus Stevens examines the political interests, relationships, and practices of two of the era's most prominent politicians as well as the political landscapes they inhabited and informed. Both men called Lancaster County, Pennsylvania, their home, and both were bachelors. During the 1850s, James Buchanan tried to keep the Democratic Party alive as the slavery debate divided his peers and the political system. Thaddeus Stevens, meanwhile, as a Whig turned Republican, invested in the federal government to encourage economic development and social reform, especially antislavery and Republican Reconstruction.

Considering Buchanan and Stevens's divergent lives alongside their political and social worlds reveals the dynamics and directions of American politics, especially northern interests and identities. While focusing on these individuals, the contributors also explore the roles of parties and patronage in informing political loyalties and behavior. They further track personal connections across lines of gender and geography, and underline the importance of details such as who regularly dined and conversed with whom, the complex social milieu of Washington, the role of rumor in determining political allegiances, and the ways personality and failing relationships mattered in a hothouse of national politics fueled by slavery and expansion.

The essays in *The Worlds of James Buchanan and Thaddeus Stevens* collectively invite further consideration of how parties, personality, place, and private lives influenced the political interests and actions of an age affected by race, religion, region, civil war, and Reconstruction.

The Worlds of James Buchanan and Thaddeus Stevens

CONFLICTING WORLDS

NEW DIMENSIONS OF THE AMERICAN CIVIL WAR

T. Michael Parrish, Series Editor

THE WORLDS OF
JAMES BUCHANAN
AND
THADDEUS STEVENS

PLACE, PERSONALITY, AND POLITICS
IN THE CIVIL WAR ERA

EDITED BY
MICHAEL J. BIRKNER, RANDALL M. MILLER,
AND JOHN W. QUIST

Louisiana State University Press   Baton Rouge

Published by Louisiana State University Press
Copyright © 2019 by by Louisiana State University Press
All rights reserved
Manufactured in the United States of America
First printing

Designer: Barbara Neely Bourgoyne
Typeface: Adobe Caslon
Printer and binder: Sheridan Books

Map by Mary Lee Eggart

Library of Congress Cataloging-in-Publication Data
Names: Birkner, Michael J., 1950– editor. | Miller, Randall M., editor. | Quist, John W.,
    1960– editor.
Title: The worlds of James Buchanan and Thaddeus Stevens : place, personality, and politics
    in the Civil War era / edited by Michael J. Birkner, Randall M. Miller, and John W. Quist.
Description: Baton Rouge : Louisiana State University Press, [2019] | Series: Conflicting
    worlds : new dimensions of the American Civil War | Includes bibliographical references
    and index.
Identifiers: LCCN 2018053648 | ISBN 978-0-8071-7081-6 (cloth : alk. paper) | ISBN
    978-0-8071-7154-7 (pdf) | ISBN 978-0-8071-7155-4 (epub)
Subjects: LCSH: United States—History—1815–1861. | United States—History—Civil War,
    1861–1865. | United States—Politics and government—19th century. | Buchanan, James,
    1791–1868—Political and social views. | Stevens, Thaddeus, 1792–1868—Political and social
    views. | Legislators—United States—19th century—Biography. | Politicians—United
    States—19th century—Biography.
Classification: LCC E415.8 .W67 2019 | DDC 973.7—dc23
LC record available at https://lccn.loc.gov/2018053648

To

MICHAEL F. HOLT

MERTON L. DILLON

J. MILLS THORNTON III

Mentors and exemplars of historical scholarship

Mr. Buchanan is a constituent of mine, and until he attempted to make Kansas a slave State, and uphold the doctrines of slavery in his messages, he and I were on intimate terms. Since then we have never spoken to each other.

—THADDEUS STEVENS in congressional debate, January 27, 1862.
Congressional Globe, 37th Cong., 2nd Sess. 495.

CONTENTS

Contents

PREFACE

This book grew out of a two-day national symposium, The Worlds of James Buchanan and Thaddeus Stevens, held at LancasterHistory.org in Lancaster, Pennsylvania, September 18–19, 2015. The third in a series of Buchanan-related conferences sponsored by LancasterHistory.org (formerly the Lancaster County Historical Society) over the past two decades, it accommodated a larger compass of interest than Buchanan and antebellum politics alone.[1] The working premise of the symposium was to examine the ways place and personality informed politics during the Civil War era by looking especially, though not exclusively, at the worlds of Buchanan and Stevens, both bachelors with strong ties to Lancaster but whose lives and politics diverged widely. Afterward, we invited the presenters to revise their works for publication. As we came to understand the scope and direction of the book based on the symposium presentations, responses to them, and the subsequently revised papers, we engaged other scholars to contribute essays that extended the inquiries. The result is this book.

NOTE

1. Two books resulted from the two previous symposia: Michael J. Birkner, ed., *James Buchanan and the Political Crisis of the 1850s* (Selinsgrove, PA: Susquehanna University Press, 1996); and John W. Quist and Michael J. Birkner, eds., *James Buchanan and the Coming of the Civil War* (Gainesville: University Press of Florida, 2013).

ACKNOWLEDGMENTS

This volume is the product of many hands. It began in discussions at Lan-casterHistory.org with Thomas Ryan and Patrick Clarke, who wanted to build on the work of their previous two symposia to offer a wider scope of inquiry about the worlds of James Buchanan and Thaddeus Stevens. Their wise counsel and encouragement did much both to facilitate the conference and focus our thinking about where a resulting publication project might go in emphasis and interest. The support of LancasterHistory. org in every facet of organizing, sponsoring, and hosting the symposium ensured its success. So, too, the generous support of Margaret J. Neff, Mr. and Mrs. Rick Rodgers, the Wilbur S. & Sally J. Smith Foundation, Mr. and Mrs. Daniel B. Strickler Jr., and the National Endowment for the Humanities made the Lancaster meeting possible. We thank them all for providing the resources and encouragement that laid the groundwork for this publication. The book, in turn, benefited again from the support of LancasterHistory.org and from funding for illustrations that came from Gettysburg College and Saint Joseph's University.

Also important to this project were historians Judith Giesberg, Leigh Fought, Emma Jones Lapsansky-Werner, and Louise Stevenson, whose insights at and after the symposium informed the book in critical ways. We also profited from the good counsel and support of Louisiana State University Press, especially editor Rand Dotson, who believed in the project from the beginning and guided it through the publication process, and from the press's anonymous reviewer, whose interest and encouragement moved the book in a good direction. Special thanks also go to T. Michael Parrish, who seized on the idea for this volume and invited it into his series.

In doing the background research necessary to edit the essays and prepare the work, we benefited from the help and support of librarians and staff at Gettysburg College, Saint Joseph's University, Shippensburg University, the University of Pennsylvania, Haverford College, and the Historical Society of Pennsylvania. To all we extend our thanks.

We dedicate this book to our mentors—Michael F. Holt, Merton L. Dillon, and J. Mills Thornton III—who taught us much about nineteenth-century American history and what it means to be responsible historians.

The Worlds of James Buchanan and Thaddeus Stevens

INTRODUCTION

One of the persistent problems in studying the Civil War era is sorting out and determining the extent to which combinations of principles, partisanship, and personalities directed and drove the politics of the age. Historians have emphasized one factor over others in trying to understand the coming apart of the old party system, the coming together of a new party, and the coming of the war, and then the consequences of that struggle in shaping postwar politics. The recent spate of biographies of prominent figures—not only, and of course, Abraham Lincoln, but also Stephen A. Douglas, Frederick Douglass, William H. Seward, Edwin M. Stanton, and Ulysses S. Grant, among others—has shed light especially on northerners and the political worlds they inhabited. Other major works tracking the history of political parties have pointed more to ideology and partisan interest than personality as the critical forces informing political issues and loyalties. Whatever the emphasis or mix, historians still debate how, why, and with what effect such elements made the politics of the age so unstable and made possible new political coalitions.

At the same time, historians have been increasingly attentive to the varieties and vagaries of political loyalties based on place. Whatever the discipline of party systems, locality counted in deciding on which issues and interests to press. New England Democrats, Whigs, and Republicans had different styles and priorities than their border-state counterparts, for example. Some of that was a difference in culture and economy, some a matter of proximities, such as the distance from "the South" physically and socially. Recent scholarship on border-state politics has shown that proximity mattered, whether in family and commercial ties that mitigated sectional differences or in borders between "free" and "slave" states that exacerbated them, especially regarding the issue of fugitive slaves.

The *Worlds of James Buchanan and Thaddeus Stevens* takes up such questions and concerns by focusing on two of the nation's most prominent politicians and the political and social worlds they occupied, affected, and sometimes imagined. Both men were from Lancaster County, Pennsylvania, where they had gained success in business pursuits and had been weaned on border-state politics, and bachelors, which affected their social rootedness. Both were successful lawyers before entering politics and had lives that spanned identical decades: Buchanan was born in 1791, less than a year before Stevens, and Stevens died in 1868, less than three months after Buchanan. Yet they diverged dramatically in ideology, interest, and personality to the extent that place seemed hardly to matter in explaining their character, concerns, and conduct. At the same time, both men regarded Lancaster County as their "home" even as they lived elsewhere, especially in Washington, where separate social circles and national political issues kept them apart. By the 1850s, Buchanan was in many ways "the old public functionary," looking backward in trying to keep alive the Jacksonian Democracy he had done much to build as the slavery issue tore at the party systems, while Stevens was the forward-looking Whig-turned-Republican, willing to invest the federal government with new powers for economic development and social reform, especially antislavery, and then later for Republican Reconstruction. Buchanan's border-state experiences and, more so, his lifelong loyalty to the Democratic Party drew him to southerners as friends and allies; his political fortunes rose and fell with southern Democrats. Stevens's border-state experiences drew him to Whiggish ideas about an active government promoting economic growth and development and to righting the wrong of slavery, which to his mind was both a moral outrage and a drag on progress. Buchanan's and Stevens's lives mirrored those of many others of their day and place. Considering their lives and their political and social worlds thus offers an opportunity to discover the dynamics and directions of American politics, especially northern interests and identities. It is the subject of this book.

Left: James Buchanan (1791–1868). Sketch by unknown artist, drawn
February 16, 1866, at Buchanan's home, Wheatland, in Lancaster, Pennsylvania.
Courtesy LancasterHistory.org, Lancaster PA.

Right: Thaddeus Stevens (1792–1868). Painting by unknown artist, ca. 1867.
Courtesy National Portrait Gallery, Washington, DC.

Several themes run through this volume. One is the importance of
personal relationships and personality in reflecting and affecting political
ideas and allegiances. Any student of politics understands that equation,
but the essays herein track the personal connections across lines of gender
and geography and point to a new appreciation for elementary, though
essential, facts of political association: for example, with whom one ate
and conversed on a regular basis, the social isolation of Washington,
and the role of rumor in defining, and undermining, relationships and
political loyalties. Much has been written on the petticoat politics of the
capital, but much less is known about the world of men without women,
whether as husbands away from their wives at home while serving in
Washington or as bachelors living in separate quarters with other men.
At the same time, the predominance of men in the capital has obscured
the ways women influenced political interests, in part through close male-
female friendships that allowed them a political voice beyond their own
families.

Another theme is the constancy of a westward vision, even compulsion, driving a politics of Manifest Destiny for Democrats, Whigs, and Republicans alike that persisted from the antebellum period through Reconstruction. No party had a monopoly on wanting the West. Whether illusion or delusion, the West promised renewal and reward. It was worth fighting for and fighting over, and men did just that. That story is well known, but several essays in this book suggest a dynamics of westward thrust that went beyond partisan interest and cast both Buchanan and Stevens as westward directed in their politics. Both men and their respective political friends, regardless of party, insisted on asserting federal power to secure the West. Yet on land issues, in both the West and the South, principle, partisanship, and personality mattered. When race factored into thinking about who should gain land and what protections the government would provide for them, it proved a combustible mix that disrupted politics and destroyed political friendships.

Yet another theme is the instability of national political institutions caused by the aggressive expansionism of the era; the convulsions of the slavery controversy; the antiparty attitudes coming from radicals of various religious, reform, and regional interests; the self-serving politics of ambitious chieftains; and the social and psychological strains of failing relationships. Here, too, personality counted. For example, the clashing ambitions and egos of Buchanan and Douglas did much to hasten the coming apart of the Democratic Party. And Buchanan's difficulties with erstwhile political "friends" who were disappointed when the rewards fell short of what they thought was their due revealed a stubbornness on all sides that hardened rivalries within the party.

All that said, such instability did not create a new politics, as some historians have argued. However much the collapse of the so-called Second Party System and the rise of the Republican Party in the 1850s reordered political identities, writing an epitaph for the old politics altogether misses the continued vitality and centrality of parties as the principal means of organizing and directing political loyalty and behavior. The sectional politics that subsumed everything else at the national level did not drive away older interests and issues that informed politics at the local level or create new methods of party discipline or electioneering. New party labels and coalitions did not necessarily lead to the abandonment of old allegiances and relationships. Indeed, close examinations of politics at the state level reveal examples of state and local party organizations able to sustain loyalties enough through habit, patronage, and social compatibility to win elections and continue to reward friends and followers. Any new politics of ideology could not survive long without attention to the old politics of personal association and reward and disciplined organizing from the local level upward.

Such themes and concerns as noted above do not encompass all that informed and shaped the worlds of Buchanan, Stevens, and their contemporaries. The essays in this book compose no comprehensive overview of the politics and personalities of the Civil War era, nor do they suggest that an emphasis on parties, personality, place, and private lives can explain the political interests and actions of the age—hardly so, when factors of race, religion, and region loomed large and when a civil war almost turned politics inside out. But collectively, they do invite further consideration of such factors as being at least influential and sometimes decisive.

POSSESSING THE POWER

The Role of Force in James Buchanan's Caribbean Policy

AMY S. GREENBERG

Scholars agree that James Buchanan was one of the great expansionist voices of the antebellum era. During his nearly fifty years in public office, he served as minister to both Russia and England, chairman of the Senate Committee on Foreign Relations, secretary of state, and president, rising to office on an aggressively expansionist platform and pursuing the acquisition of foreign territories with a singlemindedness that, in retrospect, can only be read as tragic given the domestic crises at hand. He pushed for the annexation of Texas, for ports on the Pacific coast, for safe transit across Central America and Mexico, and for US control of the Caribbean. In 1854 he and two fellow diplomats in Europe coauthored a secret memorandum to President Franklin Pierce that advocated for war against Spain in order to acquire Cuba, an island "as necessary to the North American republic as any of its present members." The Ostend Manifesto, as it was known, became a sensation once it was leaked to the press but did nothing to prevent Buchanan's nomination and election as president two years later.[1]

While in office, Buchanan helped make America's destiny manifest. His "purposeful and calculated" expansionist policies offered a distillation of the "consuming nationalism" of his era, according to one admiring biographer. "The basic difference between James Buchanan and most of his contemporary expansionists was not in the rhetoric of Manifest Destiny and its ideology of limitless boundaries, but in the obvious fact that, in positions of high office, Buchanan orchestrated some of that rhetoric into deliberately planned policies."[2]

But to say he was great is not to say he was good. The Ostend Manifesto asserted that "every law, human and divine," supported the conclusion that "we shall be justified in wresting" Cuba "from Spain if we possess the power." Wresting Cuba from Spain simply because the United States was the stronger opponent? While Americans are hardly united over the proper role of force in international relations, particularly when it comes to national security, the majority opinion, now as in 1854, runs counter to the proposal that might makes right when it comes to foreign policy.[3]

Of course, the United States did not take Cuba from Spain in 1854. The manifesto was met with widespread outrage and repudiated by President Pierce. The theft of Cuba was no simple matter; many Americans believed the prospect of stealing territory from a European power unsavory, regardless of what "destiny" might suggest. It is worth noting, however, that Americans in 1854 had far less perspective on the evolution of aggressive expansionism than we do today. From our vantage point, Buchanan's arguments in favor of stealing Cuba seem bizarre in part because, with the exception of the wedge of Arizona and New Mexico acquired from Mexico in 1854 with the Gadsden Purchase, the contiguous United States was complete in 1848 at the close of the US–Mexican War. We know Cuba will remain Spanish territory until its independence. Why did Buchanan not realize this?[4]

Over the years, a number of scholars have argued that the ideology of Manifest Destiny, the conviction that God had singled out the United States for almost unlimited territorial expansion, was not heartfelt. That it was a rather transparent justification for stealing land from Indians and Mexicans, and that no one really believed in it, is clear from the precipitous drop in discussions of America's destiny after the United States acquired the great ports of the Pacific coast in the mid-1840s: Puget Sound from joint control with England, and San Francisco from Mexico. "Manifest Destiny persists as a popular term in American historical literature to explain the expansion of the United States to continent wide dimensions," writes one skeptic. "Like most broad generalizations, it does not bear close scrutiny." Another has argued that "from the outset Manifest Destiny—vast in program, in its sense of continentalism—was slight in support. It lacked national, sectional, or party following commensurate with its bigness."[5]

The first point, that Manifest Destiny provided a convenient excuse for theft, is inarguable. Indians and Mexicans had land Americans wanted; the fancy phrase "Manifest Destiny" put a gloss on the misappropriation of their territory.[6] But the second idea, that Manifest Destiny lasted only as long as it needed to and no longer, is fairly easy to refute. Anyone hoping to find evidence that this ideology had staying power even after the annexation of a third of Mexico at the close of the US–Mexican War need look no further than Buchanan's public and private utterances.

Buchanan grew increasingly invested in Manifest Destiny at the conclusion of that war, the exact opposite of what one would expect were that ideology in decline after the acquisition of what is now the western third of the United States. He also became increasingly willing to use force in the name of expansion. This essay will consider the evolution of Buchanan's views on Manifest Destiny from 1844 through the close of his presidential career, not only to lay to rest the idea that Manifest Destiny was in decline but also to provide a new perspective on an aspect of Buchanan's career that has been the object of a great deal of derision and perplexity—his obsession with Cuba. While many things that Buchanan did during his career can be attributed to political opportunism, his focus on Cuba while president cannot: He was pledged to a single term, and his dream of a Caribbean empire was clearly out of step with much of the entire northern portion of the country. A close examination of Buchanan's changing views of the role of force in American foreign policy reveals a larger social context that linked manhood and expansion in a manner that ultimately proved destructive not only to his presidency but also to the union of the United States.[7]

Buchanan was one of the very first Democratic politicians to promote Manifest Destiny. Indeed, in the spring of 1844, more than a year before an expansionist newspaper coined the phrase, the then-senator publicly expressed his conviction that "Providence has given to the American people a great and glorious mission to perform, even that of extending . . . liberty over the whole North American continent. . . . What, sir! Prevent the American people from crossing the Rocky Mountains? You might as well command Niagara not to flow. We must fulfill our destiny."[8] He fully supported the annexation of Texas in 1845, in part because he bought into the argument of fellow Democrat Robert J. Walker that Texas could prove a dumping ground for slaves, that its admission to the Union would "whiten" the upper South as slaves moved to economically more productive land and ultimately to Mexico, where, in Buchanan's words, "they would find a climate more congenial to their nature." It was a nonsensical argument that had surprising traction among proslavery northern Democrats.[9] Buchanan became President James K. Polk's secretary of state in 1845, mere months after Texas became the twenty-eighth state in the Union.

Despite Buchanan's early identification of and with Manifest Destiny, he was initially a remarkably cautious secretary of state who "stood almost alone in the cabinet for moderation and compromise" with England over the Oregon Country.[10] Polk had campaigned on the promise to take all of Oregon from England ("Fifty-four Forty or Fight") and showed little interest in backing down from that promise until Buchanan convinced him that annexation of the entire jointly controlled territory would lead to war with England.

Buchanan's fears of a military conflict were misplaced but sincere. He repeatedly urged compromise until the moment Polk agreed to split the territory with England. At this point Buchanan, in a moment of "play acting," tried to distance himself from the division of Oregon at the same time that he urged British officials to accept the proposed treaty. His goal of not alienating potential northern expansionist voters was transparent to the entire cabinet.[11] His attitude toward Oregon was indicative of his overall approach to expansionism as secretary of state: extreme caution that he often tried to obscure from the public. Buchanan wanted to add territory to the United States, lands that he expected, like the waters of Niagara, to flow naturally to the Union. War for territory, though, placed the Union at risk, and Buchanan was no risk taker. Indeed, his caution in matters of war drove Polk to exasperation: "Mr. Buchanan is an able man, but is in small matters without judgment, and sometimes acts like an old maid."[12] Was the president, in this statement, referring obliquely to the secretary of state's bachelor status? It is impossible to say, but Buchanan was clearly not of the same mind as Polk about the privileges due the United States in its relations with foreign nations.

Amid negotiations with England over Oregon, Polk sent four thousand soldiers, half of the regular army, into a region contested by newly annexed Texas and the neighboring Republic of Mexico. At the same time he had Buchanan draft a memorandum to his agent in Mexico, John Slidell, offering that country up to $25 million, and the settlement of debts outstanding, for the purchase of California. Mexico refused to negotiate, in large part because four thousand armed men were poised to invade its territory. Polk surely understood that marching his army through land that Mexico claimed would lead to the sort of international incident that would enable him to go to Congress, announce that a war had commenced, and request money and volunteers to redeem US honor.[13]

Unfortunately, this incident was slow in coming. On Saturday, May 9, 1846, Polk called his cabinet together and told them "that in my opinion we had ample cause of war" because of the insults given the United States by Mexico, specifically its treatment of rebuffed agent John Slidell, "and that it was impossible that we could stand in *statu quo*." The majority of the cabinet accepted Polk's argument that the United States could declare war on Mexico without direct military provocation, yet Buchanan remained on the fence, voting with the majority in favor of war but in opinion leaning toward caution. When Polk received news the very next day of a Mexican attack on Major General Zachary Taylor's forces, he again called his cabinet together; this time the vote in favor of declaring war was unanimous.[14]

The cabinet got straight to work implementing plans for the long awaited conflict. Polk's first action was to request "all the orders and letters of instruction to our [naval] squadrons in the Pacific & Gulf of Mexico" and ask that these be read to the cabinet. Polk "desired to refresh" his memory about the exact orders that he had given Commander J. D. Sloat when, back in the president's third month in office, he had ordered

Sloat to immediately seize San Francisco and other ports in California if war should break out.[15]

The secretary of state, however, was unwilling to advocate for taking land from Mexico. Polk could have hardly been clearer about his territorial ambitions, but Buchanan drafted a message to the great powers of Europe disavowing interest in conquering territory, which he then presented to the cabinet. The message stated "that in going to war we did not do so with a view to acquire either California or New Mexico or any other portion of the Mexican territory." Yet Buchanan surely knew that gaining such lands, specifically California, was precisely the point of the war. Polk told him "that though we had not gone to war for conquest, yet it was clear that in making peace we would if practicable obtain California and such other portion of the Mexican territory as would be sufficient . . . to defray the expenses of the war. . . . It was well known that the Mexican government had no other means of indemnifying us."

This was not what Buchanan had hoped to hear. The secretary of state insisted that war "with England as well as Mexico, and probably with France also," would be the result, "for neither of these powers will ever stand by and [see] California annexed to the U.S." Growing ever more animated, Polk responded, "I would meet the war which either England or France or all the Powers of Christendom might wage, and . . . I would stand and fight until the last man among us fell in the conflict" before ever agreeing to Buchanan's pledge.[16] The men argued for two hours, with the rest of the cabinet lining up behind the president. Finally, at close to 11:00 P.M., Polk rose and demanded that Buchanan strike out the offending paragraphs of his message, at which point a clearly angry secretary of state left the room. This was a singular example of Polk having to bluntly exert his will within his cabinet. Buchanan clearly feared England and France more than his chief executive in this matter.[17]

At a cabinet meeting six weeks later, he tried once again to convince Polk of the folly of dismembering Mexico. When Secretary of the Treasury Robert Walker argued in favor of annexing everything north of latitude 26° north (including most of Sonora, Chihuahua, Durango, and Baja California, as well as a good portion of Nuevo Léon and Tamaulipas; in total a third of modern-day Mexico), Buchanan protested. "If it was the object of the President to acquire all the country North of 26° . . . , it should be known," he insisted. And should this occur, "the opinion of the world would be against" the United States, "especially as it [the seized territory] would become a slave-holding country." Walker responded "that he would be willing to fight the whole world sooner than suffer other Powers to interfere in the matter." Polk agreed with his belligerent secretary. "I remarked that I preferred the 26° to any boundary North of it."[18] No one in the cabinet questioned Buchanan's assumption that any lands taken from Mexico would become slave territory. This is really a bit odd when one considers that slavery had, at that point, been abolished in Mexico for twenty years. What they were talking about was establishing slavery among a free (if subjected to the United States) population.

That was Buchanan in the summer of 1846, arguing against taking portions of Mexico on the grounds of international law and the reputation of the United States abroad. "The opinion of the world would be against us," he argued. Sixteen months later, in the fall of 1847, with the United States in occupation of Mexico's capital, his views had changed. As a presidential candidate, Buchanan now declared that annexing all of Mexico was "that destiny which Providence may have in store for both countries."[19] When President Polk received a draft of the treaty of Guadalupe Hidalgo, which would ultimately bring the war to a close, Buchanan, along with Walker, insisted that he reject it and demand more land from Mexico.[20] When Buchanan tried to talk him out of submitting the agreement to the Senate for ratification, insisting on the need for a greater territorial cession, Polk chastised him, reminding the presidential hopeful that, at the start of the war, Buchanan had been opposed to taking any territory from Mexico at all. He attributed his secretary of state's change of view to politics, virtually sighing to his diary that night, "No candidate for the Presidency ought ever to remain in the Cabinet."[21]

Perhaps Polk was right that Buchanan was taking a more aggressive position, so to speak, in order to gain the Democratic presidential nomination. He showed a great deal more caution as secretary of state during this time than his public utterances might suggest. When white Yucatecos turned to the United States for protection in April 1848 during the Caste War, Buchanan argued against annexing the Yucatan on the grounds that it would jeopardize the final resolution of the war with Mexico.[22]

But even after losing the Democratic nomination to Lewis Cass, Buchanan continued to publicly advocate for an ever-larger nation. And as he left Washington in 1849 at the close of his cabinet term with the great ports of the Pacific secured, Buchanan wrote his replacement: "We must have Cuba. We can't do without Cuba. . . . We shall acquire it by a coup at some precipitous moment. Cuba is already ours. I feel it in my finger tips."[23] This is notable for several reasons. First, Buchanan seemed to have dropped any scruples about how these actions would appear to the rest of the world. Second, he had begun to adopt the pugilistic viewpoint, if not yet language, of Polk and Walker, who threatened to fight the world if they did not get their way. And third, this marked the beginning of his obsession with the Caribbean.

Buchanan's expansionism was avid, sustained, and frankly more than a bit out of step with his constituency in Pennsylvania. While one could argue that there was at least some support for the annexation of Texas in Pennsylvania, certainly more than in New England, in point of fact Polk only won the great commonwealth's electoral votes because vice-presidential nominee George Mifflin Dallas asserted that, if elected, Polk would fearlessly protect Pennsylvania industry despite his public support for a low tariff. As for the proposal that the United States should absorb all of Mexico, it generated little enthusiasm outside of Philadelphia.[24] But both of these issues paled with that of the annexation of Cuba, a slave society that threatened to upset the balance of power in the United States if it entered the Union.

Buchanan lobbied for the acquisition of Cuba throughout the 1850s, most notably while serving as minister to England, when he and two other diplomats penned the Ostend Manifesto after the US minister to Spain, Pierre Soulé of Louisiana, bungled negotiations over the sale of the island. Buchanan's disregard for the views of the rest of the world in this document contrast starkly with the restraint he showed at the outset of the US–Mexican War. The United States, he argued, "can afford to disregard the censures of the world" when taking Cuba from Spain. Such censures were nothing new. The nation had been "exposed" to such criticism "so often and so unjustly" in the wake of other acquisitions, despite the fact that they were all fair and legal. From Louisiana in 1803, to Florida in 1819, and to the 1836 revolution of Mexican Texas and its subsequent annexation, "the United States have never acquired a foot of territory except by fair purchase, or, as in the case of Texas, upon the free and voluntary application of the people of that independent State, who desired to blend their destinies with our own." Even California and New Mexico, wrestled from Mexico just six years earlier, were "no exception to this rule, because, although we might have claimed them by the right of conquest in a just war, yet we purchased them for what was then considered by both parties a full and ample equivalent."[25]

Indeed, the United States paid Mexico $30 million at the close of the war, which was almost the exact amount it had refused to accept for that land prior to the conflict, a fact Buchanan certainly knew because, as the secretary of state, he had drafted the memorandum to Slidell containing the offer. In any case, the editor of the Ostend Manifesto made clear his decided opinion that there was little point in having the United States worry about the world's censure at this point in its glorious territorial march. Regardless of the view of the rest of the world, "national honor" fully vindicated war against Spain. Why? Because earlier that year Spanish officials in Havana had confiscated the cargo of an American steamer for violations of port protocol. "The flag of the United States" had been insulted. This canard was eerily similar to Polk's arguments in favor of war with Mexico before "American blood was shed on the American soil": Mexico had insulted the United States by rejecting the country's representative and by refusing to pay claims due American citizens. These were excuses that Buchanan was far from comfortable with in 1846. In 1854, however, they seemed to him perfectly sound. The question in his mind was no longer what Europe would think, but whether the United States had the power to take what was not its own. And Buchanan not only believed it did but also took it for granted.[26]

It is difficult to overestimate the severity of the backlash against the Ostend Manifesto, even after its repudiation by the Pierce administration.[27] In 1856 the preeminent northern printmaking firm Currier and Ives produced two Buchanan prints that reflect the views of many voters in the North, that Manifest Destiny in the Caribbean had devolved into highway robbery conducted by and in support of violence-prone slaveholders.

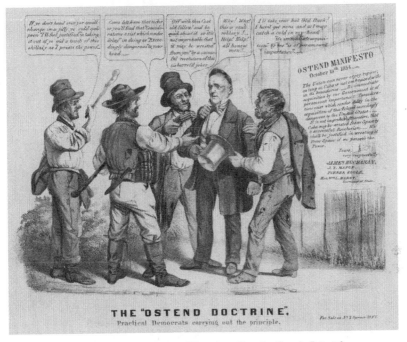

The "Ostend Doctrine": Practical Democrats Carrying Out the Principle.
Lithograph by N. Currier, 1856.

The first lithograph, *The "Ostend Doctrine": Practical Democrats Carrying Out the Principle,* represents thugs robbing Buchanan while repeating lines from the manifesto. A ragged Irishman holding a club warns, "If ye don't hand over yer small change in a jiffy ye ould spal-peen 'I'll feel justified' in taking it out of ye wid a touch of this shillaly as 'I pozziz the power,'" while another hoodlum, flaunting a large revolver, warns, "Off with this Coat old fellow! and be quick about it or 'it is not improbable that it may be wrested' from you 'by a successful revolution' of this six barrel'd joker." Buchanan cries out, "Why! Why! this is rank robbery! Help! Help! all Honest men!" The actual text of the manifesto hangs in the background.

The second print, *A Serviceable Garment—Or Reverie of a Bachelor,* shows a poverty-stricken Buchanan as a hopeful Democratic presidential candidate, sewing a patch that says "Cuba" on his very worn coat. He says:

A Serviceable Garment, or Reverie of a Bachelor. Lithograph by N. Currier, 1856.

"My Old coat was a very fashionable Federal coat when it was new, but by patching and turning I have made it quite a Democratic Garment. That Cuba patch to be sure is rather unsightly but it suits Southern fashions at this season."

One should pause at this phrase, "Southern fashions." Currier and Ives clearly see the consistency of Buchanan's dream of a Caribbean empire as directly related to his dream of the presidency. When he speaks about annexing all of Mexico, or Cuba, or invading Mexico, he was speaking not to northerners but to southerners, the constituency whom he (rightly) believed held his political future in their hands. This thesis makes a great deal of sense in the context of the 1856 presidential election. But it makes much less sense after Buchanan won that election, when there appeared to be no decrease in his desire for Caribbean territory.

In the beginning of his presidential term, Buchanan's secretary of state, Lewis Cass, wrote that the United States "requires more land, more territory upon which to settle, and just as fast as our interests and our destiny require additional territory in the North, or in the South, or on the Islands of the Ocean, I am for it."[28] This was a pretty fair statement of the approach Buchanan took to territorial acquisition during his presidency. He sought to establish an American protectorate over parts of northwestern Mexico, even asking Congress in 1859 for permission to raise an army to invade that country "for the purpose of obtaining indemnity for the past and security for the future."[29] Depending on one's perspective, this was either remarkably forward thinking of Buchanan—as the United States would set up many protectorates in Central and South America, in fact if not in name, starting in the late nineteenth century—or somewhat misguided, given the domestic problems he should have been addressing: the financial panic of 1857, violence in Kansas, the *Dred Scott* decision, and the 1850 Fugitive Slave Act.

Buchanan's failure to lead, or even react, to events in the South after Lincoln's election is well known.[30] Rather than face the crisis at home, he kept his mind set on Cuba (in particular) and the Caribbean and Mexico (in general). So avid was Buchanan's expansionism that his biographer Jean Baker asserts that in contrast to southerners, who were only interested in territory amenable to slavery, and those few northerners who thirsted for "Free Soil" (but only "Free Soil") annexations, Buchanan was exceptional in that he "fought for territory everywhere."[31]

This is not exactly true. As president, Buchanan chose not to assist the American filibuster William Walker, who was desperate to reestablish power in Nicaragua after being forced out of the isthmus in 1857 by a Costa Rican–led army.[32] Nor is there evidence that he supported annexing Hawaii in the 1850s after King Kamehameha's agents approached President Pierce about that possibility.[33] But for the most part, Baker is right. During his final message to Congress in December 1860, Buchanan asked for $30 million to buy Cuba, despite the fact that there was no evidence that Spain was interested in selling. Lawmakers refused to allow either his proposal to invade Mexico or his final quixotic effort to acquire Cuba to come to the floor for a vote.[34]

❧

So how does one explain Buchanan's transformation from a secretary of state unwilling to annex Mexican territory during the supposed highwater mark of Manifest Destiny to a president who continued to pursue Cuba as the Union collapsed? Pledged to serving only a single term, there was no clear political reason for him to adopt policies he did not himself believe in once in office. Yet this was precisely when his obsession with the Caribbean became most evident—and most damaging.

Buchanan's increasingly aggressive approach to territorial annexation was in part driven by what Robert E. May has described as "Southern dreams of a Caribbean empire." As opportunities for slavery expansion to the west were cut off, southerners turned their attention farther south. Mass immigration to the North had left the South outnumbered in the House of Representatives, which worried southerners concerned about slavery's future. After the Missouri Compromise of 1820 prohibited slavery in the territories north of latitude 36°30′ north (with the exception of the state of Missouri), southerners began to look south for new territory. Expansion in that direction could bring additional slave states into the Union, strengthening the power of the South. It also promised an opportunity for nonslaveholding white yeoman farmers, who made up the bulk of the southern population, to gain slaves and land, which would strengthen the institution of slavery as well.[35]

While Buchanan was not himself southern, he identified with that wing of his party and adopted policies that promoted the interests of the expansionist South. The importance of extending southern slavery into the Caribbean in the 1850s has been overshadowed by the rise of sectionalism, but in fact the specter of such expansion was a major factor in increasing sectionalism. As Robert May shows in his book *Slavery, Race, and Conquest in the Tropics,* the Republican Party was convinced that southerners were intent on bringing Cuba, Mexico, and parts of Central America into the Union as slave states.[36]

But perhaps equally important to the evolution of Buchanan's Caribbean policy were transformations in masculine norms in the antebellum era that imbued territorial acquisition with a decidedly gendered hue. The period in question was one of increasingly bombastic and violent utterances of supporters of aggressive expansionism; the threats by both Polk and Walker to fight the world if it dared to interfere with the United States were hardly fringe sentiments. Between the 1840s and the start of the Civil War, Manifest Destiny and a particularly aggressive or martial form of manhood became mutually reinforcing: Manifest Destiny was empowered by the rise of a martial ideal of manhood, and the idea that the best expression of American manhood was violent and aggressive was in turn reinforced by the easy victory of the United States in its war of aggression against Mexico.[37]

Although territorial expansion in the early American republic had never proceeded peacefully, the expansionism of the 1840s achieved a new level of pugnacity. Up until the 1830s, Americans justified taking land from "savages" because they were not farming and "improving" their land by constructing permanent structures on it. But after the ethnic expulsion of the civilized Cherokees—a tribe that both farmed and improved their land—in the 1830s, race became the determining factor in this equation. Increasing numbers of "Anglo-Saxon" Americans believed their claims to North America to be superior to those of any racially "impure" peoples.[38]

Transformations in race relations within the United States in the 1830s were central to the intensifying drive to expand its boundaries. The last vestiges of colonial slavery did not disappear in the northern states until the 1840s. Gradual emancipation in the North turned slavery into a purely sectional phenomenon, not only putting southerners on the defensive about their "peculiar institution" but also leading to social unrest on the other side of the Mason-Dixon Line. The newly elevated status of northern freedmen, along with the increasing size of free-black urban communities, led to an upsurge in northern racism in the 1830s and 1840s.

One reason for this development was that white workingmen in the North faced increased competition from free African Americans and surging numbers of immigrants drawn to the United States by declining conditions in Europe. Between 1840 and 1860, almost 4.5 million European immigrants arrived in the United States, the largest influx in US history relative to the country's total population. Many of those newcomers were Catholics from Ireland and Germany, resulting in a notable increase in anti-Catholicism and fears among Protestants of an attempted European-led Catholic takeover of the US political system. The working conditions of laboring men also declined due to the beginnings of the Industrial Revolution and the devaluing of many traditional artisanal skills.[39]

Workingmen faced new challenges to their cultural values along with decreasing wages in the 1830s and 1840s. An emerging middle class embraced temperance and church attendance, rejecting the heavy drinking and rowdy male camaraderie that was once the norm in artisan workshops of the early republic and among some immigrant groups. By the 1830s, these behaviors were seen by many in the middle class as uncouth. They also began to idealize women for their supposed moral superiority to men. A new ideology of domesticity insisted that women and men were essentially different beings and suited to different spheres of influence. Men's realm was the public world of work and politics; women's was the home. But what was new was the elevation of women by middle-class sensibilities to a place of equality with men in religion and family matters, while women asserted that their domestic virtue entitled them to exert their influence beyond the home and into society. This empowerment through the ideology of domesticity helped spark the first women's rights movement in the 1840s.[40]

All these changes left workingmen—who based their self-worth on their physical strength, traditional labor skills, and dominance over both women and nonwhites—on the defensive. By raising women to a level of equality in the home, domesticity threatened to remove one of the few prerogatives available to men whose working lives were increasingly unrewarding. Manifest Destiny promised these laborers upward mobility and an escape from declining job conditions through landownership on the frontier. In reality, few urban workers moved west. Virtually all settlers there were farmers who had already found at least moderate success working the land. It was simply too expensive to purchase land and equipment, not to mention surviving until the first harvest, for laborers or poor farmers to start a western farm.[41]

Manifest Destiny obscured this painful truth. Proponents repeatedly claimed that cheap land, beautiful women, and a better life were free for the taking by the man willing and able to fight for them. Former Texas president Sam Houston, at this time a US senator, made this connection directly in a speech he delivered at a political rally in favor of taking all of Mexico just before the conclusion of the war. He recommended that American men "take a trip of exploration" to Mexico "and look out for the beautiful *senoritas,* or pretty girls, and if you should choose to annex them, no doubt the result of this annexation will be a most powerful and delightful evidence of civilization." But he also made clear that it would not be love that ultimately led to annexation, but war. "As surely as tomorrow's sun will rise and pursue its bright course along the firmament of heaven, so certain it appears to my mind, must the Anglo Saxon race pervade the whole Southern extremity of this vast continent," Houston thundered.

The Americans regard this continent as their birth-right. The seed of all their settlements has been sown in blood and watered by blood. The pioneers who went forward into the wilderness poured out their heart's blood to prepare the country for their [posterity]; their scalps were taken by the Indian; they sacrificed their life's blood to acquire the possessions which we enjoy. If all these difficulties and sacrifices did not terrify the bold pioneer, the success of centuries only tends to confirm what they began, and nothing can prevent our mighty march. . . . [W]e have a powerful authority for wars in the conduct of the people of Israel, who were led by Divine power to possess themselves of the lands of the Ammonites, and smite them with the edge of the sword. This same mandate from God guides us in this war, and gives success to our army; and I think will continue to guide and to prosper America.[42]

Travel writers, musicians, and politicians made the same promises about land, love, and a generally easier life in California, Texas, Mexico, and even Central America.

Aggressive or violent expansionism in the heyday of Manifest Destiny was also encouraged by scientific racism. In order to "prove" that Anglo-Saxons were destined to dominate lesser races, leading scientists of the antebellum era, many from the South, posited theories of racial difference that expanded on earlier ideas of a racial hierarchy. This logic was used not only to justify slavery but also to promote Manifest Destiny. Contemporary race theory similarly suggested that through the sexual union of white men and Latin American women, Mexico might be whitened, since Anglo-Saxon characteristics would overpower nonwhite characteristics in the resulting generation. In the literature of Manifest Destiny, Mexican women were repeatedly represented as sexually desirable, hardworking, and, unlike the newly empowered women of the United States, easily dominated. Race theory promised that what Senator Houston called "annexation" between white US soldiers and Mexican women would result in Anglo-Saxon hegemony in the newly acquired western territories.[43]

Aggressive territorial expansion offered men the promise of asserting their martial virtues, dominating supposed racial inferiors, and—by dint of their physical strength and courage—winning fertile land of their own, docile women for their brides, and an empire for the United States. These sentiments came to the fore during the US–Mexican War. "Uncle Sam's Song to Miss Texas," for instance, was a popular ditty sung by soldiers marching through Mexico and in taverns back home. Addressing "star-eyed" Texas, envisioned here as an attractive "Indian gal," singers threatened:

> If Mexy, back'd by secret foes,
> Still talks of taking you, gal,
> Why we can lick 'em all, you know,
> An' then annex 'em too, gal;
> For Freedom's great millenium,
> Is working airth's salvation,
> Her sassy kingdom soon will come,
> Annexin' all creation.[44]

In a period when workingmen, Democrats, and slaveholders were quick to fight, or to threaten to fight, upon the slightest provocation, Manifest Destiny offered rewards. Not surprisingly, aggressive expansionism was supported by those who embraced physical domination by individuals and nations. These martial men believed that the masculine qualities of strength, aggression, and even violence better defined a true man than did the firm and upright behavior of restrained individuals, though at times even embracing the "chivalrous" ideals of knighthood or other models of manhood from the past.[45] By the 1840s, the Democratic Party embraced an aggressive expansionist discourse and was, in turn, embraced by these martial men.

Initially, James Buchanan was not one of those, like Polk or Walker, who endorsed physical domination and the willingness to fight. He was not a slaveholder, not a southerner, and not a military man. But the vast territorial acquisitions resulting from the US–Mexican War, which transferred 1,193,061 square miles of Mexican territory (including Texas) to the United States at a cost of thirteen thousand American—and at least twenty thousand Mexican—lives, inflamed the desires of Democratic expansionists, who envisioned their country soon encompassing Sonora, Mexico; Cuba; Nicaragua; and lands even farther afield. They saw the successful conclusion of the war as legitimating a hemispheric destiny for the United States. And they seemed to justify the attitude that might makes right. While it is certainly true that "many Americans saw the United States' victory [over Mexico] as fulfillment of their 'Manifest Destiny,'" there is ample evidence that many other Americans believed that northern Mexico was just the beginning of US territorial expansion southward.[46]

For many, the US–Mexican War served to enflame expansionist desire, seemingly fulfilling the proclamations of the most rabid exponents of Manifest Destiny and offering a precedent for further dramatic gains. During the war, Ralph Waldo Emerson predicted that "Mexico will poison us." But even he had privately mused that "the strong British race . . . must also overrun . . . Mexico and Oregon."[47] Easy victory over Mexico empowered a martial vision of manhood in the United States, one that valorized strength and the ability to dominate others, one that soon made compromise between northerners and southerners increasingly difficult to achieve or even fathom.

Before the war, the expansionist *United States Democratic Review* regularly suggested that "the whole of this vast continent is destined one day to subscribe to the Constitution of the United States." In the early 1850s the paper pictured the southern boundary of the country "moving downward on the two sides, from California and from Texas, and in a less decided manner, extending, as it were, a penumbra over the West Indies." By the close of the 1850s, the *Democratic Review* was even more emphatic that "Mexico and Cuba . . . be numbered among the United States of America. That this is to be the certain destiny of this people, notwithstanding the delay occasioned by diplomacy, no well-informed person entertains the shadow of a doubt."[48] The possibility that Nicaragua, Cuba, or even distant Hawaii could become a new state seemed far more likely after the dramatic (if ill-gotten) gains of the 1840s than it had before. Manifest Destiny was not in "eclipse" in the 1850s. If anything, the 1850s were, as Albert K. Weinberg has put it, "the heyday of 'spread-eagleism,'" when the "lack of luck rather than boldness limited the decade's achievements." The war with Mexico only in retrospect marked an end to antebellum territorial expansion. At the end of the 1840s, it seemed rather to open the door to it.[49]

In the 1850s Buchanan set aside his concerns about the "censures of the world," concerns that occupied him in 1846 to the degree that he was willing to contradict his commander in chief, not once, but twice. By 1848, European censure made absolutely no difference when the United States dismembered Mexico, as victory over that country seemed to prove that might does make right in foreign policy. To argue otherwise was a sign of weakness, or, as Buchanan put it at the start of his presidential term,

THE BEWILDERED OLD WOMAN.

MRS. J. B.—"SAKES ALIVE! I KNOW NO NORTH, NO SOUTH, NO EAST, NO WEST—NO NOTHING! AND WHO ON EARTH'S GOING TO TAKE THIS PLAGUY MESSAGE?

The Bewildered Old Woman. From *Vanity Fair,* January 7, 1860.

"expansion is in the future the policy of our country, and only cowards fear and oppose it." He was no longer the "coward" he had been in the Polk cabinet. But his martial expressions of manhood had more currency in the South, where domination over slaves was a part of life, than in the North. This helps explain why his bluster was not better received by the majority of Americans as well as the reaction of Currier and Ives to his statements in the Ostend Manifesto, which would have struck President Polk as perfectly sensible, indeed as echoes of what he, himself, had stated.[50]

The US–Mexican War seemed to prove that "landlust" combined with power could translate into territorial acquisition. For James Buchanan, this conflict offered other lessons as well: that a man who possessed the power of the presidency was entitled to use it; that it was, in fact, his responsibility to use it; and that Polk's pugilistic approach was the right and proper approach to foreign relations. So Buchanan pushed for Cuba and pushed for war against Mexico—because he had the power.

In the long run, however, Buchanan's efforts did nothing to transform his public persona into a martial man, as suggested in a *Vanity Fair* cartoon from 1860. *The Bewildered Old Woman* mocks Buchanan's supposed neutrality on the eve of war by reminding readers of his authorship of the Ostend Manifesto, a message that continued to plague him. "Sake's Alive!" the cartoonist has "Mrs. J. B." exclaim, "I know no North, no South, no East, no West—no Nothing! And who on earth's going to take this plagy message?"[51] Buchanan could adopt Polk's language, but at least for northerners, a pugilistic demeanor with regards to Cuba did nothing to dispel the notion that he was still, in Polk's earlier words, "an old maid."[52]

James Buchanan's transformation from a lone voice in the Polk cabinet urging caution in the realm of international affairs to a president with almost a monomania on the subject of annexing Cuba, all in just ten years, perhaps tells us less about his failure to judge the tenor of the times than one might think. Indeed, views and actions that seem, in retrospect, inexplicably misguided make a great deal of sense within the politics of slavery focused on a southern Caribbean empire and a martial political culture that celebrated domination.

NOTES

1. The diplomatic dispatch James Buchanan, Pierre Soulé, and John Mason wrote in Ostend, Belgium, was dubbed the Ostend Manifesto once it arrived in Washington, DC. It was published by the US Congress as *The Ostend Conference, &c, Message from the President of the United States,* 33rd Cong., 2nd Sess., 1855, H. Exec. Doc. 93, 127–32. On Buchanan's

role as editor of the manifesto, see Frederick Moore Binder, *James Buchanan and the American Empire* (Selinsgrove, PA: Susquehanna University Press, 1994), 200. Although Mason and particularly Soulé helped write the manifesto, this essay will refer to it as Buchanan's because of his position as editor.

2. Binder, *James Buchanan and the American Empire,* 10.

3. "Ostend Manifesto," in *Manifest Destiny and American Territorial Expansion: A Brief History with Documents,* ed. Amy S. Greenberg (Boston: Bedford Books / St. Martin's, 2012), 126–27. On the diversity of views of the use of force in American diplomacy today, see Alexander George, "The Role of Force in Diplomacy: A Continuing Dilemma for U.S. Foreign Policy," in *Managing Global Chaos,* ed. Chester A. Crocker, Fen Osler Hampson, and Pamela Aall (Washington, DC: US Institute of Peace, 1996), 209–22; and Eben Kaplan, "U.S. Political Parties and Foreign Policy," last updated October 31, 2006, Council on Foreign Relations, https://www.cfr.org/backgrounder/us-political-parties-and-foreign-policy, accessed July 27, 2016.

4. Greenberg, *Manifest Destiny and American Territorial Expansion,* v, 128.

5. Norman A. Graebner, "Empire on the Pacific," in *Patterns of American History,* ed. Alexander DeConde and Armin Rappaport, 2 vols. (Belmont, CA: Wadsworth, 1965), 1:352; Frederick Merk (with the collaboration of Lois Bannister Merk), *Manifest Destiny and Mission in American History: A Reinterpretation* (New York: Alfred A. Knopf, 1963), 216. See also Norman A. Graebner, *Empire on the Pacific: A Study in American Continental Expansion* (New York: Ronald, 1955), vi, 217, 218. Michael Morrison's contention that, "although Manifest Destiny was not in eclipse, to a growing number of Americans in 1851 expansion no longer appeared to promote automatically the ideals of liberty and emancipation" is reasonable. But for Buchanan and his followers, it is not true that "caution and introspection began to overshadow the sense of boundlessness of the previous decade." Morrison, *Slavery and the American West: The Eclipse of Manifest Destiny and the Coming of the Civil War* (Chapel Hill: University of North Carolina Press, 1997), 133.

6. See Greenberg, *Manifest Destiny and American Territorial Expansion.*

7. For a more positive assessment of James Buchanan's foreign policy, as well as an argument in favor of the national appeal of Cuba, see John M. Belohlavek, "In Defense of Doughface Diplomacy: A Reevaluation of the Foreign Policy of James Buchanan," in *James Buchanan and the Coming of the Civil War,* ed. John W. Quist and Michael J. Birkner (Gainesville: University Press of Florida, 2013): 111–33.

8. James Buchanan, "Speech, March 12, 1844, on the Oregon Question," in *The Works of James Buchanan: Comprising His Speeches, State Papers, and Private Correspondence,* ed. John Bassett Moore, 12 vols. (Philadelphia: J. B. Lippincott, 1908), 5:477. The phrase "Manifest Destiny" was first used in "Annexation," in *United States Magazine and Democratic Review* 17 (1845): 5–10.

9. Moore, *Works of James Buchanan,* 6:15; Robert J. Walker, *Letter of Mr. Walker, of Mississippi, Relative to the Reannexation of Texas* (Philadelphia: Mifflin and Parry, 1844), 13–15; Frederick Merk (with the collaboration of Lois Bannister Merk), *Fruits of Propaganda in the Tyler Administration* (Cambridge, MA: Harvard University Press, 1971), 21–26. Jane

McManus Storm Cazneau made similar arguments in the *United States Democratic Review* and in *The King of Rivers* (New York: Charles Wood, 1850).

10. Binder, *James Buchanan and the American Empire*, 79.

11. David Pletcher, *The Diplomacy of Annexation: Texas, Oregon, and the Mexican War* (Columbia: University of Missouri Press, 1973), 412.

12. James K. Polk, *The Diary of James K. Polk during his Presidency, 1845–1849*, 4 vols. (Columbia, TN: James K. Polk Memorial Assoc., 2005), 4:355.

13. Amy Greenberg, *A Wicked War: Polk, Clay, Lincoln, and the 1846 US Invasion of Mexico* (New York: Knopf, 2012), 76–102.

14. Polk, *Diary*, 1:354; Pletcher, *Diplomacy of Annexation*, 384.

15. Polk, *Diary*, 1:393.

16. Polk, 397–98.

17. Polk, 399.

18. Polk, 496.

19. App. to Cong. Globe, 30th Cong., 1st Sess., 197 (1848).

20. Polk, *Diary*, 3:348.

21. Polk, 350.

22. Binder, *James Buchanan and the American Empire*, 130–34.

23. Moore, *Works of James Buchanan*, 8:361.

24. Greenberg, *Wicked War*, 60; On the "All Mexico" movement, see John Douglas Pitts Fuller, *The Movement for the Acquisition of All Mexico, 1846–1848* (Baltimore: Johns Hopkins University Press, 1936).

25. "Ostend Manifesto," 126–27.

26. "Ostend Manifesto," 126–27. On failed negotiations to buy New Mexico and California before the war, see Pletcher, *Diplomacy of Annexation*, 287–91.

27. Peter H. Smith, *Talons of the Eagle: Dynamics of U.S.–Latin American Relations*, 2nd ed. (New York: Oxford University Press, 2000), 24–25.

28. Willard Carl Klunder, *Lewis Cass and the Politics of Moderation* (Kent, OH: Kent State University Press 1996), 289–90 (quote, 289).

29. Moore, *Works of James Buchanan*, 12:250.

30. For an excellent overview of historiographical assessments of Buchanan's reaction to the secession crisis, see "Introduction: Bum Rap or Bad Leadership?," in Quist and Birkner, *Buchanan and the Coming of the Civil War*, 2–19. It says a great deal about Buchanan's perspective that, at the end of his presidential term, he insisted that his administration had been "eminently successful in its foreign and domestic policy, unless we may accept the sad events which have recently occurred. Those no human wisdom could have prevented." Buchanan to James Gordon Bennett, March 11, 1861, quoted in Binder, *James Buchanan and the American Empire*, 275.

31. Jean H. Baker, *James Buchanan* (New York: Times Books, 2004), 36.

32. Robert E. May has argued that Buchanan worked diligently to prevent filibusters, even at the expense of his support in the South. May, "James Buchanan, the Neutrality

Laws, and American Invasions of Nicaragua," in *James Buchanan and the Political Crisis of the 1850s,* ed. Michael J. Birkner (Selinsgrove, PA: Susquehanna University Press, 1996), 123–45.

33. Proclamation of King Kamehameha, December 8, 1854, Official Dispatches, Archives of Hawai'i, Honolulu reel 6; Robert E. May, "Manifest Destiny's Filibusters," in *Manifest Destiny and Empire: American Antebellum Expansionism,* ed. Sam W. Haynes and Christopher Morris (College Station: Texas A&M University Press, 1997), 146–48, 168.

34. Elbert B. Smith, *The Presidency of James Buchanan* (Lawrence: University Press of Kansas, 1975), 78.

35. Robert E. May, *The Southern Dream of a Caribbean Empire, 1854–1861* (Baton Rouge: Louisiana State University Press, 1973).

36. Robert E. May, *Slavery, Race, and Conquest in the Tropics: Lincoln, Douglas, and the Future of Latin America* (New York: Cambridge University Press, 2013).

37. On the relationship between manhood and expansionism, see Amy S. Greenberg, *Manifest Manhood and the Antebellum American Empire* (New York: Cambridge University Press, 2005).

38. On the role of race in Manifest Destiny, see Reginald Horsman, *Race and Manifest Destiny: The Origins of American Racial Anglo-Saxonism* (Cambridge, MA: Harvard University Press, 1981).

39. Greenberg, *Manifest Destiny and American Territorial Expansion,* 17, 69–71.

40. Greenberg, *Manifest Manhood,* 7–9.

41. Greenberg, *Manifest Destiny and American Territorial Expansion,* 18; John Mack Faragher, *Women and Men on the Overland Trail,* rev. ed. (New Haven, CT: Yale University Press, 2001), 20–22.

42. "The Great War Meeting at Tammany Hall: Tremendous Gathering of the People—Shall the Whole of Mexico Be Annexed?," *New York Herald,* January 30, 1848, 1.

43. Horsman, *Race and Manifest Destiny.*

44. "Uncle Sam's Song to Miss Texas," in *The Rough and Ready Songster* (New York: Nafis and Cornish, 1848), 54–55.

45. On "chivalry," see Nancy Isenberg, *Sex and Citizenship in Antebellum America* (Chapel Hill: University of North Carolina Press, 1998), 141–47.

46. Carol and Thomas Christensen, *The U.S.–Mexican War* (San Francisco: Bay Books, 1998), v.

47. Ralph Waldo Emerson, *The Journals and Miscellaneous Notebooks of Ralph Waldo Emerson,* vol. 9, *1843–1847,* ed. Ralph H. Orth and Alfred R. Ferguson (Cambridge, MA: Harvard University Press, 1971), 74.

48. Robert E. May, *Manifest Destiny's Underworld: Filibustering in Antebellum America* (Chapel Hill: University of North Carolina Press, 2004), 18, 52, 91–101; William Prince diary, September 22, 1851, Beinecke Rare Book and Manuscript Library, Yale University, New Haven, CT; "Territorial Aggrandizement," *United States Democratic Review* 17 (October 1845): 247; "The Line of Political Knowledge," *United States Democratic Review* 32 (March

1853): 280; "Abrogation of the Clayton-Bulwer Treaty," *United States Democratic Review* 42 (December 1858): 442. See also "The Monroe Doctrine Versus the Clayton and Bulwer Treaty," *United States Democratic Review* 32 (March 1853): 199.

49. Luis G. Zorilla, *Historia de las relaciones entre México y los Estados Unidos de América, 1800–1958,* 2 vols. (Mexico City: Editorial Porrúa, 1977), 1:368–94; Thomas David Schoonover, *Dollars over Dominion: The Triumph of Liberalism in Mexican–United States Relations, 1861–1867* (Baton Rouge: Louisiana State University Press), 5–6; Albert K. Weinberg, *Manifest Destiny: A Study of Nationalist Expansionism in American History* (1935; repr., Chicago: Quadrangle Books, 1963), 190.

50. Weinberg, *Manifest Destiny,* 201.

51. *The Bewildered Old Woman, Vanity Fair,* January 7, 1860.

52. Polk, *Diary,* 4:355.

THE BACHELOR'S MESS

James Buchanan and the Domestic Politics of Doughfacery in Jacksonian America

THOMAS J. BALCERSKI

During the decade of the 1830s, the Democratic Party of Andrew Jackson and his successor, Martin Van Buren, dominated Washington politics. In both the House of Representatives and the Senate, Jacksonian Democrats held a numerical majority and directed the legislative agenda. Yet the era was rife with political controversies, among them the veto of the recharter of the Second Bank of the United States, the nullification crisis and the Force Bill, the controversy over the reception of abolitionist petitions and the resulting "gag rule," the issuance of the Specie Circular, and the subsequent Panic of 1837. The many arguments over policy and politics precipitated the rise of a permanent opposition party—the Whigs. "America had known parties before," historian Harry Watson has observed, "but the earlier competition between Federalists and Democratic-Republicans had been amateurish compared to the rivalry between well-established and increasingly sophisticated organizations that came to dominate virtually all aspects of American politics in the 1830s and 1840s." The Second Party System, born of this bitter stew of political and personal differences, defined the course of electoral politics over the next two decades.[1]

The divisions produced by the legislative contest of the 1830s also shaped the contours of domestic politics in Washington. Through the institution of the congressional boardinghouse, or mess, Democrats forged personal friendships with other politicians that extended beyond the purely political. These "boardinghouse families," as they came to be called, stood in as proxies for the domestic, as well as the affective, needs of congressmen away from families back home. To survive these unusual conditions of domestic life, one historian has argued, most congressmen "essentially lived as bachelors." An unexpected corollary followed from this: since unmarried politicians knew how to navigate the idiosyncrasies of life in bachelor's quarters, lifelong bachelorhood could well prove a political advantage in the Washington boardinghouse. Bachelors, in essence, were ideally suited for the domestic politics of the capital.[2]

The congressional career of James Buchanan of Pennsylvania exemplified this bachelor's advantage. Without the burdens of a family, Buchanan freely formed political and personal friendships with like-minded politicians, relationships that often intensified through the medium of the Washington boardinghouse. Once elected to the US Senate in 1834, he organized a boardinghouse group based on one salient personal commonality: bachelorhood. In this vein, Buchanan declared to a Pennsylvania friend, "I shall be delighted to welcome you to the Bachelor's mess." The invitation, though seemingly ordinary, revealed more than a passing pronunciation—the identification of the "Bachelor's mess" supports the longstanding view that "mess group affiliation was recognized as a mark of identification among legislators," so much so that "some boardinghouse groups were given distinctive names." But in the charged climate of 1830s Washington, Buchanan's group practiced a noticeably partisan and sectional form of politics that promoted Jacksonian aims and protected the institution of slavery from abolitionist assaults. For the new Pennsylvania senator, participation in the Bachelor's mess also meant embracing a new status: a "northern man with southern principles."[3]

The study of Buchanan's congressional years has long noted his role as a foot soldier in the cause of the Jacksonian Democracy. Historians and biographers have highlighted how Buchanan promoted a higher tariff to protect domestic manufacturing, sustained the "gag rule" that banned antislavery petitions from being accepted by the US Senate, and tried to bridge the growing distance between the sectional wings of the Democ-

James Buchanan of Pennsylvania. Engraving by John Sartain, 1840.
Courtesy Prints and Photographs Division, Library of Congress, Washington, DC.

racy. For this and other actions taken during his Senate years, historians have variously labeled him as "the consummate doughface," as "the most prominent doughface allying with slaveholders," as a "safe candidate" for higher office to southern Democrats, and as part of a generalized southern conspiracy to maintain the "slave power" in the affairs of the federal government. Nevertheless, few have sufficiently explained exactly how or why Buchanan embraced southern principles in the 1830s. As such, political historians have minimized the importance of his associations with southern Democrats in the Bachelor's mess. Biographical studies of Buchanan's congressional years have been naturally more attentive to his various congressional associates, but none has fully explored the connections between his publicly stated political views and his intimate personal friendships with southern Democrats—or for that matter, the process by which he became a doughface.[4]

The lack of scholarly attention to the domestic politics of Buchanan's congressional years derives from the difficult task of reconstructing his intimate personal and political relationships forged with fellow Democrats in the Washington boardinghouse. Less troubled by the conjectural work required by such a topic, the writer John Updike framed how historians understand Buchanan's personal life. In his novel *Memories of the Ford Administration* (1992), Updike detailed the domestic life shared by Buchanan and his messmates, surmising at one point that they enjoyed "the leathery, cluttered, cozy, tobacco-scented bachelor quarters where, emerging from separate bedrooms and returning from divided duties, they often shared morning bacon and evening claret." While Updike ultimately hedged on the question of Buchanan's sexuality, he nonetheless highlighted his failure to marry and by extension questioned the nature of the friendships with his congressional messmates. Subsequent Buchanan biographers have followed suit, assuming, whether implicitly or explicitly, that his bachelorhood represented, at best, a personal failing of manhood and, at worst, a coded sexual preference for men. Other critics have gone further, asserting definitively "Buchanan's homosexuality" or, more judiciously, that Buchanan was "likely gay." The controversy continues apace in popular and scholarly circles and is unlikely to reach a definitive resolution.[5]

This essay takes a different approach and conceives the domestic politics of James Buchanan's Bachelor's mess as constituting a powerful partisan strategy in Jacksonian America. A multitude of Democratic congressmen joined the mess during these years, including William Rufus King of Alabama, Edward Lucas of Virginia, Bedford Brown of North Carolina, Robert C. Nicholas of Louisiana, and John P. King of Georgia. Dominated by southern Democrats, the Bachelor's mess cannot be understood outside of the sectional politics of the early Second Party System. Indeed, the informal group remained most politically potent while the Democratic Party held power in Washington during the 1830s. Its members collectively controlled two major Senate committees: Buchanan chaired Foreign Relations, of which both William Rufus King and John Pendleton King had been members, and William Rufus King was the chair of Commerce. Nicholas and Buchanan both sat on the Senate Finance Committee, while William Rufus King served as presi-

William Rufus King of Alabama. Portrait by unknown artist, ca. 1837.
Courtesy Selma Dallas County Public Library, Selma, Alabama.

dent pro tempore for six years. In an era when the US Senate numbered anywhere between forty-eight and fifty-two members, Buchanan's group represented a critical voting bloc.

But more than politics animated the personal relationships within this group of bachelors. The messmates also developed intimate friendships with one another that sustained them through difficult political and personal episodes and that outlasted their congressional service. Moreover, the relationships formed in the mess were representative of the kinds of intimate male friendships that blossomed among nineteenth-century politicians in Washington. Taken together, they illustrate the domestic politics of boardinghouse groups, the nature of intimate male friendships among politicians, and the powerful political effect of bachelorhood in Jacksonian America.[6]

Bachelors were not uncommon in Jacksonian America. Several factors help explain this: the elimination of bachelor taxes in frontier communities, nascent bachelor subcultures in cities, and a growing societal acceptance of the unmarried. Although historians have proclaimed the late nineteenth century to be an "age of the bachelor," the roots of its normalization and mainstream acceptance may be traced to earlier decades. In his study of bachelorhood in the early American republic, one scholar found that by midcentury, new developments in American society had "created the bachelor as a legal identity, a cultural ideal, and a lived experience" and made him "a permanent fixture of American society." By the 1830s, such men were publishing newspapers, forming their own social clubs, and participating in an emergent literary sensibility. Henry David Thoreau embraced his moniker as "America's bachelor uncle." Bachelors, it seemed, were everywhere.[7]

Yet among congressional officeholders in early America, marriage held a widely acknowledged political value. The wife of a politician aided her husband in uncountable ways, from the more traditional management of the household to the arrangement of social gatherings for her husband's political friends and their respective families. In its most overtly political form, such marriages approached a powerful cross-collaboration between an elected husband and his unelected wife. In the Washington of the 1830s, the marital partnership of Congressman James K. Polk of Tennessee and his wife, Sarah Childress Polk, presented one such power couple, while the continued presence of the indomitable Dolley Madison reminded the unmarried politician of the immense practical advantages of a socially adept and politically active partner. Toward that end, the newly arrived unmarried congressman received additional attention from capital society that gravitated him toward the altar. In some cases these men became prime targets to assume the related social obligations, and given that the work of politicians required their attendance at receptions, balls, and parties of all kinds during a congressional session, the occasions for such escorts were numerous. Through the fulfillment of these social obligations, an entering congressional bachelor might well conclude his years of service as a married man.[8]

Table 2.1. Washington Boardinghouses of James Buchanan, 1834–1841

Congressional Session	Boardinghouse and Messmates
23rd Congress, 2nd Session (Dec. 1, 1834–Mar. 3, 1835)	*Saunder's, E St., near the General Post Office* Bedford Brown (S), NC James Buchanan (S), PA William R. King (S), AL Edward Lucas, VA
24th Congress, 1st Session (Dec. 7, 1835–July 4, 1836)	*Mr. Saunders, 7th St.* William R. King (S), AL Edward Lucas, VA *Mr. Guest, 10th St., private residence near F St.* James Buchanan (S), PA
24th Congress, 2nd Session (Dec. 7, 1836–Mar. 3, 1837)	*Mrs. Galvin, No. 2, C St.* James Buchanan (S), PA William R. King (S), AL Robert C. Nicholas (S), LA Edward Lucas, VA
25th Congress, 1st Session (Sept. 4–Oct. 16, 1837)	*Mr. Ironside, 7th St.* James Buchanan (S), PA William R. King (S), AL John P. King (S), GA Robert C. Nicholas (S), LA
25th Congress, 2nd Session (Dec. 4, 1837–July 9, 1838)	*Mr. Ironside, 7th St.* James Buchanan (S), PA William R. King (S), AL Robert C. Nicholas (S), LA
25th Congress, 3rd Session (Dec. 3, 1838–Mar. 3, 1839)	*Mrs. Ironside, E St., between 9th and 10th Sts.* James Buchanan (S), PA Robert C. Nicholas (S), LA William R. King (S), AL
26th Congress, 1st Session (Dec. 2, 1839–July 21, 1840)	*Mrs. Ironside, E St., between 9th and 10th Sts.* James Buchanan (S), PA William R. King (S), AL Robert C. Nicholas (S), LA William S. Ramsey, PA

Table 2.1. *continued*

Congressional Session	Boardinghouse and Messmates
26th Congress, 2nd Session	*Mrs. Ironside, E St., between 9th and 10th Sts.*
(Dec. 7, 1840–Mar. 3, 1841)	James Buchanan (S), PA
	William R. King (S), AL
	Robert C. Nicholas (S), LA
	William H. Roane (S), VA

Source: Perry M. Goldman and James S. Young, eds., *The United States Congressional Directories, 1789–1840* (New York: Columbia University Press, 1973).

Nevertheless, marriage had proven a highly divisive issue in the partisan wars of the era. During the campaign preceding the 1828 election, nothing had enraged Andrew Jackson more than attacks against the legitimacy of his marriage to Rachel Donelson Robards. Her untimely death in late 1828 embittered Jackson even further against his enemies and likely reinforced his inherent tendency to defend women subjected to political attacks. The marriage of his secretary of war, John Eaton, to the much younger widow Margaret "Peggy" O'Neal—under circumstances similar to Jackson's own marriage—caused the new president to defend the virtue of the younger woman. The ensuing "Petticoat Affair," in which cabinet wives refused to accept the new Mrs. Eaton into polite society, caused one of the greatest internal controversies of the Jackson administration.[9]

The discord of the Petticoat Affair affected the domestic politics of the boardinghouse families. Prior to Buchanan's arrival in Washington, William Rufus King had replaced messmates Willie P. Mangum of North Carolina and John Bell of Tennessee (who both turned Whig) with Democrats Bedford Brown of North Carolina and Edward Lucas of Virginia. In the ensuing months, the group of King, Brown, and Lucas sought to identify an additional messmate whose Jacksonian principles were unwavering and, just as important, whose personal qualities made him a congenial social companion. In 1834 they turned to Buchanan and relocated to Saunder's boardinghouse on E Street, near the post office. For his part, Buchanan well knew the practical necessity, political potential, and personal benefits of belonging to a partisan congressional mess. While a member of the House of Representatives (1821–31), he had lived exclusively with fellow Federalists and then, after his conversion to the Democratic Party, with fellow Democrats from the middle Atlantic region. Now at Saunder's, all four messmates were staunch Jacksonians, and significantly, three of the four were also bachelors.[10]

The bachelor Democrats who gathered together at Saunder's boardinghouse shared much in common politically, even as they differed significantly in their personality and appearance. Born in 1786 in Sampson County, North Carolina, near Fayetteville, William Rufus King had attended the University of North Carolina and soon after advanced as a public man. Elected to the state house of commons in 1808, he was then sent to the US House of Representatives in 1811, one of the youngest men ever chosen for that body. A fierce War Hawk during the War of 1812, he subsequently served abroad as secretary to the foreign legations in Italy and Russia. Upon his return to the United States, King headed southwest as part of the great cotton boom and settled in the new town of Selma, Alabama. First chosen for the US Senate in 1819, he served continuously until his appointment as minister to France by President John Tyler in 1844. Of the group, King may have been the most congenial; the pioneering female journalist Anne Royall reported that the "sweetness of his manners and the generosity of his heart renders him not only the idol of Washington, but of all those who have the honor of his acquaintance." Yet King was still a bachelor, a fact noted in another contemporary publication that described him as an "old gentleman, a bachelor, who wears a prim wig, and is precise in his manners, as well as his notions of legislation." By the time that he first formed a mess with Buchanan in 1834, King was already firmly established as both an old-fashioned bachelor and a spokesman for national unity in the Democratic Party.[11]

By contrast, Senator Bedford Brown of North Carolina presented a roughhewn appearance and embodied the frontier in his manners. The two southerners had much in common: King and Brown originally hailed from North Carolina; both had attended the University of North Carolina; and both achieved success from a young age in politics. But in 1816 Brown married and began his career as a planter-politician and father of seven. Although he was interested primarily in local issues, a vacancy occasioned his selection for the US Senate in 1829. Reflecting on the turbulent decade of the 1830s, Martin Van Buren noted that Brown was "an old and constant friend of Genl. Jackson and my own, one on whom as much as any other man, we relied for support of our respective administrations in the Senate." A contemporary described him as possessing a "dignity . . . so studied that it was a little pompous." However seemingly incompatible his personality with his bachelor messmate, Brown displayed an unwavering commitment to Jacksonian principles and a fierce loyalty to his political and personal friends.[12]

If King and Brown represented one discrete pair entering the new arrangement at Saunder's boardinghouse, Lucas and Buchanan formed the other. Born in Shepherdstown, Virginia (today West Virginia), in 1790, Edward Lucas, like Buchanan, graduated from Dickinson College. Along with his college friend, Lucas had likewise "got[ten] into drinking bouts sufficiently rowdy to come to the attention of the faculty." After graduation, Lucas returned home and fought during the War of 1812. In time, he established a prosperous legal and mercantile career. Next came stints in the Virginia House of Delegates, followed by election in 1833 to the US House of Representatives, which made him the only such member of that body in the new mess. Regardless, Lucas was an ardent Jacksonian, and he was forty-three and unmarried upon his entry to Washington society.[13]

Of the foursome lodging at Saunder's boardinghouse, James Buchanan seems to have been the most personally agreeable. Washington contemporaries found that the forty-two-year-old Buchanan presented a physically appealing personage, with polished manners and an instantly likable personality. Typical was a description by Democratic congressman John Fairfield of Maine, who called Buchanan "a great favorite of mine." He wrote, "I liked him the first time I put my eye upon him." Buchanan still cut an attractive figure, and Fairfield found him to be "rather tall & large—light complexion—and a fine, open, manly, ingenious face. . . . [H]is voice is clear, rather strong and very pleasant." The senator was witty and possessed a fine public-speaking voice. Yet Buchanan was also beginning the transition into middle age, during which time he received his iconic nickname "Old Buck." A Philadelphia newspaper reported that he was "a bachelor, probably on the wrong side of forty"; in fact, Buchanan was only thirty-nine when that article was printed. In the years ahead, the signs of this transformation became more apparent: his blonde hair began to turn white, his waistline increased, and his old-fashioned style of dress looked increasingly out of date. "He is a bachelor, and always wears a white cravat," a reporter noted dryly.[14]

How had the mess arrangement come to pass? Of the new quartet, the connection between William Rufus King and Brown was longstanding—they were already messmates from the previous session. But did Buchanan and King already know one another? In the most basic sense, the answer is yes, since they had served in opposite chambers in the Capitol from 1822 to 1831 and almost certainly met in passing. The two might also have met each other socially during their overlapping years in Washington, perhaps at one of the many formal receptions hosted by First Lady Elizabeth Kortright Monroe or at a ball arranged by Louisa Catherine Adams. Neither man mentioned the other in his correspondence, however, prior to the formation of this mess. Even if the two men had known one another, the strongest association between Buchanan and his new messmates came through his old college classmate and intimate friend Lucas. Whatever the specifics, all four messmates shared an unwavering commitment to the Democratic Party.[15]

The Washington world of the Bachelor's mess was in many respects a primitive one. Since Buchanan first arrived in Washington decades earlier, the city had grown in population (from just over twenty-four thousand people, enslaved Africans Americans included, in 1810 to over forty thousand by 1830) and in the number of its buildings (from the "Seven Buildings" of the 1790s to many dozens of structures by the 1830s). Still, one resident reminisced that "the streets were deep with mud in wet weather and thick with dust at other times." Few fashionable neighborhoods existed, though Dolley Madison's drawing room stood out as a center of social life in the young city. That situation began to change in 1837, when larger, more stately residences appeared on C Street (along with the Patent Office, a grand edifice in the neoclassical mold, and the Treasury Building, also of Palladian design). Soon thereafter, new homes were erected on F Street—only recently made into a proper road—near the Executive Mansion, including several permanent dwellings for prominent political figures; John Quincy Adams, the ex-president, resided there as did members of the cabinet. Jacksonian Washington, one historian of the capital observed, "bore the air of a city without driving ambition."[16]

Into the 1840s, boardinghouses most commonly accommodated congressmen while in Washington. For the reasonable rate of around ten dollars a week, individuals could obtain single rooms within a shared house that might contain as many as a dozen other bedrooms, each often furnished with little more than a bed, dresser, and nightstand. In the era before indoor plumbing, the boarders relied on servants, often enslaved African Americans, to meet the everyday needs of ablution. Yet there was an essential communal element to the boardinghouse. The meals, the most important of which was dinner, were served on average between three and six o'clock, with a menu that featured an assortment of meats, fish, berries, and pies. Alcoholic beverages such as wine, brandy, and madeira commonly accompanied meals, though boarders provided these items at their own expense. The messmates commonly congregated in the shared parlors, especially around the fireplaces in the colder months, to discuss politics and the social doings in the capital. Since many boardinghouses featured the mixed company of men and women, such gatherings could be quite formal. From these parlors, social calls were made and returned around the Capitol Hill neighborhood. The Washington boardinghouse differed from those elsewhere in that its inhabitants were the country's leading elected officials.[17]

The domestic confines of the Washington boardinghouse offered the opportunity to forge intimate friendships with other middle-aged men. Most typically, such male relationships formed in youth, usually in the all-male spaces of college or the sphere of fraternal associations. Rising marital prospects often precipitated a decline in the intimacy of these friendships. Yet the development of intimate male friendships among older bachelors faced comparatively few obstacles. The college dormitory–like atmosphere of the boardinghouses provided an important setting for congressmen to find commonalties, often regardless of political party. While such domestic contact did not necessarily lead to the kinds of close friendships formed during youth, a mess that brought together congressmen with similar political views and personal temperament afforded the opportunity to develop such relationships. The combination of Democrats and bachelors at Saunder's boardinghouse produced just such a congeries of intimate companionship.[18]

With his mess established and the Democracy squarely in control of Congress, Buchanan turned to the state of affairs in late 1834. The tariff debates and the bank wars of the prior years had passed, but new questions about fiscal policy, slavery, and foreign relationships lay ahead. When the short session of the lame-duck Congress ended in March 1835, the messmates at Saunder's boardinghouse returned to their respective states. When the newly elected Twenty-Fourth Congress met for its first session in December 1835, the messmates went their separate ways: Brown and Buchanan tried to join a mess with Democratic senator Garret Wall of New Jersey at Mr. Birth's boardinghouse on Third Street, while William Rufus King and Lucas wanted to return to Saunder's boardinghouse. The group was not necessarily committed to resuming its previous arrangement.[19]

Personal considerations dictated the dissolution of the original group of Democratic messmates. Buchanan considered Wall, with whom he had become friendly years earlier, to be among the most intimate of his political and personal friends. As he recounted many years later to Wall's son, "With the exception of Col. [William Rufus] King, I never was in terms of more intimate personal & political association with any friend than with your excellent father." But Buchanan encountered a stumbling block in making the arrangements at Birth's boardinghouse: Wall wanted to bring his wife and children with him, and they could not find an appropriate establishment to house the enlarged group. Just before the new congressional session, Buchanan received a letter from John Pendleton King of Georgia "urging me to unite with King of Alabama, Brown of N. Carolina, & himself in forming a mess." Yet such was not Buchanan's desire, as he ruefully admitted to Wall: "The truth is I had wished to form such a mess & to include yourself; but I could not bring them to act specifically on the subject." In the same letter he further outlined his reasons for forming a smaller group, referring to his early years in the House: "I cannot live in a large mess & would reluctantly go into one where there were members of the House." His indecision continued for weeks, forcing him to secure a private residence.[20]

With another session of Congress approaching in December 1836, Buchanan once again attempted to arrange lodgings in the capital. Affairs seemed unsettled through the fall. Subsequently, William Rufus King asked Buchanan to "oblige me by securing a residence for *us*, I cannot say what are [John Pendleton] King's arrangements. I have requested him to write you, and say whether he will live with gentlemen or [bring] himself as usual." Buchanan acceded to William Rufus King's request, for he wrote a Lancaster confidant, "I have engaged to take lodgings for Mr. King the President pro tempore of the Senate & myself." The October 1836 letter from King to Buchanan—the earliest to survive between the two men—suggests that their friendship had grown more personally intimate over the prior year. In an earlier letter (now missing), Buchanan had written King about an "annual pilgrimage" to the mountain resort at Bedford Springs, where Pennsylvania politicians gathered en masse to discuss politics and enjoy a "gay & agreeable time." In response King teased his messmate about a flirtation with one unnamed young woman: "Miss L—, the romping rosy girl you saw at the springs, who would probably have been fortunate had some kind friend whispered in her ear, 'that old Bachelors are mighty uncertain.'" The mention of the flirtation with "Miss L—" was unusual for Buchanan, for he usually confined his discussion of such matters in letters to women. But with King, he had become comfortable enough to share stories of his romantic pursuits.[21]

To start the second congressional session in December 1836, the trio of James Buchanan, William Rufus King, and Edward Lucas reunited at Mrs. Galvin's boardinghouse on C Street. In addition, Robert Carter "Cary" Nicholas, a sugar planter from Terrebonne Parish, Louisiana, joined the mess. Like Lucas, Nicholas originally hailed from a wealthy Virginia family. An 1803 graduate of the College of William and Mary, the slaveholding Nicholas attempted to make his fortune in Virginia but eventually decided to move farther south in 1820. Like the other men in the mess, he traveled abroad and also maintained intimate personal friendships with political actors. More significantly, Nicholas was, at age forty-three, still a bachelor.[22]

The addition of Nicholas to the group of Buchanan, King, and Lucas meant that the mess at Galvin's boardinghouse now consisted entirely of bachelors. The incipient group of the unmarried did not last long—Lucas had not stood for reelection in 1836 and returned to Virginia in March 1837. The remaining three bachelors—Buchanan, King, and Nicholas—

Robert Carter Nicholas of Louisiana. Engraving by Charles Fenderich, 1840.
Courtesy Prints and Photographs Division, Library of Congress, Washington, DC.

were determined to keep their mess at the same size. Accordingly, they reluctantly turned to Democratic senator John Pendleton King of Georgia
to fill the fourth room. Born in 1799, John Pendleton King was in many
ways the opposite of William Rufus King. A Kentuckian by birth, John
Pendleton King was an ambitious lawyer and fiercely pro-development
businessman. For his part, Buchanan apparently got along well with King
of Georgia, and indeed he had received a warm invitation to travel south
in a letter addressed to "Dear Buck."[23]

The two Kings did not always agree on every matter related to their
domestic arrangements. King of Alabama referred to King of Georgia
as "that strange fellow." Nevertheless, John Pendleton King joined the
mess—now under the care of Mrs. Ironside on Seventh Street—for the
special session of Congress in September 1837. Unlike his bachelor messmates, King of Georgia did not intend to remain in the US Senate, nor

for that matter to remain unmarried. When the short first session of Congress ended in October, he resigned his seat to pursue his interests in the emerging railroad industry. Eventually, he was replaced in the mess by William Henry Roane of Virginia.[24]

As the residences of the Bachelor's mess changed, the pair of Buchanan and William Rufus King grew increasingly intimate, and a notably playful tone entered their correspondence. In June 1837 King asked Buchanan—who was once more in the midst of a fleeting courtship with one or the other of his Lancaster neighbors—with half-serious indignation: "Are you so engrossed by the aspirations of ambition, or the hopes, and anxieties of love, that friendship can find no abiding place in your heart? Or have you been standing on your dignity; and waiting to receive the first card?" Though they had not known each other for very long, their friendship had expanded to include conversations about romantic pursuits. King had good reason to be upset with Buchanan's silence— back in Alabama, he had suffered a near-fatal carriage accident. What excuse did Buchanan have? Accordingly, he closed the letter with a terse salutation: "I hope to see you in September, till then farewell." Buchanan certainly deserved the rebuke, for while he was a dedicated correspondent with others, he habitually disregarded the need to write. Nevertheless, he continued the pattern of epistolary neglect in the years ahead, often causing much consternation on King's part.[25]

Following the end of the special congressional session in October 1837, Buchanan returned to Lancaster, where in late November he welcomed William Rufus King. This initial "flying visit" lasted less than a full day and made local Democratic citizens feel left out. "As soon as our Democratic citizens learned that he was amongst us, they immediately made arrangements for offering him a public dinner," Editor John W. Forney of the pro-Buchanan *Lancaster Intelligencer* reported, "but, much to their disappointment, they were prevented from tendering him this honor by his unexpected departure." In contrast, the anti-Buchanan *Lancaster Examiner and Democratic Herald* criticized King's visit as evidence of an underlying conspiracy between the two men. "During Mr. King's visit to this place, a year or two ago," Editor Robert W. Middleton later claimed, "Mr. Buchanan paid the greatest attention to him, and has ever since been using his influence in his behalf." The intensely partisan climate likely accounted for the discrete nature of the visit.[26]

Back in Washington, the loss of John Pendleton King had reduced the Bachelor's mess to Buchanan, William Rufus King, and Nicholas. The social dynamics also shifted, as Nicholas quickly became a favorite of both Buchanan and King. The two southerners, King and Nicholas, who served together on the Committee on the District of Columbia, often dined together with other Senate colleagues, sometimes without Buchanan's knowledge. In May 1838, for example, Buchanan learned from his sometimes drinking companion Daniel Webster that the Massachusetts senator had "asked [Mr. Nicholas] & Mr. King to dine with me on *Thursday*" and that he hoped "for the pleasure of your company at the same time." Buchanan politely accepted the invitation.[27]

On other occasions, however, Buchanan and Nicholas operated without King. In June 1838 the pair traveled to Charlottesville, Virginia, where they visited with Thomas Jefferson Randolph, grandson of the former president, for nearly a week. Then, too, the messmates operated independently of one another. Two months after his trip to Charlottesville, Nicholas could be found vacationing alongside President Van Buren, members of the cabinet, and numerous other congressmen at the White Sulphur Springs resort in the Virginia Springs region of the state. The following summer King joined Nicholas at White Sulphur Springs, where the pair mingled with other members of elite society in taking the mineral waters and enjoying the pleasant company. Through this kind of intermingling outside the capital, the members of the Bachelor's mess fused together the personal and political aspects of their lives.[28]

As the Democratic senators faced the many problems affecting the country, they increasingly spoke out on the Senate floor. Of the group, the more politically ambitious Buchanan and the highly respected King began to position themselves as the last generation of national figures capable of uniting the Democratic Party. In 1837 King declared the Senate to be "the great conservative body of this republic," where the "demon of faction should find no abiding place." Buchanan concurred: "This body is truly the conservative body of the country, and we are not to be deterred, through fear of giving offence, from marching forward in the course of our duty." The two men were building their senatorial reputations as respected and influential national figures.[29]

Related to the growing sectional divide, the bachelor messmates found common cause to oppose abolitionists' petitions. In January 1836 Whig senator Thomas Morris of Ohio introduced two such antislavery petitions to the Senate. Earlier in the House, James Henry Hammond of South Carolina had proposed a strict "gag rule" on accepting such documents. Then, Senator John C. Calhoun moved to proceed in a similar fashion regarding a petition to abolish slavery in the District of Columbia. After a brief but heated series of exchanges, the subject was postponed on Buchanan's motion. The Senate continued debating the antislavery petitions, and each time Buchanan opposed their reception. At first he moved to table the motion; later, he proposed that the Senate "receive and reject," a procedural move used until 1850. Buchanan believed that "the only mode of avoiding everlasting debate" was to avoid reading antislavery petitions.[30]

As president pro tempore of the Senate, William Rufus King was pleased with his messmate's course of action and temporarily left his presiding seat to urge his fellow senators to moderate their petitions and, by extension, to concur with Buchanan. "The course proposed by the Senator from Pennsylvania . . . would, if adopted, be the most decisive that could be pursued," he said in a rare speech on March 3, 1836. A reporter noted that King was almost too embarrassed to add anything more to the "able argument . . . so strongly and clearly enforced by his friend from Pennsylvania." The Alabama senator agreed with Buchanan on every point, adding that slaves were "well-fed, well-clothed, happy, and contented." Slavery, he insisted, must be forever protected. Undoubtedly, Buchanan had taken this point to heart. A few days later he joined King in celebrating their Senate victory over dinner, with South Carolina senators Calhoun and William C. Preston, at the residence of Mahlon Dickerson, secretary of the navy (and yet another resident bachelor of the capital city).[31]

In the winter months of early 1837, new petitions to abolish slavery in the District of Columbia continued to inflame Congress. Although he had previously favored receiving antislavery petitions from his own constituents in Pennsylvania, Buchanan opposed receiving those for abolition in the district. In fact, Buchanan declared himself "never better satisfied with his own course" on the slavery question because he "deprecated a renewed discussion of the question, which would only tend to keep up the excitement in the South and in the North, without any countervailing advantage." Nevertheless, Buchanan and King tried to block a resolution promoted by Calhoun against further "intermeddling with slavery" in the district. Buchanan hoped that his earlier resolutions might serve as a "platform for the friends of the South in the Northern States, on which they might stand and defend themselves against the assaults of the Abolitionists; and that we of the North would have gone further than we had done . . . had it not been from a dread of public opinion at home." By the late 1830s, he recognized that the politically sensitive slavery question had become too important to leave to politics as usual.[32]

Still, Buchanan's support of the gag rule has often suggested that he had always been a committed northern doughface. But the associations with his southern messmates had proven critical in convincing him of the necessity to remove slavery from debate in the Senate. More so than in his previous domestic arrangements, Buchanan's intimate associations with southerners brought him into direct contact with men whose political and personal convictions about the issue superseded his own ambivalent position on the peculiar institution. As such, the topic constantly surfaced among the messmates. At one point, William Rufus King warned Buchanan that if northern abolitionists continued in their course to end slavery, "then we will separate from them." Buchanan's Lancaster associate Thomas Elder thundered in reply, "let them withdraw and wade in blood before six months"; as always, Buchanan took a more cautious approach.[33]

As with so many aspects of his life, Buchanan's motivations to support the gag rule mixed political and personal motives. On the political front, he needed southern allies if he ever hoped to move beyond his status as Pennsylvania's favorite son and become a national candidate for his party's presidential nomination. Much as Van Buren had done before him, Buchanan hoped to present himself as a safe northern man in a party largely dominated by southern interests and larger-than-life southern politicians. But his views of slavery were shaped in more intimate ways. In the Bachelor's mess African Americans, both enslaved and free, enabled the cozy domestic arrangement. Moreover, Buchanan watched as King purchased a trio of enslaved African Americans, including a new personal valet or manservant named John Bell. From these exposures to

African Americans in the boardinghouse, the institution of slavery must have carried a personal face to Buchanan.[34]

Buchanan also encountered the slave system in other aspects of his personal life. In addition to his early interactions with his nurse, Hannah, in 1835, Buchanan purchased the freedom of Daphne Cook, age twenty-two, and her daughter Ann Cook, age five, doing so to avoid the embarrassment that must have resulted from the public knowledge that one of his family members owned slaves. Accordingly, he arranged to indenture Daphne and Ann, as provided by the manumission laws of Pennsylvania. As an added benefit to Buchanan, the Cooks performed household work at his Lancaster home. Thus, he regularly associated with both enslaved and free African Americans, all of whom served in household capacities. As such, his peculiar domestic arrangements with the southern slaveholders of the Bachelor's mess were not out of character.[35]

Much as Buchanan's obeisance for the slave system intensified through his years in the US Senate, he began to modify his views on the economic questions of the day to align them with the emerging Jacksonian orthodoxy. Even more so than the slavery question, the financial health of the nation preoccupied Congress during the summer of 1837. As Buchanan vacationed in the mountains of western Pennsylvania and King in the Virginia springs, the nation entered a severe depression. Known as the Panic of 1837, the crisis was precipitated when the Jackson administration withdrew federal funds from the Second Bank of the United States (BUS) and deposited them into various regional banks, which came to be known as "pet banks." Jackson's proclamation of the "Specie Circular," which mandated the payment of gold in the sale of public land, only worsened the monetary crisis. In response, President Van Buren proposed a sub-treasury, or independent treasury, which placed the task of funding the federal government in the hands of state-level banks, and took the unprecedented step to call Congress into an emergency session to commence in early September.[36]

As thoroughgoing administration Democrats, Buchanan and William Rufus King declared themselves publicly for the president's plan. Yet when both men returned home that summer, they found local conditions deteriorating. The withdrawal of the federal deposits from the BUS had "done us much mischief," King lamented to Buchanan. To Asbury Dickens of North Carolina, King likewise reported that the removal of the federal deposits, "once considered a master stroke of policy . . . , is now openly denounced." While King had publicly supported Jackson's decision, he now blamed Van Buren for following "a mistaken delicacy towards his predecessor" and thus failing to modify the government's policy. For his part, Buchanan faced an angry electorate, one far more connected to the financial interests than King's more agrarian constituency. While Buchanan privately blamed Van Buren for acquiescing to the "bidding of the New York Merchants," he publicly joined King in supporting the president.[37]

Anxiety over the economy continued to worsen during the summer of 1837. Buchanan determined to deliver a speech in favor of the sub-treasury plan, which he did before the full Senate on September 29. In this oration, considered "one of the best speeches of his life," Buchanan warned of a "stimulus of excessive banking" and again that the "banks are all-powerful." As the presiding officer, William Rufus King avoided making a public address on the question, but he moved along the debate where possible and consistently voted in favor of the sub-treasury plan. After weeks of charged debate, the Senate passed the Independent Treasury Bill in 1837, but the House ultimately did not agree to its provisions for another three years. For their continued support of the plan, the *Boston Courier* declared Buchanan and King to be "at the head . . . of the more moderate friends of the Administration."[38]

The moderate tendencies of the bachelor messmates were mutually reinforcing. From Buchanan's first Senate vote on a minor internal improvement matter back in January 1835, he had voted in nearly the same way as his various messmates. Among the most important of these votes was the expunging resolution of an earlier censure passed by the Senate against Andrew Jackson in March 1834. The resolution was first introduced by William Rufus King in January 1835 and finally taken to a vote in January 1837. Mutual support of other bills followed: the Distribution Act of February 1836, which allocated surplus funds from tariff duties to the states; the gag rule on the reception of abolitionist petitions during 1836 and 1837; and the creation of a sub-treasury system in 1837 to replace the BUS.[39]

Table 2.2. Percentage Correlation of Roll Call Votes
among James Buchanan with Senators in the Bachelor's Mess,
23rd Congress to 26th Congress (1834–1841)

	23rd Congress (1834–1835)	24th Congress (1835–1836)	25th Congress (1837–1839)	26th Congress (1839–1841)	Total Average % Correlation by Messmate (weighted)
William Rufus King	80.0%	78.4%	87.4%	84.5%	84.2%
Bedford Brown	75.8%	n/a	n/a	n/a	75.8%
Robert Carter Nicholas	n/a	83.5%	83.6%	75.6%	80.9%
John Pendleton King	n/a	n/a	88.0%	n/a	88.0%
William Henry Roane	n/a	n/a	n/a	83.3%	83.3%
Total Average by Session (weighted)	77.9%	81.0%	85.6%	80.6%	

Methodology: I tabulated the total number of "yes" and "no" roll-call votes of each messmate and correlated them to the votes of James Buchanan (excluding abstentions by one or both of the senators). I also tabulated the percentage of votes exactly in common (either "yes" or "no" votes), and likewise those during which Buchanan was not a messmate (indicated by "n/a"). For the total average by messmate, I weighted the average across all relevant sessions (23rd–26th Congresses). For the total average by session, I weighted the average for all the relevant members of the mess. Thus, the total averages reveal both how messmates voted with Buchanan in a given congressional session and how they voted with him across the period of living together as messmates.

Source: Keith T. Poole, NOMINATE Roll Call Data (revised from Interuniversity Consortium for Political and Social Research data set), http://www.voteview.com.

In addition to his votes on these landmark bills, Buchanan frequently voted in alignment with his various messmates on other issues. A multi-year roll-call analysis from 1834 to 1841 reveals that he accorded with his messmates, and particularly with William Rufus King, on approximately four out of every five votes (barring abstentions and missed votes). The two men did occasionally disagree on issues reflective of their different cultural origins and constituencies. For example, King consistently voted in favor of distributing federal lands, while Buchanan voted against such measures. Likewise, Buchanan supported Revolutionary War widow-pension applications and approved additional allocations to expand the collections of the Library of Congress, including the purchase of the public papers from the estate of James Madison, while King voted against these expenditures. These differences aside, Buchanan had undeniably changed from a pro-tariff, pro-bank Federalist to a proslavery, anti-bank Jacksonian populist. Similarly, King's alignment with Buchanan widened his purview from a strictly sectional approach to encompass a more wholly national, albeit strictly partisan, view of issues.[40]

Of course, the relationships formed by its various members did not necessarily determine the outcome of voting behaviors. But as their many concurring votes suggest, the various members were remarkably consistent in their voting patterns. If the Jacksonian Democrats who joined the Bachelor's mess held largely preformed political opinions, their experience living together hardened those views in the partisan climate of the 1830s. The setting provided an opportunity for members, as King wrote to Buchanan, to "unite" together around those very issues and to plot their legislative agenda. In time the Bachelor's mess functioned as an incubator for partisan unity and, by extension, helped determine the voting behavior of its members, underpinning the Jacksonian legislative program on Capitol Hill.

The Bachelor's mess had been formed by the necessity of finding suitable lodging in the capital, but in time, it had transformed into something more: a boardinghouse group that combined the intensely political aspects of the Jacksonian Democracy with the equally personal aspects of middle-aged bachelors. Bachelorhood had become an unlikely political asset to these men. As the 1830s progressed, the Bachelor's mess emerged as an important voting bloc and provided critical direction to the Jacksonian agenda in the US Senate. Together, the messmates stood united on two of the most divisive issues before the Congress: the petitions calling for the abolition of slavery and the establishment of a sub-treasury system to replace the defunct BUS. Their outspoken support of the Jacksonian agenda helped them forge coalitions with politicians from different wings of the party. By decade's end, the local supporters of Buchanan and King began to advance the two as possible presidential and vice-presidential candidates of their party. The personal union of two bachelors from Pennsylvania and Alabama might yet generate a fertile political bounty.[41]

Of the messmates, Buchanan was by far the most ambitious and ultimately benefited the most from his fraternization with the boardinghouse group. Entering the Senate in 1834, he was but a peripheral player on the Washington political scene—his association with his southern messmates marked his emergence as a power player in the national Democratic Party. As a representative from the border state of Pennsylvania, Buchanan undoubtedly thought his alliance with southern Democrats could promote his chances as a safe northern candidate for the presidency. Moreover, his positions on the questions of slavery, the tariff, and the bank were in line with southern moderates. Along the way he found himself sharing intimate friendships with men who likewise had ventured through life without getting to the altar. In this way Buchanan embodied the qualities of a northern doughface, as much for potential political advancement as for the personal satisfaction of his associations with his southern messmates. The conjoined identities of Jacksonian, bachelor, and doughface proved a potent combination in his quest for higher office.

The example of the Bachelor's mess suggests how a gendered domestic politics operated in the accumulation of political power in the nation's capital. For the first time in national politics, Buchanan and his messmates turned a previously stigmatized societal status into a useful political commonality. As such, this study of domestic politicking of unmarried Jacksonian Democrats modifies not only scholarly conceptions of how powerful partisans operated but also how boardinghouse-group associations and identities sustained those efforts. That the bachelor Buchanan seized the opportunities to form political friendships with southern Democrats suggests the multidirectional force at work: Buchanan was both instrumental in his choice of associations and effectively assumed a doughface identity in the process. Along the way he found himself sharing intimate friendships with men who likewise had ventured through life without marrying. Some would go on to wed, while others would seek political fortunes instead. For Buchanan, the domestic intimacy of the mess also paved a path forward to future electoral power—as an unmarried northern man with southern principles.

NOTES

1. On the major political issues of the Jacksonian period, see the still quite useful summary by David J. Russo, "The Major Political Issues of the Jacksonian Period and the Development of Party Loyalty in Congress, 1830–1840," *Transactions of the American Philosophical Society*, n.s., 62, no. 5 (1972): 3–51. For general overviews of the period, see Richard P. McCormick, *The Second American Party System: Party Formation in the Jacksonian Era* (Chapel Hill: University of North Carolina Press, 1966); Robert V. Remini, *Andrew Jackson and the Course of American Democracy, 1833–1845*, vol. 3 (New York: Harper and Row, 1984); Harry L. Watson, *Liberty and Power: The Politics of Jacksonian America*, 2nd ed. (New York: Hill and Wang 2006); William W. Freehling, *The Road to Disunion*, vol. 1, *Secessionists at Bay, 1776–1854* (New York: Oxford University Press, 1990); Michael F. Holt, *Political Parties and American Political Development from the Age of Jackson to the Age of Lincoln* (Baton Rouge: Louisiana State University Press, 1992); Sean Wilentz, *The Rise of American Democracy: Jefferson to Lincoln* (New York: W. W. Norton, 2005); and Elizabeth R. Varon, *Disunion!: The Coming of the American Civil War, 1789–1859* (Chapel Hill: University of North Carolina Press, 2008).

2. For the landmark study of congressional boardinghouses in the early republican period, see James Sterling Young, *The Washington Community, 1820–1828* (New York: Columbia University Press, 1963). For studies of boardinghouse culture in the early republican period that variously argue with Young, see Allan G. Bogue and Mark P. Marlaire, "Of Mess and Men: The Boardinghouse and Congressional Voting, 1821–1842," *American Journal of Political Science* 19 (May 1975): 207–30; Cynthia D. Earman, "Messing Around: Entertaining and Accommodating Congress, 1800–1830," in *Establishing Congress: The Removal to Washington, D.C., and the Election of 1800*, ed. Kenneth R. Bowling and Donald R. Kennon (Athens: Ohio University Press, 2005): 128–47; Rosemarie Zagarri, "The Family Factor: Congressmen, Turnover, and the Burden of Public Service in the Early American Republic," *Journal of the Early Republic* 33 (Summer 2013): 284–316 (quote, 296–97); and Padraig Riley, "The Lonely Congressmen: Gender and Politics in Early Washington, D.C.," *Journal of the Early Republic* 34 (Summer 2014): 243–73. For the later period, see also Rachel A. Shelden, *Washington Brotherhood: Politics, Social Life, and the Coming of the Civil War* (Chapel Hill: University of North Carolina Press, 2013).

3. James Buchanan to Peter Wager, Jan. 13, 1838, James Buchanan Letters and Documents, New York Public Library; Young, *Washington Community*, 100.

4. For a recent historiographic overview of James Buchanan's congressional career, see Jean H. Baker, "James Buchanan: The Early Political Life," in *Companion to the Antebellum Presidents, 1837–1861*, ed. Joel H. Silbey (Malden, MA: Wiley-Blackwell, 2014), 397–419. For the various historians' quotations about Buchanan, see Leonard L. Richards, *The Slave Power: The Free North and Southern Domination, 1780–1860* (Baton Rouge: Louisiana State University Press, 2000), 197; Nicholas Wood, "'A Sacrifice on the Altar of Slavery': Doughface Politics and Black Disenfranchisement in Pennsylvania, 1837–1838," *Journal of the Early Republic* 31 (Spring 2011): 75–106 (quote, 84); and William J. Cooper, *The South and*

the Politics of Slavery, 1828–1856 (Baton Rouge: Louisiana State University Press, 1978), 257. On the concept of the "slave power," see also James L. Huston, "James Buchanan, the Slavocracy, and the Disruption of the Democratic Party," in Silbey, *Companion to the Antebellum Presidents*, 421–45. For later northern men with southern principles, see also Michael Todd Landis, *Northern Men with Southern Loyalties: The Democratic Party and the Sectional Crisis* (Ithaca, NY: Cornell University Press, 2014). Notable works from Buchanan biographers include Philip G. Auchampaugh, "James Buchanan, the Bachelor of the White House: An Inquiry on the Subject of Feminine Influence in the Life of Our Fifteenth President," *Tyler's Quarterly Historical and Genealogical Magazine* 20 (January 1939): 154–66; and (April 1939): 218–34; Auchampaugh, "James Buchanan, the Squire from Lancaster: The Squire's Home Town," *Pennsylvania Magazine of History and Biography* 55 (1931): 289–300; and 56 (1932): 15–32; and Philip S. Klein, *President James Buchanan: A Biography* (University Park: Pennsylvania State University Press, 1962). For recent scholarship about Buchanan, see Michael J. Birkner, ed., *James Buchanan and the Political Crisis of the 1850s* (Selinsgrove, PA: Susquehanna University Press, 1996); and John W. Quist and Michael J. Birkner, eds., *James Buchanan and the Coming of the Civil War* (Gainesville: University Press of Florida, 2013).

5. John Updike, *Memories of the Ford Administration* (New York: Alfred A. Knopf, 1992), esp. 224–43, 314 (quote, 234). On Updike's novel, see esp. Paul Boyer, "Notes of a Disillusioned Lover: John Updike's 'Memories of the Ford Administration,'" *American Literary History* 13 (Spring 2001): 67–78. For others who extend Updike's analysis and present more controversial views of Buchanan's sexuality, see James W. Loewen, *Lies Across America: What Our Historic Sites Get Wrong* (New York: New Press, 1999), esp. 367–70 (quote, 370); Jean H. Baker, *James Buchanan* (New York: Times Books, 2004); Robert P. Watson, *Affairs of State: The Untold History of Presidential Love, Sex, and Scandal, 1789–1900* (New York: Rowman and Littlefield, 2012), esp. 227–55, 441–45 (quote, 445); and the countless number of articles and websites on the Internet devoted to the topic.

6. On the possibilities of intimate male friendships in this period, see esp. E. Anthony Rotundo, *American Manhood: Transformations in Masculinity from the Revolution to the Modern Era* (New York: Basic Books, 1993); and Richard Godbeer, *The Overflowing of Friendship: Love between Men and the Creation of the American Republic* (Chapel Hill: University of North Carolina Press, 2009). For a further discussion on friendship as a category of analysis among political actors, see Thomas J. Balcerski, "'A Work of Friendship': Nathaniel Hawthorne, Franklin Pierce, and the Politics of Enmity in the Civil War Era," *Journal of Social History* 50, no. 4 (Summer 2017): 655–79.

7. On bachelorhood in the early part of the nineteenth century, two studies are helpful: John G. McCurdy, *Citizen Bachelors: Manhood and the Creation of the United States* (Ithaca, NY: Cornell University Press, 2009), 199 (quote); and Howard P. Chudacoff, *The Age of the Bachelor: Creating an American Subculture* (Princeton, NJ: Princeton University Press, 1999), esp. 21–44. On Cavendish, see James Lees-Milne, *The Bachelor Duke: A Life of William Spencer Cavendish, 6th Duke of Devonshire, 1790–1858* (London: John Murray, 1998). For a prosopographical study of the antebellum Senate that considers marital status, see

Susan Radomsky, "The Social Life of Politics" (PhD diss., University of Chicago, 2005), esp. 469–88.

8. For the part played by the wives of politicians, see esp. Catherine Allgor, *Parlor Politics: In Which the Ladies of Washington Help Build a City and a Government* (Charlottesville: University Press of Virginia, 2000). On Sarah Childress Polk, see Amy S. Greenberg, *Lady First: The World of First Lady Sarah Polk* (New York: Alfred K. Knopf), 2019. On Dolley Madison, see Catherine Allgor, *A Perfect Union: Dolley Madison and the Creation of the American Nation* (New York: Henry Holt, 2006). On the involvement of women more broadly in antebellum politics, though largely focused on the Whig Party, see Elizabeth Varon, *We Mean to Be Counted: White Women and Politics in Antebellum Virginia* (Chapel Hill: University of North Carolina Press, 1998); and Ronald J. Zboray and Mary Saracino Zboray, *Voices without Votes: Women and Politics in Antebellum New England* (Durham: University of New Hampshire Press, 2010).

9. For a broad overview of gendered aspects of the politics in the Jacksonian era, see Nancy Morgan, "'She's as Chaste as a Virgin!': Gender, Political Platforms, and the Second American Party System," in *A Companion to the Era of Andrew Jackson*, ed. Sean P. Adams (Malden, MA: Wiley-Blackwell, 2013), 298–327. On the politicization of the marriage of Andrew Jackson in the election of 1828, see Norma Basch, "Marriage, Morals, and Politics in the Election of 1828," *Journal of American History* 80 (Dec. 1993): 890–918. On the Peggy Eaton affair, see Richard B. Latner, "The Eaton Affair Reconsidered," *Tennessee Historical Quarterly* 36 (Fall 1977): 330–51; John F. Marszalek, *The Petticoat Affair: Manners, Mutiny, and Sex in Andrew Jackson's White House* (Baton Rouge: Louisiana State University Press, 1997); Kirsten E. Wood, "'One Woman So Dangerous to Public Morals': Gender and Power in the Eaton Affair," *Journal of the Early Republic* 17, no. 2 (Summer 1997): 237–75; and Jon Meacham, *American Lion: Andrew Jackson in the White House* (New York: Random House, 2009), esp. 98–114.

10. For the best source of congressional boardinghouses during Buchanan's early years in the Senate, see the underutilized Perry M. Goldman and James S. Young, eds., *The United States Congressional Directories, 1789–1840* (New York: Columbia University Press, 1973), esp. 127, 147, 151, 157–58, 169–70, 183–84, 194–95, 206, 217, 219, 228, 230, and 281.

11. For Anne Royall's description of King, see *Paul Pry*, Aug. 4, 1832. For the characterization of King as an "old bachelor," see "Letters from Washington—No. 19," *Puritan Recorder* (Boston), June 12, 1852, enclosed in David Hitchcock to Caleb Cushing, June 18, 1852, Caleb Cushing Papers, box 61, folder 10, Library of Congress, Washington, DC (hereafter LC). On William Rufus King, the most important scholarly work remains John M. Martin, "William Rufus King: Southern Moderate" (PhD diss., University of North Carolina, 1955). Also useful are Mark O. Hatfield and Wendy Wolff, eds., *Vice Presidents of the United States, 1789–1993* (Washington, DC: US Government Printing Office, 1997), 181–87; Lewis O. Saum, "'Who Steals My Purse': The Denigration of William R. King, the Man for Whom King County Was Named," *Pacific Northwest Quarterly* 92 (Fall 2001): 181–89; and Daniel F. Brooks, "The Faces of William R. King," *Alabama Heritage* 69 (Summer 2003): 14–23.

12. David Schenck, *Personal Sketches of Distinguished Delegates of the State Convention 1861–2* (Greensboro, NC: Thomas, Reece, 1885), 19; and Martin Van Buren to Theodore Miller, June 11, 1860, in William K. Boyd, ed., "Correspondence of Bedford Brown," *Annual Publication of Historical Papers Published by the Historical Society of Trinity College* 7 (1907), 20. On Bedford Brown, see also Houston G. Jones, *Bedford Brown: States Rights Unionist* (Carrollton: West Georgia College, 1955); Brian G. Walton, "Elections to the United States Senate in North Carolina, 1835–1861," *North Carolina Historical Review* 53 (April 1976): esp. 172–74; and "Bedford Brown," in *Dictionary of North Carolina Biography*, ed. William S. Powell, 6 vols. (Chapel Hill: University of North Carolina Press, 1988), 1:240–41.

13. Philip S. Klein, "James Buchanan at Dickinson," in *John and Mary's College: The Boyd Lee Spahr Lectures in Americana* (Carlisle, PA: Fleming H. Revell, 1956), 157–79 (quote, 164). On Edward Lucas, see "Edward Lucas IV, 1790–1858," in Frederica H. Trapnell, "Some Lucases of Jefferson County," *Magazine of the Jefferson County Historical Society* 60 (December 1994): 17–34, esp. 27–28. See also Margaret Sumner, *Collegiate Republic: Cultivating an Ideal Society in Early America* (Charlottesville: University of Virginia Press, 2014), esp. 101–2.

14. John Fairfield to Anna P. Fairfield, January 7, 1836, in *Letters of John Fairfield*, ed. Arthur G. Staples (Lewiston, ME: Lewiston Journal, 1922), 65–66; *Poulson's Advertiser* (Philadelphia), December 31, 1830, reprinted in *Journal of the Lancaster County Historical Society* 35 (1931): 95; and "From Washington—Congressional Sketches," *New York Weekly Herald*, April 30, 1842. See also Klein, *President James Buchanan*, 100–104.

15. On the formal receptions and balls hosted by Elizabeth Kortright Monroe and Louisa Catherine Adams, see Allgor, *Parlor Politics*, esp. 147–89. See also Jeffrey L. Pasley, "Minnows, Spies, and Aristocrats: The Social Crisis of Congress in the Age of Martin Van Buren," *Journal of the Early Republic* 27, no. 4 (Winter 2007): 599–653.

16. For the early history of Washington and the population figures, see esp. Constance M. Green, *Washington: Village and Capital, 1800–1878* (Princeton, NJ: Princeton University Press, 1962), 21, 48, 150 (quotes); George R. Brown, *Washington: A Not Too Serious History* (Baltimore: Norman, 1930), 234; and on the C Street neighborhood, Douglass Zevely, "Old Houses on C Street and Those Who Lived There," *Records of the Columbia Historical Society, Washington D.C.* 5 (1902): 151–75 (quote, 152).

17. For more on Washington boardinghouses and hotels, see Shelden, *Washington Brotherhood*, esp. 102–10; Earman, "Messing Around"; and Young, *Washington Community*, 87–109. About boardinghouse culture more generally, see Wendy Gamber, *The Boardinghouse in Nineteenth-Century America* (Baltimore: Johns Hopkins University Press, 2007); and David Faflik, *Boarding Out: Inhabiting the American Urban Literary Imagination, 1840–1860* (Evanston, IL: Northwestern University Press, 2012).

18. On the part played by age in male friendships, see esp. Rotundo, *American Manhood*; and Thomas J. Balcerski, "'Under These Classic Shades Together': Intimate Male Friendships at the Antebellum College of New Jersey," *Pennsylvania History* 80 (Spring 2013): 169–203.

19. See the various listings in Goldman and Young, *United States Congressional Directories*, 290–94; and Klein, *President James Buchanan*, 100–104.

20. For Buchanan's comparison of King and Wall, see James Buchanan to James W. Wall, January 16, 1863, James Buchanan Papers, box 52, folder 2, Historical Society of Pennsylvania, Philadelphia (hereafter HSP). For a similar comment, see Buchanan to James W. Wall, July 14, 1860, Buchanan Papers, box 51, folder 17, HSP. For the correspondence between Buchanan and Wall, see Garret D. Wall to James Buchanan, July 27, Sept. 23, 1835, box 3, folder 18; and Buchanan to Garret D. Wall, Nov. 19, 1835, Buchanan Papers, box 52, folder 30, HSP.

21. William R. King to James Buchanan, Oct. 5, 1836, box 4, folder 9; and James Buchanan to Thomas Elder, Nov. 7, 1836, Buchanan Papers, box 45, folder 6, HSP. On Buchanan's visits to Bedford Springs, see James Buchanan to L. Harper, Aug. 6, 1851, Gilder Lehrman Collection, New-York Historical Society. On the prevalence of mineral springs during this period, see Charlene M. Boyer Lewis, *Ladies and Gentlemen on Display: Planter Society at the Virginia Springs, 1790–1860* (Charlottesville: University Press of Virginia, 2001); and Thomas Chambers, *Drinking the Waters: Creating an American Leisure Class at Nineteenth-Century Mineral Springs* (Washington, DC: Smithsonian Institute Press, 2002).

22. On the life of Robert Carter Nicholas, see Thomas L. Bayne, "Genealogica, Vol. 1," Mss1 B3448 b 1, Virginia Historical Society, Richmond; the anonymous, "Nicholas Family of Virginia and Louisiana," *Virginia Magazine of History and Biography* 57 (January 1949): 83–85; and Victor D. Golladay, "The Nicholas Family of Virginia, 1722–1820" (PhD diss., University of Virginia, 1973), esp. 427–29. The source record of Robert Carter Nicholas (referenced as Robert Carter Nicholas II by genealogists) presents conflicting evidence: while some sources cite Nicholas as born in 1793 and as the son of George Nicholas, he was most likely born in 1787 to Wilson Carey Nicholas and, keeping with this chronology, graduated from the College of William and Mary in 1803. See note on the Nicholas family bible, Bayne's "Genealogica," and the listing of the class of 1803 in *Catalog of Graduates of William and Mary* (1859).

23. John P. King to James Buchanan, April 2, 1837, Buchanan Papers, box 5, folder 12, HSP. On King, see Josephine Mellichamp, "John P. King," in *Senators from Georgia* (Huntsville, AL: Strode, 1976), 107–9. For mentions of King's later activities, see W. K. Wood, "The Georgia Railroad and Banking Company," *Georgia Historical Quarterly* 57 (Winter 1973): 544–61.

24. William R. King to James Buchanan, June 2, 1837, Buchanan Papers, box 5, folder 12, HSP. On the messmates' various moves, see Goldman and Young, *United States Congressional Directories*, 304, 318, 330, 344, 358. For other notable Washington residences during this time, see Hal H. Smith, "Historic Washington Homes," *Records of the Columbia Historical Society, Washington, D.C.* 11 (1908): 243–67.

25. William R. King to James Buchanan, June 2, 1837, Buchanan Papers, box 5, folder 12, HSP.

26. "Senator King of Alabama," *Lancaster (PA) Intelligencer*, reprinted in the *Washington Daily Globe*, Dec. 1, 1837; "Buchanan's Influence," *Lancaster (PA) Examiner and Democratic Herald*, Mar. 11, 1840.

27. For references to drinking between Daniel Webster and James Buchanan, see Webster to Buchanan, March 21, 1835, Buchanan Papers, box 3, folder 15, HSP. For the dinner invitation, see Webster to James Buchanan, May 29, 1838, Buchanan Papers, box 6, folder 8, HSP.

28. On Buchanan's trip to Virginia, see James Buchanan to Thomas J. Randolph, February 20, 1838, James Buchanan Papers, box 1, folder 20, Dickinson College Library; "Charlottesville, June 8," *Virginia Free Press* (Charlestown), June 6, 1838; and "White Sulphur Springs," *Lewisburg (VA) Enquirer,* Aug. 17, 1838, reprinted in *Virginia Free Press* (Charlestown), Aug. 30, 1838. For King's trip to Virginia, see William R. King to James Buchanan, June 20, 1839, Buchanan Papers, box 7, folder 5, HSP. On the Virginia Springs, see Lewis, *Ladies and Gentlemen on Display.*

29. *Congressional Debates,* 24th Cong., 2nd Sess., 618–19; "Remarks, March 1, 1839, on the Resolutions Concerning the Maine Boundary," in *The Works of James Buchanan: Comprising His Speeches, State Papers, and Private Correspondence,* ed. John Bassett Moore, 12 vols. (Philadelphia: J. B. Lippincott, 1908), 5:108.

30. App. to Cong. Globe, 25th Cong., 2nd Sess., 34–39 (1838). On the gag-rule debates, see Daniel Wirls, "'The Only Mode of Avoiding Everlasting Debate': The Overlooked Senate Gag Rule for Antislavery Petitions," *Journal of the Early Republic* 27 (Spring 2007): 115–38, esp. 125–29. For Buchanan's involvement in the disenfranchisement of free African Americans in Pennsylvania, see Wood, "'Sacrifice on the Altar of Slavery,'" 75–106.

31. *Congressional Debates,* 24th Cong., 1st Sess., 715; William Rufus King, "Slavery in the District of Columbia," App. to Cong. Globe, 24th Cong., 1st Sess., 142 (1836); Mahlon Dickerson Diary, Mar. 7, 1836, Mahlon Dickerson Papers, box 4, folder 1, New Jersey Historical Society, Newark.

32. "Remarks, March 2, 1836, on Petitions for the Abolition of Slavery in the District of Columbia," "Remarks, February 6, 1837, on Memorial Praying for the Abolition of Slavery in the District of Columbia," and "Intermeddling with Slavery," January 10, 11, 1838, all in Moore, *Works of James Buchanan,* 3:9, 205, 356.

33. Remarks of William R. King, Dec. 18, 1837, *Niles' National Register,* December 30, 1837, 275; Thomas Elder to James Buchanan, December 23, 1837, Buchanan Papers, box 2, folder 20, HSP.

34. On the purchase of John Bell, see the account of Bessie Hogan Williams, ca. 1917, in Henry P. Johnston, *William R. King and His Kin* (Birmingham, AL: Featon, 1975), 295.

35. On the African American community in Washington, DC, see Mary Beth Corrigan, "The Ties That Bind: The Pursuit of Community and Freedom among Slaves and Free Blacks in the District of Columbia, 1800–1860," in *Southern City, National Ambition: The Growth of Early Washington, D.C., 1800–1860,* ed. Howard J. Gillette Jr. (Washington, DC: American Architectural Foundation, 1995), 69–90. On Buchanan's role in the sale of enslaved people in the 1830s, see Klein, *President James Buchanan,* 100–101.

36. On the Panic of 1837, see esp. Jessica M. Lepler, *The Many Panics of 1837: People, Politics, and the Creation of a Transatlantic Financial Crisis* (New York: Cambridge University Press, 2013).

37. William R. King to James Buchanan, June 2, 1837, Buchanan Papers, box 5, folder 12, HSP; King to Asbury Dickens, June 1, 1837, Misc. Mss. Collection, box 1, LC; James Buchanan to Eliza Violet Blair, June 3/7, 1837, Buchanan Papers, box 46, folder 2, HSP.

38. James Buchanan to Eliza Violet Blair, June 3/7, 1837, Buchanan Papers, box 46, folder 2, HSP; "Speech, September 29, 1837, on Making Public Officers Depositories," in Moore, *Works of James Buchanan,* 3:266, 270; J. T. Buckingham, ed., "The Government and the Country," *Boston Courier,* April 6, 1840. See also Cong. Globe, 25th Cong., 1st Sess., 85 (1837).

39. For the record of the various votes, see from *Congressional Debates:* Wabash River improvement vote, January 2, 1835, 23rd Cong., 2nd Sess., 90; expunging resolution vote, January 16, 1837, 24th Cong., 2nd Sess., 504; surplus revenue vote, February 19, 1836, 24th Cong., 1st Sess., 577–78; abolition of slavery votes, March 11, 1836, 24th Cong., 1st Sess., 804; and February 9, 1837, 24th Cong., 2nd Sess., 740; and sub-treasury measures votes, 25th Cong., 1st Sess., passim.

40. See table 2.2. For a study that utilizes roll-call analysis of congressional boarding-houses, see Bogue and Marlaire, "Of Mess and Men." For a comparison to congressional voting behavior in the 1840s, see Joel H. Silbey, *The Shrine of Party: Congressional Voting Behavior, 1841–1852* (Pittsburgh: University of Pittsburgh Press, 1967). See also Alan G. Bogue, *Clio & the Bitch Goddess: Quantification in American Political History* (Beverly Hills, CA: Sage, 1983); and Keith T. Poole and Howard Rosenthal, *Congress: A Political-Economic History of Roll Call Voting* (New York: Oxford University Press, 1997).

41. For more on this subject, see Thomas J. Balcerski, *Bosom Friends: The Intimate World of James Buchanan and William Rufus King* (New York: Oxford University Press, 2019).

STEPHEN A. DOUGLAS, FREE-SOILER

A Counterfactual Analysis of Party Reformation in the 1850s

DOUGLAS R. EGERTON

His head was enormous. Whatever else people noticed about Senator Stephen A. Douglas, they noticed his head. Republican Charles Francis Adams Jr. took an immediate dislike to the Illinois Democrat, describing the five-foot-three-inch-tall Little Giant as a "squab, vulgar little man," but he admitted that Douglas possessed an "immense, frowsy head." Journalist Murat Halstead sneered that the stocky senator was growing ever more so, "his waist becoming still more extensive." But the reporter, too, was drawn to the cranium. Douglas "*has* an immense head," he marveled. In "height, and breadth and depth, you cannot find its equal in Washington." Few observers outdid Henry Flint, an ardent supporter who would write Douglas's 1860 campaign biography. "His massive head rivets undivided attention," Flint gushed. "It is the head of the antique, with something of the infinite in its expression of power: a head difficult to describe, but better worth description than any in the country." In a century when phrenologists carefully measured heads and believed that skull size determined intelligence and even moral aptitude, Douglas's prodigious cranium, Flint bragged, housed "a brain of unusual size." Friend and foe alike conceded that he was a political tactician of the first order.[1]

Flint was not wrong to regard his friend as one of the most astute political operators of the 1850s. Born in Vermont and raised by his widowed mother in western New York, Douglas, armed with letters of introduction and a gift of $300 from his stepfather, set out for Illinois at the age of twenty. When asked by his mother when she might see him again, he allegedly answered, "On my way to Congress." Within the year, Douglas was appointed state attorney for Morgan County, and two years after that, in 1836, he won a seat in the Illinois assembly. Elevated to the US Senate in 1847 after a stint as Illinois secretary of state and two terms in the US House of Representatives, Douglas quickly earned the enviable reputation as a man who would one day reside in the Executive Mansion. In 1850 he revived Henry Clay's moribund compromise package by shrewdly chopping the Kentucky senator's omnibus bill into five separate pieces of legislation. Although still a freshman senator, Douglas emerged as the spokesman for those rising Democrats who embraced the "Young America Movement," aspiring politicians who hoped to bury divisive arguments over slavery and instead ride to power by harnessing the spirit of aggressive expansionism and appealing to patriotic notions of national might.[2]

Having replaced the aged Clay as the master of the Senate, Douglas was nearly rewarded with his party's presidential nomination in 1852, despite the fact that he was only thirty-nine. His obvious eagerness for the presidency, together with a very crowded field of candidates as well as the Democrats' troublesome rule that candidates earn the support of two-thirds of the convention's delegates, cost him the prize that year. After Douglas edged out his chief rival, former secretary of state James Buchanan of Pennsylvania, on the thirtieth and thirty-first ballots, the Virginia delegation advanced Franklin Pierce of New Hampshire as a compromise candidate. The party rallied behind Pierce on the forty-ninth ballot. Privately dismayed by his hapless handlers, Douglas was content to wait until 1856. No president had been reelected since Andrew Jackson in 1832, and the Whigs, he predicted, were destined to vanish due to their "lack of confidence in the virtue of the people."[3]

Optimistic that his chance would come, Douglas and his Illinois supporters evidently failed to analyze the Baltimore convention's vote or understand what it meant for his future platform. The first calls for a Douglas nomination had started in California, a free state and also a reliably Democratic stronghold throughout the 1850s. Douglas also matched

1848 nominee Lewis Cass of Michigan in drawing votes from twenty-one state delegations, while Buchanan drew votes from only fifteen states. Buchanan, however, received his strongest support from the South, and it was a united Virginia delegation that finally handed the nomination to Pierce. When it came to the fate of the Mexican Cession lands, most southerners evidently preferred Buchanan's advocacy of extending the Missouri Compromise line—which in 1820 pertained only to the Louisiana Purchase territory—to the Pacific over Douglas's vague promises of popular sovereignty in the Southwest. The senator had performed surprisingly poorly in Indiana and other midwestern states apart from his adopted Illinois, although several New England delegates indicated that he, rather than Buchanan, would have been their choice were favorite-son Pierce not a candidate. As one of Douglas's earliest biographers observed, the balloting should have "convinced him that narrow, sectional policies and undue favor to the South would never land him in the White House." To capture the presidency, the senator needed, in short, to "grow in the national confidence, and not merely in the favor of a single section." Sadly, for his career, Douglas failed to grasp that warning.[4]

So why did the man known as the "Little Wizard of the West," this man of immense brain, commit what was perhaps the greatest political blunder of the nineteenth century? As the chairman of the Senate Committee on Territories, Douglas hoped to achieve two goals—and initially, he supposed that the first would lead inexorably to the second, which was the president's chair. As did most Democrats and more than a few Whigs, Douglas believed that his republic was one day destined to stretch from coast to coast and from pole to pole. But the senator planned to use his seat and influence to open the western frontier in a way that enriched his state, his chief political supporters, and his own purse. As were several of his principal Illinois backers, Douglas was a major investor in real estate just west of Chicago. If he organized a rail line toward San Francisco, Chicago could trade with California and beyond. The previously near-worthless prairie lands he and his associates owned could quadruple in value as a result. To that end, in March 1853 he and Illinois congressman William Richardson, who chaired the House Committee on Territories, drafted legislation to organize what remained of the Louisiana Purchase region into one vast Kansas Territory. A handful of old Jacksonians fretted about the venture's cost and constitutionality, but Douglas swatted down such complaints with appeals to national greatness. Settlers would follow the railroad west, he promised, creating profitable farms and towns while transforming the West into "one of the most densely-populated and highly-cultivated portions of America."[5]

When it came time to cast a vote, senators from Mississippi and Texas rose to express their opposition, and a stunned Douglas watched as the Senate voted to table his bill. "Mr. Douglas made an ineffectual attempt to take up the Nebraska Territory bill," one editor reported, but the legislation as then crafted appeared doomed. Congress adjourned the next day, not to meet again until the following fall. *What* happened next has been well documented. Less examined is *why* Douglas, a politician considered so astute, such a master of the Senate, so fortunate to be dealing with a weak and controllable president, and so in touch with the pulse of his constituents committed a blunder that was to reshuffle the nation's two-party system, bring a longtime foe out of political retirement, and cost him the republic's highest office.[6]

Before returning to Illinois during the recess, Douglas paid a call on the so-called F Street mess, a Washington boardinghouse group comprising a quartet of powerful southern Democratic senators: David Rice Atchison of Missouri, Andrew Pickens Butler of South Carolina, James Murray Mason of Virginia, and Douglas's future presidential rival, Robert M. T. Hunter, also of Virginia. Atchison's and Mason's biographers emphasize that the four bluntly warned Douglas that they would continue to oppose his bill so long as the thirty-three-year-old agreement banning slavery from the lands north and west of Missouri remained on the books. Douglas's vision of yeomen farmers flooding into the new territory was their nightmare, for within a few years these free lands would have the requisite populations to apply for admission as free states. Thanks to the Compromise of 1850, Atchison observed, northern influence had theoretically increased in Washington—although California's two Democratic senators typically voted with their native South—and Douglas's bill would only render their "species of [human] property [even more] insecure." In fact, as early as November 1852, Douglas had briefly abandoned popular sovereignty and assured a colleague that he now desired to see "the old compromise line extended, first to the Rio Grande, then to the Pacific." But Atchison was demanding the chance to spread slavery into the upper Midwest, not merely the Southwest, and the fact that Douglas was willing to guarantee planters not just access but control over southern California and what would become all or parts of three other states suggests that he did not see the coming firestorm clearly. Pierce had campaigned just that fall on the promise to maintain the 1850 agreement, yet only weeks after the election, Douglas had changed his mind yet again: "I am now for its repeal."[7]

Perhaps Douglas spoke with sensible advisors during the summer and fall of 1853, because when Congress resumed its deliberations in December, he sought to satisfy Atchison's demands that "slaveholder and non-slaveholder" be placed "upon terms of equality" in the Kansas Territory by saying as little as possible about unfree labor in the region. Portions of the Mexican Cession had been resolved in 1850 with only one vague reference to slavery on the basis of "popular sovereignty," and Douglas was content to allow white settlers, as opposed to distant legislators, settle the issue when the time came for statehood. On January 4, 1854, Douglas introduced a second version of his bill, which now divided the region into two territories: Kansas in the south and Nebraska in the north. Settlers had the option to retain or abolish slavery "as their constitution may prescribe at the time of admission." As chairman, the senator also produced a report questioning the constitutionality of the 1820 prohibition and endorsing the conciliatory "language of the Compromise measures of 1850." For politicians anxious to avoid taking a public position on the explosive question of slavery expansion, popular sovereignty had the virtue of appearing to follow the revered tradition of Jeffersonian localism. "Our chief source of safety is found in the doctrine of the inviolability of states' rights," observed one supportive editor.[8]

Senator Douglas quickly discovered that his intentionally vague language still failed to appease southern fire-eaters. In a drunken tirade on the floor of the Senate, Atchison shouted that no prudent slaveholder would carry his expensive human property into a property if it appeared likely that antislavery settlers could later pack a constitutional convention and abolish his capital investment. The Missourian hoped to witness Kansas "sink into hell" before letting it become a free state. Senator Archibald Dixon, a Kentucky Whig who thought it unwise to allow southern Democrats to outflank him on the issue, seconded Atchison and demanded that Douglas rewrite his bill. Unless the proposal clearly and unequivocally repealed the Missouri Compromise, Dixon warned, he would feel compelled to draft a rival bill that did. By this date, Douglas understood that overturning the now-thirty-four-year-old prohibition on slavery in the American Midwest would cause "a hell of a storm" across the North, but he believed that he had little choice. Still hoping not to use the explosive term "repealed" in his bill, Douglas instead sought refuge in utter duplicity. In his third version the senator slyly suggested that the doctrine of congressional restriction adopted in 1820 had been "superseded by the principles" of popular sovereignty embedded in the Compromise of 1850 and so was "inoperative and void." This final version explicitly permitted territorial settlers to decide upon slavery while lifting and incorporating his earlier statements regarding the popular-sovereignty sections of the 1850 agreement from his earlier report.[9]

The final touch necessary was the endorsement of President Pierce. Washington insiders knew that the New Hampshire Democrat, still mourning the death of his son Benjamin, who had been killed in a railway accident just after the 1852 election, was so easily persuaded on any course of action that his support was worthless unless put in writing. Early on the morning of Sunday, January 21, 1853, Douglas, Atchison, and Democratic congressman John C. Breckinridge of Kentucky called on the president. Since Pierce and his devout wife, Jane, rarely accepted visitors on the Sabbath, Douglas also urged Secretary of War Jefferson Davis to join the group. After a meeting of several hours in the Executive Mansion library, Pierce agreed to support the repeal of the 1820 ban but emphasized the seriousness of Congress doing so. Although an expansionist, he instead recommended an alternative bill that left the question of slavery in the West up to the US Supreme Court. But Douglas bluntly insisted that the president endorse their course of action in writing. Pierce finally did so but declined to use the word "repeal." Even so, the final version of Douglas's bill, revised yet again with the assistance of Breckinridge and introduced on January 23 as the Kansas-Nebraska Act, was now a Democratic measure and so officially required the support of all party members.[10]

As he had warned Atchison, Douglas expected a political firestorm in the North, though one he could survive. He would have four more years to mend fences in Illinois before having to defend his seat in the Senate, and one of the virtues of popular sovereignty, he believed, was that it deferred the final battle over a territory's status to some future and distant date. As did many politicians who foolishly conflated slavery with cotton, Douglas suspected that midwestern soil would prove inhospitable to unwaged labor. Thus the ultimate result of his bill would be more free states, though without recourse to a Wilmot Proviso-like ban that would infuriate southerners. The process of political settlement in Kansas, he suspected, would be both peaceful and uneventful, and so, as biographer Martin H. Quitt recently remarked, "the controversy would fade from the country's concern."[11] In short, Douglas believed that he could yet achieve all of his goals. The Kansas-Nebraska Act became the law of the land on May 30, 1854, with Pierce's signature; less noticed, Douglas then prepared to introduce his railroad bill. The feckless Pierce, all understood, would not be the party's nominee in 1856; even if denied the prize that year, a decisive Senate victory in 1858 would certainly propel Douglas toward the nomination in 1860, when he would still be only forty-seven years of age, making him the country's youngest president. But that, of course, did not happen.

Unfortunately for Douglas, to start with, the immediate consequences of the act's passage were far worse than he ever imagined. Setting out on a speaking tour across the North, the senator soon discovered just how bad the damage was. In Trenton, New Jersey, where he planned to discuss wage issues with labor leaders, Douglas instead found himself hooted off the stage and hounded by an angry mob all the way back to the train station. Previously friendly editors compared him to Judas and Benedict Arnold for selling out his northern constituents. Abolitionist Frederick Douglass took especial pleasure in reporting that an "effigy of Senator Douglas was found suspended from a tree on Genesee Street [in Auburn, New York], this morning, with the words 'Stephen Arnold Douglas hung for treason' attached." The senator himself observed another such effigy hanging from a tree in Cleveland. Even in Chicago, the Little Giant's attempts to defend his course were met with boos, hisses, and so many interruptions that, cursing, he finally quit the stage. "The framers and supporters of this bill, may see written across it their own political death warrant," editorialized one Massachusetts editor. "Whatever Mr. Douglas may have once thought, he may say now [that] the comfort of a retirement lives in this."[12]

Two years later, when the Democrats met in Cincinnati to choose their standard bearer in the presidential election, Douglas discovered that the fury over the repeal of the Missouri Compromise had yet to dissipate. As the spokesman for the West, the selection of Cincinnati should have worked in the senator's favor, as 1856 was the first time the Democrats had met outside of the original thirteen states. But the balloting confirmed what Douglas should have learned from the 1852 convention. On the sixteenth ballot, after Pierce withdrew from consideration and the Cass forces realized that they stood no chance, Douglas received 73 votes from slave-state delegates compared to Buchanan's 47, a reversal of four years previous, when the Pennsylvanian enjoyed greater southern support than his Illinois rival. But while his capitulation to the F Street mess had enhanced Douglas's clout among slaveholders, it hurt him badly among delegates from both New England and his own Midwest, where Buchanan bested him 28 to 13 and 41 to 19, respectively. As the editor of the *New Orleans Daily Creole* observed, "the unpopularity of Mr. Buchanan" did not stop him from winning the nomination. "That gentleman was not the favorite of the Democracy, [as] Douglas stood head and shoulders above him in the hearts of the majority of his party." But Buchanan had the good luck of being posted abroad during the 1854 legislative debacle. "It would not do to run 'the Little Giant,'" the editor sighed, "for the author of the Kansas-Nebraska bill was not the Atlas to carry on his back the world of Northern indignation without sinking under it."[13]

The national returns that fall confirmed the damage. Although Buchanan received 171 electoral votes to a combined 122 for his two rivals, he won only 45.3 percent of the popular vote, making him the first minority president since Zachary Taylor and handing him the lowest popular vote since John Quincy Adams's 1824 showing. In Douglas's Illinois Buchanan bested Republican John C. Frémont by only four percentage points; although he captured Illinois's 11 electoral votes, Buchanan's popular count of 105,348 was smaller than the combined Republican and American Party tally of 133,633. Much to Douglas's dismay, his old Illinois ally William A. Richardson, who had helped shepherd the Kansas Bill through the House, lost his bid for governor to Republican William H. Bissell, a former anti-Kansas Democrat who refused to accept the repeal of the 1820 ban on slavery in the Midwest.[14]

But let us suppose a different course, one that did not turn previous supporters against the senator, one that did not cleave the Democracy in two, and one that did not result in a Republican triumph in 1860. Let us suppose that journalist Murat Halstead was right and that Douglas's "immense head" housed the brain of a first-rate political tactician, which was certainly the general consensus prior to 1854. More than fifty years ago, Glyndon G. Van Deusen speculated on how the course of history might have been different had Henry Clay endorsed the Wilmot Proviso in 1848. Instead of losing the nomination to Louisiana general and planter Zachary Taylor, Clay might have received the support of the West and the North, transforming the Whigs into a free-soil party and "antedating Republicanism by half a dozen years." Counterfactual analysis, of course, functions best when it refrains from flights of historical fancy and instead serves as a useful reminder that policymakers have always had options, that had other choices been pursued, the series of events that naturally followed would also be changed. The past was never carved in stone—nor were the political disasters wrought by Douglas inevitable.[15]

What if Douglas had realized early on that caving to the demands of the F Street mess would not only *not* lead to the presidency in 1856 but also, in fact, forever cost him the prize? The Illinois senator was clearly an impatient man in a hurry and not much given to the long game, but let us begin this exercise with the assumption that he was as clever as conventional wisdom had it and understood that he had options, if perhaps not immediate ones. Instead of attempting to appease the militant proslavery wing of his party, what if Douglas instead had sought to rally free-soil Democrats behind his leadership, isolate the extreme fire-eaters, and capture the presidency as a western man of northern principles? In one of his final speeches, delivered in late April 1861 in Springfield, Douglas confessed an error. He had "lean[ed] too far to the southern section of the Union against my own." He had tried to placate southern demands only to be repaid by slaveholders who wished "to destroy the best government the sun of heaven ever shed its rays upon." The potential to adopt that position existed seven years before, but Douglas failed to see it.[16]

Adopting a free-soil position in what remained of the Louisiana Purchase would not, it is important to note, have required Douglas to shed the public racism that earned him the enmity of abolitionists such as Frederick Douglass. As Fergus Bordewich has remarked about the senator, although passionately "democratic with respect to the rights of white men, he was deeply and irremediably racist when it came to blacks." But for most of the 1850s, lower North and midwestern free-soilers made it clear that they spoke for the right of white pioneers to settle the territories as yeomen farmers. That was particularly true of the so-called "Barn-burner" antislavery Democrats, many of whom found themselves without a political home after Free-Soil Party's nominee John Hale captured a disappointing 4.9 percent of the popular vote in 1852. The *Hartford Courant* spoke for many of them when assuring its readers that they wished to shield the West "from the pestilential presence of the black man." As Pennsylvania's David Wilmot—the former Democratic congressman whose famous 1846 proviso sought to exclude slavery from the Mexican Cession—insisted in speech after speech, he felt "no morbid sympathy for the slave." Rather, his objective was "to preserve to free white labor a fair country, a rich inheritance, where the sons of toil, of my own race and color, can live without the disgrace which association with negro slavery brings upon free labor." No less than Democratic Party activist John Van Buren, the son of the former president, insisted that he opposed the extension of slavery into the West because "you cannot induce the white labouring man to work beside a black slave." Douglas's racist pronouncements, sadly, were routinely repeated by northern antiextension politicians on both sides of the political aisle.[17]

After all, once Douglas broke with Buchanan and denounced the proslavery Lecompton Constitution, no less than *New York Tribune* editor Horace Greeley, a former Whig turned Republican, recommended that his partisans back Douglas in the Senate race of 1858, despite having once denounced the Illinois Democrat as "a lying villain" for the Kansas-Nebraska Act. Greeley was not alone. Senator Henry Wilson of Massachusetts, a former "Conscience" Whig turned Free-Soiler turned Republican, also endorsed Douglas in 1858, as did his state's *Springfield Republican* editor Samuel Bowles. In fact, the senator's 1856 marriage to twenty-year-old Adele Cutts, the great-niece of Dolley Madison, led abolitionist Lucy Stone to believe that Douglas might be supportive of women's issues. Stone invited Douglas to attend the 1859 Chicago Women's Rights Convention, prompting Frederick Douglass to rebuke her for honoring "a man already notorious for holding [black] women in bondage." The senator responded by insisting that his support for popular sovereignty in the territories mirrored his belief that white women should "obtain the liberty of governing yourselves in your own way." The black Douglass's animosity notwithstanding, these potential free-soil supporters existed in far greater numbers four years earlier, before the Little Giant alienated them by overturning the Missouri Compromise.[18]

Douglas and his handlers might also have paid greater attention to the Democratic Party's arcane convention rules. Unlike the Republicans or the Whigs before them, since 1832 the Democrats had required a two-thirds supermajority to win their presidential nomination, and that high bar, of course, would damage Douglas's chances in 1860. But aiding him in his quest for the presidency was the fact that each state was granted as many votes in party conventions as it had in the Electoral College; thus Massachusetts, a state the Democrats had yet to carry, possessed thirteen votes at the 1856 Baltimore meeting, while reliably Democratic Mississippi could claim only seven. As a result, the more populous North controlled roughly 60 percent of the delegates. The supermajority requirement effectively barred southern slaveholders from the nomination, so proslavery delegates were reduced to supporting the least-objectionable northern "doughface." Since Buchanan was not the only northern Democrat to endorse the extension of the Missouri line, Douglas would probably never be the first choice of southern extremists. Some delegates, admittedly, rallied to his cause at the 1856 convention, but as several journalists commented as early as 1852, Douglas was merely "acceptable to southern delegates." The reality was that nothing he might do over the ensuing years could much erase their doubts. Ironically, popular sovereignty offered slaveholders only a gambler's chance of securing land in the West, and even the most militant fire-eater conceded that a territorial legislature, at the moment of statehood application, enjoyed the right to abolish a proslavery settler's expensive human property. In popular sovereignty, ironically, Douglas had crafted a policy that was despised by both free-soilers and fire-eaters. Since he could never please both, the electoral math—for both his party and for the nation—indicated that

72

he would have been far wiser to have resisted the F Street mess and its demands.[19]

A longtime political model for a different course existed as close as neighboring Missouri, where aged Democratic senator Thomas Hart Benton denounced the repeal of the 1820 ban as likely to produce violence in the western territory and lead to "the destruction of the peace of the country." As did the far younger Wilmot, Benton spoke for the old Jacksonian champions of white yeomanry, and although the *Washington Union* damned his position on Kansas as that of "a Whig adjunct and abolition ally," the senator was hardly the sort of antislavery man that William Lloyd Garrison would recognize. As early as 1848, his public position was "for keeping free territory clear of negroes," whether free or enslaved. Elected in 1821 as one of Missouri's first senators after the compromise elevated it to statehood, Benton was obviously desirous of maintaining the old agreement, but he was not the only politician from a slave state to proclaim free-soil principles. Whig senator George Badger of North Carolina announced that he could "not vote for the Douglas Nebraska bill, because the faith of the South is plighted to the Missouri compromise." As Jean Baker has observed, even as late as 1861, secession was hotly contested in portions of the South. But instead of working to isolate fire-eaters and win over moderate southerners, Douglas sought to placate them at the cost of alienating potential supporters such as Badger.[20]

The damage wrought on both his party and his presidential aspirations was swift and easy to calculate had Douglas bothered to do so. Before the 1854 elections, northern Democrats held ninety-two congressional seats, while their southern counterparts possessed sixty-seven. But Kansas-Nebraska and its consequences cost northern Democrats dearly; those who defended Douglas's bill often lost their bids for reelection, while others quit politics or their party in protest. By 1860, northern Democrats retained only thirty-two seats, a stunning loss of sixty positions, while southern Democrats picked up only two. These were not just congressmen lost to the party but critical allies and convention delegates Douglas would need in 1856 and 1860. The chief consequence of the bill, of course, was the battle over the Lecompton Constitution, and while Douglas's opposition to that fraud saved his Senate seat in 1858, it tore his party apart. As Michael Landis has recently noted, in the swing state of Pennsylvania, anti-Lecompton Douglas men often ran as third-party candidates against regular Democratic nominees, thus handing close elections to Republicans. But, then, had there been no repeal of the 1820 compromise in the first place, there would have been no "Lecompton swindle," as one furious Indiana Democrat dubbed it, to fight over.[21]

In this instance, the astute move for Douglas coincided with what was best for his state and for his country. Instead of pressuring Pierce into supporting the F Street mess's demand—and again, Pierce thought it politically unwise to explicitly state that the bill would overturn a thirty-four-year-old agreement—he might have pushed the president into endorsing a free-soil program, albeit one sold to voters through racist rhetoric. Astonishingly, Pierce believed that the major opponents for Douglas's final bill would be Whigs. But even after the president reluctantly announced its passage as a party issue, northern Democrats divided almost evenly, with forty-three voting in favor and forty-five against the measure. In their 1852 platform, Democrats had promised not only to uphold the 1850 compromise but also to "resist all attempts at renewing, in Congress or out of it, the agitation of the slavery question, under whatever shape or color the attempt may be made." And this was an era when platforms mattered. In fact, Pierce had reminded Douglas that their party had done well in 1852, even in New Hampshire, by affirming their support for the Fugitive Slave Act. But the wrong lesson was learned. Tearing down a decades-old pact was hardly tantamount to defending a law that even Illinois attorney Abraham Lincoln conceded was perfectly constitutional. The obvious lesson Douglas missed was the political wisdom in defending white privilege to American voters.[22]

A prudent counselor would have encouraged the Illinois senator to appeal to northern racism with a full-throated defense of the Fugitive Slave Act—a ploy used by candidate Buchanan—while laboring to isolate extreme elements in his own party. Douglas had, in fact, nearly done so as early as the summer of 1851, when he named Senator Hunter as his proposed running mate. Although a militantly proslavery member of the F Street mess, the ambitious Hunter promptly signed on. As John M. Belohlavek has observed, both Pierce and advisor Caleb Cushing "had some philosophical difficulties with [Douglas's revised] proposal and feared the conflagration it might provoke," so lobbying the president to support his original Kansas Bill was far from impossible. Douglas might also have called in his political debts—during the 1852 election, he had spoken in behalf of Democratic candidates in twenty-three states—to push a free-soil version of his bill through Congress. To the extent that he appeared to be the frontrunner for the nomination in 1856, few young politicians, including those from the upper South, would have willingly defied the man who might soon control federal patronage and a veto pen.[23]

Had Douglas pursued a different course in 1853 and 1854, to return to the point of a counterfactual exercise, the remaining six years of the decade would surely have looked very different. Like Pierce, Douglas believed that his final Kansas-Nebraska Bill would damage the Whigs, and it did: only two southern Whigs supported their northern brethren in voting nay, while not a single northern Whig cast a yes vote. But the anger over Kansas, of course, promptly led to the emergence of a powerful new free-soil coalition of the Republicans. Although both William H. Seward and Lincoln were reluctant to abandon their dying party—a hesitancy shared by Ohio Democrat Salmon P. Chase—ambitious young congressmen from both parties loudly championed a new political formulation. "New and important issues must be met by new organizations," argued the editor of the influential *National Era,* while James Simonton, the respected correspondent for the *New York Times,* and the *Tribune*'s Greeley insisted that it was crucial to have a new anti-Kansas party created by the 1856 elections. Seward finally came around and endorsed Republican nominee John C. Frémont. Although Buchanan carried the day, Frémont captured eleven states to Buchanan's nineteen, while former president Millard Fillmore won only Maryland. Never had a brand-new party done so well in its first national outing or immediately emerged as a country's new second party. All that was thanks to Douglas.[24]

By turning on the fraudulent proslavery Lecompton Constitution—a maneuver necessary to salvage his Senate seat in 1858—Douglas managed to convince the F Street mess and their fire-eater allies that he was seizing back the prize of Kansas, having handed it to them three years earlier. His opposition to the proposed territorial constitution, together with his August 27, 1858, statement in Freeport, Illinois, in which he flirted with free-soilism by reminding his constituents that "slavery cannot exist a day or an hour anywhere, unless it is supported by local police regulations," cost him the support of southern Democrats and further fractured an already splintered party. By 1860, though the goodwill of a failed president as badly wounded as Buchanan was perhaps not worth much to Douglas politically, after their contentious December 3, 1857, meeting at the Executive Mansion over Lecompton, even the prospect of a tepid endorsement was not to be. After hearing Buchanan warn that "no Democrat ever yet differed from an administration of his own choice without being crushed," Douglas let the aged Pennsylvanian know that he was no Old Hickory: "Mr. President, I wish you to remember that General Jackson is dead, sir." Douglas never again visited the mansion so long as Buchanan resided there.[25]

The story of the disastrous Charleston Democratic convention of April 1860 has been told often enough to not require a full analysis here. Unknowable, of course, is whether Douglas could have successfully isolated enough fire-eaters to obtain the necessary two-thirds majority for the nomination. Curiously, it did not occur to August Belmont, the New York banker who acted as Douglas's "National Chairman," to seek an alliance with the ambitious Senator Hunter, whose name Douglas had floated as a potential vice-presidential nominee in 1851. On the first ballot, Douglas stood at 145.5 delegates, with James Guthrie of Kentucky at 35, Hunter at 42, and Tennessee's Andrew Johnson at 12. With Hunter or even Guthrie as an ally rather than a rival, Douglas might have captured the nomination. Most of the New England delegates stood behind him and "non-intervention," as they preferred to style popular sovereignty. But often forgotten is that, due to his ever-shifting policies, Douglas's territorial plans were anathema not merely to lower South Democrats but also to disaffected Democrats in his own state. Frederick Douglass, who despised the Illinois senator as much as did any fire-eater, took great glee in reporting that the "anti-Douglas Democracy of Illinois have issued a circular announcing that they will elect delegates to the Charleston convention, in opposition to the Douglas faction."[26]

In defeat, Douglas found his soul, at long last, and adopted positions toward his southern critics that he should have embraced six years before. Although initially optimistic about his chances, assuring one correspondent in early July that his campaign's momentum was "gaining every day," Douglas's confidence vanished on October 9, when Pennsylvania voters, who had supported Buchanan in 1856, flocked to the polls and handed the governor's chair to a Republican by thirty thousand votes. "Mr. Lincoln is the next President," he informed those who were traveling with him on a campaign swing through New England. "We must try to save the Union. I will go South."[27]

In perhaps the only truly principled act of Douglas's political life, the defeated senator wished his southern brethren to understand that if northern voters were not united on territorial policy, they were on the question of secession. Speaking in Norfolk, Virginia, before "an immense crowd" of nearly six thousand people, Douglas said almost nothing about popular sovereignty, focusing instead on a question put to him by the editor of the *Norfolk Argus* asking if the election of a Republican justified secession. It was the simple duty of the president "to enforce the laws" passed by Congress, Douglas shouted, and as a member of the Senate, he "would do all in [his] power to aid the government." The new chief executive, he warned, "whoever he may be, should treat all attempts to break up the Union, by resistance to its laws, as Old Hickory treated the nullifiers in 1832." If Lincoln violated his oath, Douglas added, there was the remedy of impeachment. But the "mere inauguration of a President" could not "justify the revolution of secession," and northern Democrats would insist that the victor in November 1860 be sworn in on the fourth day of March 1861.[28]

On several occasions Douglas, typically the most combative of candidates, was far kinder to his Republican opponent than southern members of his own party were toward him. At one stop as he traveled the North by train, he spoke of Lincoln by name. "He is a clever fellow," the senator admitted, "a kindhearted, good natured, amiable man." The two had battled for "so long that [Douglas had] respect for him" and lacked "the heart to say anything against Abe Lincoln." When somebody from the crowd shouted in response that Lincoln was good for little besides splitting rails, Douglas defended the Republican candidate, laughing that as a young man he too had worked with wood, constructing "bureaus and secretaries." At another, Douglas found that the majority of those in his audience were Lincoln supporters. As the Democrat sought to explain his positions, a group of young men who "stood before him" gave three cheers "for Lincoln and three groans for Douglas." The weary candidate replied that he hoped "no democrat insulted Mr. Seward as he passed through the country" on a campaign swing for Lincoln. Despite the fact that northern Democrats disagreed with Seward on policy, he added, "they paid him the respect due to him as the distinguished leader of the republican party." When the hecklers kept up their jeers, Douglas lost all patience. "I came here not to insult, or say ought against any man," he snapped. "Mr. Lincoln is my personal friend, and I am his." At a time when former Alabama congressman William Lowndes Yancey was stumping across the North, denouncing Lincoln's party as "the negro party" and branding Douglas "an abolitionist," the Illinois senator's honest words of friendship for his longtime foe was a most unusual act of statesmanship.[29]

So toxic was southern rhetoric against both Lincoln and Douglas that the two Illinois politicians grew closer still as election day approached. As early as July, Thurlow Weed, Seward's longtime handler, speculated that Douglas probably preferred a Republican victory "to that of Breckinridge or [Constitutional Union Party candidate John] Bell," and that was probably true. The fact that hindsight reminds us of just how absolutely necessary a Lincoln triumph that fall was, however, should not blind us to the fact that Stephen Douglas would most likely have been the victor in 1860 had he ignored the threats of the F Street mess. Had Douglas really been "the Little Wizard of the West," or had he found his courage—and his voice—seven years before, the entire course of the ensuing decade might have been far different.[30]

NOTES

1. Charles Francis Adams Jr., *An Autobiography* (Boston: Houghton Mifflin, 1916), 47; Murat Halstead, *Three against Lincoln: Murat Halstead Reports the Caucuses of 1860*, ed. William B. Hesseltine (Baton Rouge: Louisiana University Press, 1960), 170; Henry M. Flint, *Life and Speeches of Stephen A. Douglas* (New York: Derby and Jackson, 1860), 18.

2. Roy Morris Jr., *The Long Pursuit: Abraham Lincoln's Thirty-Year Struggle with Stephen Douglas* (New York: HarperCollins, 2008), 11–12.

3. Eric H. Walther, *The Shattering of the Union: America in the 1850s* (Lanham, MD: Rowman and Littlefield, 2004), 4; James L. Huston, *Stephen A. Douglas and the Dilemmas of Democratic Equality* (Lanham, MD: Rowman and Littlefield, 2007), 98.

4. The best analysis of the Baltimore convention's vote remains Allen Johnson, *Stephen A. Douglas: A Study in American Politics* (New York: Macmillan, 1908), 203–6.

5. Robert W. Johannsen, *Stephen A. Douglas* (New York: Oxford University Press, 1973), 392; Alice Elizabeth Malavasic, *The F Street Mess: How Southern Senators Rewrote the Kansas-Nebraska Act* (Chapel Hill: University of North Carolina Press, 2017), 78–79.

6. *Amherst (MA) Farmer's Cabinet,* March 10, 1853; *Pittsfield (MA) Sun,* March 10, 1853. One possibility, of course, is that Douglas was not as brilliant a Washington tactician as his contemporaries believed. Indeed, historians tend to confuse overt political ambition with a successful mastery of the craft. As Daniel Walker Howe once observed of Henry Clay: "As a politician, he was forever blundering. . . . Clay has been overrated as a politician and underrated as a statesman." Howe, *The Political Culture of the American Whigs* (Chicago: University of Chicago Press, 1979), 124.

7. Michael F. Holt, *The Fate of Their Country: Politicians, Slavery Extension, and the Coming of the Civil War* (New York: Hill and Wang, 2004), 93–94; William E. Parrish, *David Rice Atchison of Missouri* (Columbia: University of Missouri Press, 1961), 142–43; Robert Y. Young, *Senator James Murray Mason: Defender of the Old South* (Knoxville: University of Tennessee Press, 1998), 53; Stephen A. Douglas to Parmenas Turnley, November 30, 1852, in *The Letters of Stephen A. Douglas,* ed. Robert W. Johannsen (Urbana: University of Illinois Press, 1961), 255.

8. Holman Hamilton, *Prologue to Conflict: The Crisis and Compromise of 1850* (Lexington: University of Kentucky Press, 1964), 172–74; Stephen Douglas to editor of the *San Francisco National,* August 16, 1859, in Johannsen, *Letters of Stephen A. Douglas,* 458–59; Michael A. Morrison, *Slavery and the West: The Eclipse of Manifest Destiny* (Chapel Hill: University of North Carolina Press, 1997), 142–43.

9. Larry Gara, *The Presidency of Franklin Pierce* (Lawrence: University Press of Kansas, 1991), 91; William W. Freehling, *The Road to Disunion,* vol. 2, *Secessionists Triumphant, 1854–1861* (New York: Oxford University Press, 2007), 61–62; Louis Howland, *Stephen A. Douglas* (New York: Charles Scribner's Sons, 1920), 194–95; Gerald M. Capers, *Stephen A. Douglas, Defender of the Union* (Boston: Little, Brown, 1959), 94; Robert Russel, "The Issues in the Congressional Struggle over the Kansas-Nebraska Bill," *Journal of Southern History* 29 (May 1963): 196; *St. Albans (VT) Messenger,* February 23, 1854.

10. Johannsen, *Douglas,* 414–15; William C. Davis, *Jefferson Davis: The Man and His Hour, a Biography* (New York: HarperCollins, 1991), 247–48; William C. Davis, *Breckinridge: Statesman, Soldier, Symbol* (Baton Rouge: Louisiana State University Press, 1992), 115; Sean Wilentz, *The Rise of American Democracy: Jefferson to Lincoln* (New York: W. W. Norton, 2005), 672; Roy F. Nichols, *Franklin Pierce: Young Hickory of the Granite Hills,* 2nd ed. (Philadelphia: University of Pennsylvania Press, 1958), 334; Nicole Etcheson, *Bleeding Kansas: Contested Liberty in the Civil War Era* (Lawrence: University Press of Kansas, 2006), 14.

11. Martin H. Quitt, *Stephen A. Douglas and Antebellum Democracy* (New York: Cambridge University Press, 2012), 124.

12. Walther, *Shattering of the Union,* 50; *Frederick Douglass' Paper,* March 31, 1854; *Barre (MA) Patriot,* February 24, 1854.

13. Johnson, *Douglas,* 277; *New Orleans Daily Creole,* October 31, 1856.

14. Howland, *Douglas,* 247; Huston, *Douglas,* 121.

15. Glyndon G. Van Deusen, *The Jacksonian Era, 1828–1848* (New York: Harper and Row, 1959), 254. The model for such an analysis is Gary J. Kornblith, "Rethinking the Coming of the Civil War: A Counterfactual Exercise," *Journal of American History* 90 (June 2003): 76–105.

16. Damon Wells, *Stephen Douglas: The Last Years, 1857–1861* (Austin: University of Texas Press, 1974), 287–88; Howland, *Douglas,* 368; *New York Tribune,* May 1, 1861.

17. Fergus M. Bordewich, *America's Great Debate: Henry Clay, Stephen A. Douglas, and the Compromise That Preserved the Union* (New York: Simon and Schuster, 2012), 377; Eric Foner, *Free Soil, Free Labor, Free Men: The Ideology of the Republican Party before the War* (New York: Oxford University Press, 1970), 60–61; Kenneth M. Stampp, *The Imperiled Union: Essays on the Background of the Civil War* (New York: Oxford University Press, 1980), 108–11; David M. Potter, *The Impending Crisis, 1848–1861,* completed and ed. Don E. Fehrenbacher (New York: Harper and Row, 1976), 203.

18. Mitchell Snay, *Horace Greeley and the Politics of Reform in Nineteenth-Century America* (Lanham, MD: Rowman and Littlefield, 2011), 115, 125; Leigh Fought, *Women in the World of Frederick Douglass* (New York: Oxford University Press, 2017); *Douglass' Monthly,* October 1859.

19. *Brattleboro (VT) Weekly Eagle,* March 8, 1852; *Amherst (MA) Farmer's Cabinet,* May 27, 1852; *Barre (MA) Gazette,* May 28, 1852; *Barre (MA) Patriot,* June 4, 1852. On the antiquated and contradictory rules for Democrats, see Douglas R. Egerton, *Year of Meteors: Stephen Douglas, Abraham Lincoln, and the Election That Brought on the Civil War* (New York: Bloomsbury, 2010), 66–67.

20. William Nisbet Chambers, *Old Bullion Benton: Senator from the New West* (New York: Little, Brown, 1956), 335, 402–5; *Barre (MA) Gazette,* February 3, 1854; Jean H. Baker, *James Buchanan* (New York: Times Books, 2004), 7. Sean Wilentz observes that Benton wished to keep the territories "lily-white." Wilentz, *Rise of American Democracy,* 671.

21. Freehling, *Road to Disunion,* 2:318; Michael Todd Landis, *Northern Men with Southern Loyalties: The Democratic Party and the Sectional Crisis* (Ithaca, NY: Cornell University Press, 2014), 206–7.

22. Huston, *Douglas,* 105; Michael F. Holt, *Franklin Pierce* (New York: Times Books, 2010), 79–80. Nor was Douglas as wedded to popular sovereignty as most historians suspect. Jean H. Baker notes that Douglas's proposed 1861 amendment to deny blacks the right to vote, which they enjoyed in New England, violated the localism inherent in popular sovereignty. Baker, *Affairs of Party: The Political Culture of Northern Democrats in the Mid-Nineteenth Century* (Ithaca, NY: Cornell University Press, 1983), 186.

23. Landis, *Northern Men with Southern Loyalties,* 48; Chris DeRose, *The Presidents' War: Six American Presidents and the Civil War That Divided Them* (Guilford, CT: Lyons, 2014), 65. John M. Belohlavek, *Caleb Cushing and the Shattering of the Union* (Kent, OH: Kent State University Press 2005), 254–55; *Pittsfield (MA) Sun,* June 17, 1852.

24. Freehling, *Road to Disunion,* 2:558–59; William E. Gienapp, *The Origins of the Republican Party, 1852–1856* (New York: Oxford University Press, 1987), 88–90; Walter Stahr, *Seward: Lincoln's Indispensable Man* (New York: Simon and Schuster, 2012), 162–63.

25. Some scholars doubt that those words passed between Douglas and Buchanan on December 3, 1857, suggesting that the senator invented the story when he spoke in Milwaukee in October 1860 in hopes of encouraging wavering Democratic voters that he would be a strong, Jackson-like chief executive. As early as April 2, 1858, however, the *Milwaukee Sentinel* had quoted Henry Raymond of the *New York Times*, writing from Washington, as its source for this story. In describing the meeting, Raymond reported that Buchanan warned "that he must take the liberty of reminding him of the fate of Rives and Tallmadge, who rebelled against the policy of Gen. Jackson. 'Permit me, Mr. President,' Douglas replied—'permit me to remind you that General Jackson is dead.'" The *New York Evening Post* (April 7, 1858), the *Montpelier Vermont Watchman* (April 2, 1858), and the *Manchester (NH) Union Democrat* (April 20, 1858) picked up the tale, with the last reporting that "Douglas men tell [the] story" and mention Buchanan's threat to deal with party "traitors." The *Union Democrat* was loyal to Buchanan, however, and editorialized that Douglas "may account himself lucky if he meets a better fate" than Senators Rives or Tallmadge. So far from being a Douglas-created fiction to make Buchanan appear weak, at least this proadministration editor believed that the president had come out of the meeting looking resolute. For a thorough examination of the provenance and veracity of the Buchanan-Douglas story, see the following chapter by Matthew Pinsker.

26. *Official Proceedings of the Democratic National Convention at Charleston, 1860* (Cleveland: Nevins' Print, Plain Dealer Job Office, 1860), 90–91; *Amherst (MA) Farmer's Cabinet*, June 22, 1859; *Frederick Douglass' Paper*, April 29, 1859.

27. Stephen A. Douglas to Charles Lanphier, July 5, 1860, in Johannsen, *Letters of Stephen A. Douglas*, 498; Robert W. Johannsen, "Stephen A. Douglas' New England Campaign, 1860," *New England Quarterly* 35 (June 1962): 186; Potter, *Impending Crisis*, 441.

28. *National Intelligencer* (Washington, DC), October 31, 1860; *Hartford (CT) Courant*, October 25, 1860.

29. Johannsen, "Douglas' New England Campaign," 176–77; *Niles (MI) Republican*, October 20, 1860 (I am grateful to John Quist for bringing this episode to my attention); *National Intelligencer* (Washington, DC), September 23, 1860; *San Francisco Bulletin*, October 9, 1860; Eric H. Walther, *The Fire-Eaters* (Baton Rouge: Louisiana State University Press, 1992), 76–77; *Madison Wisconsin Patriot*, August 9, 1860; *Albany Evening Journal*, October 11, 1860; *Washington (DC) Constitution*, October 13, 17, 1860.

30. Thurlow Weed to Abraham Lincoln, July 29, 1860, Papers of Abraham Lincoln, Library of Congress, Washington, DC.

"GENERAL JACKSON IS DEAD"

Dissecting a Popular Anecdote of
Nineteenth-Century Party Leadership

MATTHEW PINSKER

President James Buchanan delivered an icy stare to Senator Stephen A.
Douglas as they sat across from each other inside the White House on
Thursday morning, December 3, 1857. The "Little Giant" had just refused
a direct request from "Old Buck" about the growing Lecompton controversy. The new Congress was assembling, and everybody had been
talking for weeks about the fate of slavery in Kansas Territory. The main
question was whether national Democrats in Washington were going to
accept the "Lecompton swindle," allowing proslavery forces in Kansas
to essentially stack the deck for an upcoming constitutional referendum
that they had manipulated shamelessly and then scheduled with dubious authority. Under pressure from southern Democrats, the president
was prepared to acquiesce, but the Illinois senator, author of the original
Kansas-Nebraska Act of 1854, had just revealed to him that he would not.
This was not the illustration of popular sovereignty that he had imagined
for the territory. It was a tense moment. "Mr. Douglas," Buchanan finally
observed, "I do wish you to remember that no democrat ever yet differed
from an administration of his own choice without being crushed," adding
ominously, "beware of the fate of Tallmadge and Rives." Defiant as ever,

President James Buchanan (*center*) and his cabinet, ca. 1859. Clockwise, from top: Secretary of the Treasury Howell Cobb, Postmaster General Joseph Holt, Secretary of the Navy Isaac Toucey, Attorney General Jeremiah S. Black; Secretary of the Interior Jacob Thompson; Secretary of War John B. Floyd; and Secretary of State Lewis Cass. Montage of photographs courtesy Mathew Brady Collection, National Archives, Washington, DC.

Douglas stood up in the face of that implicit threat and replied coolly, "Mr. President, I wish you to remember that General Jackson is dead, sir." That striking scene has been recounted many times over the years by nineteenth-century historians and biographers. Yet it is better understood as an example of self-serving political fiction than any kind of transcript for real political drama. This was a memorable story, for sure, but one that was told with a strategic purpose *after the fact*—first by a mysterious leak in the spring of 1858 and then again, with ever-more-elaborate detail from Douglas himself, in two combative speeches during the 1860 presidential campaign. The beleaguered candidate's unexpected degree of open betrayal then compelled the incumbent president to deny the whole story in public. It was all wildly unprecedented. For this reason, the "General Jackson is dead" insult reveals even more about the pivotal 1860 election contest than it does about the earlier Lecompton crisis.

Such a complicated, evolving anecdote also illustrates a great deal about the challenges of writing antebellum political narrative. Scholars have used this story for years without fully fact-checking its sources. There are many possible explanations for this oversight, but mainly it is because historians, like the participants themselves, are often prone to oversimplify for the sake of making a dramatic point. Naturally, dissecting such an episode does kill much of the drama within it, but what remains is significant nonetheless. The alleged Douglas retort provides both a case study in narrative methodology and also a pathway toward a more nuanced view about one of the most consequential feuds in American political history.

There is no denying that some of the finest historians in the field have relished using this particular anecdote, even sometimes adding their own minor embellishments in ways that seem to owe more to Shakespeare than to Herodotus. In his magisterial volume on the breakup of the Democratic Party, Roy Nichols claims to know that both men were in "dictatorial moods" that December morning. Allan Nevins begins his colorful account with what he imagines as a "frigid" handshake between the politicians. "Douglas stormed into the White House," is how James McPherson frames the famous encounter in *Battle Cry of Freedom* (1988). Buchanan biographer Philip Klein implies that he knows the exact pacing of the private interview, detailing how the bitter rivals discussed the Lecompton problem "dispassionately at first" but then "with increasing impatience and rancor." In the course of summarizing their conversation, Douglas biographer Robert Johannsen goes deep inside his subject's mind, emphasizing the Illinois senator's shock "at being so peremptorily ignored" on Kansas matters. Klein has a dignified Buchanan rising to deliver his memorable threat about the now-obscure political figures Nathanial P. Tallmadge and William C. Rives. Nevins suggests that it was the Little Giant who must have "tossed his mane of black hair angrily" as he stood in defiance of the embattled president. Every leading scholar seems to quote Douglas's nifty line about Andrew Jackson being dead, even those few, like David Potter or Kenneth Stampp, who quietly acknowledge some uncertainty surrounding its exact phrasing. "I wish you to remember that General Jackson is dead, Sir," really has become the "retort," as Jean Baker describes it, "that in different forms and with different subjects has resonated throughout American history."[1]

The original source material for these scholars comes almost exclusively from a hastily improvised Douglas campaign speech delivered in Milwaukee, Wisconsin, on October 13, 1860. This effort represented his only extended firsthand public commentary on the affair. In those remarks he did not describe any "frigid" handshakes or "tossed" manes of hair, but the candidate did regale his audience with the colorful lines quoted at the outset of this essay. The full text of the Douglas statement then quickly appeared in several friendly Democratic newspapers, presumably provided by the senator's longtime traveling assistant (and shorthand transcription expert) James B. Sheridan. Over the years, some scholars have reviewed these accounts themselves, but most appear to have relied on excerpted versions of the speech that appeared in the 1880s and 1890s, when it was brought back into circulation through two major postwar political studies. Longtime Democratic newspaper editor Jeriah Bonham relayed part of the Douglas version in his memoir, *Fifty Years Recollections* (1883), though he mistakenly placed the speech in Chicago. More significantly, former Lincoln aides John G. Nicolay and John Hay included an even lengthier excerpt from the Milwaukee speech in their influential 1890 multivolume biography of Abraham Lincoln.[2]

Modern historians do not often quote from the initial public reports about the Buchanan-Douglas meeting, probably because they offer almost none of the dramatic details that Douglas shared in Milwaukee in 1860. They also convey a far more uncertain impression of the encounter.

The *New York Herald* provided the most widely reprinted contemporary dispatch about the affair, transmitted by telegraph on the very day that it occurred. "Judge Douglas and the President to-day had a full and free interchange of opinion on the Kansas question," claimed the *Herald*'s Washington correspondent, "without, it is understood, being able to arrive at the same conclusion in regard to the line of policy which justice and duty required each to pursue." Despite this allusion to intraparty conflict, the report from this leading Democratic newspaper then pointedly described the "interview" as "courteous" before claiming that the men had "parted as friends."[3] In a separate story within the same column, the paper also observed, with apparent authority, that Douglas "intends to suspend judgment until he sees what position the President takes in his message, and all the facts upon the subject are laid before the Senate," predicting that only then would he "take an early occasion to define his position."[4] Numerous Democratic newspapers carried some version of these initial dispatches.

The Republican press was naturally far more willing to stoke the flames of discord. Both the *New York Tribune* and the *Chicago Tribune* almost immediately interpreted the Buchanan-Douglas meeting as a clear sign of growing division within the Democratic ranks. "Senator Douglas and the President had a conference this morning on Kansas affairs," wrote Horace Greeley's correspondent on Thursday afternoon, December 3, 1857, "but without any satisfactory result." According to that account, "Senator Douglas denounced the Convention and maintained the whole [Lecompton] Constitution ought to be submitted to the people." This dispatch concluded, "The Democratic camp is troubled again." In Chicago the Republican paper commented almost gleefully on the apparent disagreement over Kansas policy expressed at the "interview," where each man was "absolute in his position." On this point the *Chicago Tribune* could barely contain its enthusiasm. "Has Douglas at last rebelled?" it asked. "Has he mustered the courage to brave the lion in his lair?"[5]

This was the critical question, but the answer, at least coming out of the meeting itself, was more muted than one might expect given all of the later stormy retellings of the encounter. On Friday the *New York Herald*'s correspondent confirmed that Douglas seemed concerned but was holding his fire. "Judge Douglas denies that he has broken ground with the administration on the Kansas question," came the definitive-sounding report. "He says he disapproves much that has been done, but will wait until he sees the Message and hears all sides before determining definitely upon his course of action. He hopes all differences will be healed."[6]

Here was coded language for political truce, not war. Buchanan and Douglas were circling each other warily, but the full open breach between them had not yet occurred. It is important to recall that these two party leaders had spent much of the previous year working in harmony on the knotty Kansas question despite their lingering personal antipathy as previous rivals. They were also both heavily invested as leaders in getting the nation and their party past the sectional troubles regarding the territory's future. If they now disagreed over the proposed state's flawed constitutional process, no matter how sharply, then each politician was still pragmatic and experienced enough to realize that no good would come from an open feud about it. Of course, they might well have threatened and insulted each other anyway inside the confines of the White House—nobody can know for sure—but even so, that would have meant practically nothing to these Washington veterans. They needed each other, and they knew it. That was the essential message that Douglas appeared to be trying to convey through the pages of the *New York Herald.*

In his own stiff, halting manner, President Buchanan tried to reciprocate. He devoted nearly one-fifth of his annual message delivered to Congress on Tuesday, December 8, to the subject of Kansas, even though he grumbled near the end that, in his opinion, the troubled territory had "for some years occupied too much of the public attention." What consumed most of the president's verbiage was a paean to Douglas's original territorial-organizing legislation and its "great doctrine of popular sovereignty."[7] This was an internal peace overture of sorts, one that Buchanan and his advisors clearly hoped would placate the Illinois senator even as they ignored his warnings about endorsing the dubious constitutional referendum. Even though some Douglas supporters leapt at this rhetorical offering when they read the message, it was not nearly enough.[8] The senator himself wasted no time in announcing right after the official reading that he "totally dissent[ed]" from the president's position on the Lecompton matter and that he would speak from the Senate floor about it on the following day.[9]

Delivered on Wednesday, December 9, that speech, which Douglas biographer Robert Johannsen calls "probably the most significant of his career," marked the actual open breach with Buchanan, though even then, it is important to realize, it was not yet an irreparable one.[10] Both sides continued to labor in the subsequent months to overcome their differences. The Lecompton matter was complicated by a number of technical factors—whether or not the original convention had authority to draft a state constitution, how exactly that constitution should be submitted to eligible voters within the territory, and finally, and most explosively, whether or not the property rights of existing slaveholders could somehow be protected even if territorial voters rejected any future for slavery in the new state. All of those factors had played into the "swindle" at Lecompton, but the complex nature of these issues made the crisis an inherently negotiable one—at least for national Democrats like Buchanan and Douglas, who were no longer beholden to a strong antislavery faction in their party after the tumultuous realignment of 1854 that had given birth to the Republican Party.

So for the time being, Douglas remained as chairman of the Senate Committee on Territories and retained much of his influence on Capitol Hill despite his open rupture with Buchanan. Though still a leading senator, he probably held his greatest sway during this period over Democratic forces in the House, where the combined anti-Lecompton votes of Republicans and a cohort of northern Democrats still held a shaky majority. This reality then compelled the president and his men to attempt to forge some kind of compromise measure. Hence, the English Bill emerged in the spring of 1858, a proposal drafted by Representative William English, a Democrat from Indiana, which shifted the debate away from the controversial December referendum and toward a plan for a new territorial vote tied to a land-grant issue. There were also other key compromise initiatives floated during this period, including one from Senator John Crittenden of Kentucky that Douglas supported, but ultimately it was the English Bill that prevailed. For weeks and months, however, it was unclear exactly how these matters would shake out and whether or not Douglas might be able to find common ground with the president and the national party.

That was how the dramatic story of the private Buchanan-Douglas meeting from December got a new lease on life. On Wednesday, March 24, 1858, editor Henry J. Raymond reported to the *New York Times* from Washington in a fascinating column about the Kansas question that included an entirely new set of details about the earlier White House encounter. Raymond began his dispatch by noting that "nobody, in or out of Congress, talks or thinks of anything else" besides "the fate of Lecompton." He claimed this was not really because of the slavery issue per se, but rather the result of all the stratagems over "*party* divisions, or *party* supremacy," which he believed were "at the bottom of most of it." Raymond concluded that the president had made a near-fatal error by insisting upon Lecompton as a party measure and was now on the verge of feeling its defeat as "a death-blow to his Administration." By contrast, Douglas appeared to the Republican journalist as almost indifferent to Buchanan's fate and thoroughly unbowed by the "marked bitterness" being directed toward him from southern Democrats. To punctuate this point about the Little Giant's unwillingness to appear either "mealy-mouthed" or "overfastidious," Raymond then described for his readers some vague "interviews" between the senator and president during "an early stage of his defection," in which "the latter remarked to him that it was very perilous for a public man to put himself in opposition to his party—and that he must take the liberty of reminding him of the fate of Rives and Tallmadge, who rebelled against the policy of Gen. Jackson. 'Permit me, Mr. President,' Douglas replied, 'permit me to remind you *that General Jackson is dead*.'" This outright defiance, according to Raymond, was "very much the tone which the Illinois Senator has taken throughout this contest."[11]

That last characterization may or may not have been true, but these were certainly provocative new details of the Buchanan-Douglas feud that Raymond was now sharing with the public. The journalist did not provide any sources for this intimate scene, but the implication was that he got such confidential information from the senator himself, or at least from one of his trusted advisors. The question is, why would tongues from the Douglas camp have become loosened by March 1858, especially in front of a Republican journalist? Perhaps it was an accident, someone just blurting out the literal truth of what had happened one night while drinking in Washington. More likely, however, if Douglas or one of his aides had really been the source behind Raymond's reportage, then it was probably because they were boasting, intentionally inflating (or perhaps even inventing) the General Jackson retort in order to enhance the senator's image at a key moment in this ongoing partisan saga.

But there is an equally plausible scenario that suggests it was Raymond who might have been the one guilty of reshaping this anecdote for partisan purposes. The Buchanan-Douglas feud represented an enormous opportunity for Republicans. Leading party newspaper editors from the East, such as Raymond and Greeley, were practically salivating at the prospect of drawing the Little Giant out of the Democratic Party. Their obvious interest in the Illinois senator had been the subject of intense parlor discussions for months and a particular source of concern to Lincoln. From Springfield, he was asking sharply, for example, "What does the New-York Tribune mean by it's [*sic*] constant eulogising, and admiring, and magnifying [of] Douglas?"[12] Raymond was somewhat less openly admiring of Douglas than Greeley, but he was just as invested in flipping him. Thus, by late March 1858, with the Lecompton debate at a critical juncture and with growing signs that Democrats were trying to find grounds for mutual accommodation, a shrewd Republican journalist like Raymond might well have felt plenty of motivation to rekindle the embers of that high-level dispute, even at the cost of a little political fiction.

One clue that suggests some level of script doctoring by Raymond was the pointed reference to "the fate of Rives and Tallmadge, who rebelled against the policy of Gen. Jackson." This was not such an uncommon usage in that era, but the way it was framed here was oddly wrong. Rives and Tallmadge had been two respected conservative Democrats from the 1830s and 1840s. Rives had been the more prominent figure, a member of the Virginia gentry who had once studied law under Thomas Jefferson, served in Congress, and then joined the Jackson administration as the US minister to France before entering the Senate in 1832. Tallmadge was an experienced New York politician who had begun his senatorial career in Washington just one year after Rives had joined the upper chamber. Both men sometimes defied President Jackson, such as over his Specie Circular in 1836, but they bickered much more openly with his successor, Martin Van Buren.[13]

Van Buren biographer Donald Cole provides an especially sophisticated account of the conservative Democratic realignment in the late 1830s. Cole situates Rives and Tallmadge and their conservative allies in a four-way policy battle that erupted in late 1837 over Van Buren's independent-treasury proposal, with John C. Calhoun and his hard-money faction on one extreme and probank Whigs, led by Daniel Webster and Henry Clay, on the other. The conservative Democrats occupied a middle ground, preferring the old Jacksonian pet banks to the new president's alternative. For a time, they frustrated administration efforts by voting occasionally with the Whigs.[14] Naturally, tensions mounted, and by 1839, Rives and Tallmadge had officially switched party affiliations, as much from local forces in their respective states, however, as from any irreconcilable conflict with the administration. With some hiccups (Virginia was without a senator for over a year in the early 1840s), they were able to continue in office as US senators, caucusing with the Whigs until 1844 and 1845, long after both Jackson and Van Buren had departed Washington. Ex-senator Tallmadge subsequently held an appointment as governor of Wisconsin Territory, and Rives even enjoyed a second stint in Paris during the early 1850s as US minister under the Taylor and Fillmore administrations. Their "fate" as party bolters had not really been so dire, nor was it the result of any action by Jackson.

True, both men were out of elective office by the 1850s, and their subsequent careers had exposed them to a degree of disdain from regular politicos. Tallmadge had become a noted spiritualist (claiming direct communication from the aura of the late Webster no less), and Rives, somewhat more quietly, was on his way toward becoming a respected historian, author of a soon-to-be published multivolume biography of James Madison.[15]

Perhaps more than anything else, that explains why these two figures had become a kind of editorial punchline in the 1850s whenever Democratic newspapermen were trying to discourage party bolting.[16] Yet that is also why this seems suspiciously like something that Raymond might have found as useful source material if he was trying to come up with a credible (but fictional) line for a Buchanan threat. The problem is that he had Old Buck invoking Rives and Tallmadge, then Douglas responding with a reference to General Jackson. But it was Van Buren, not Jackson, who tangled with the disloyal senators. Besides, neither president had really done much to destroy the careers of those men anyway. Raymond was only a teenager living in upstate New York during the original controversy over the independent-treasury proposal, so he probably just did not understand or even remember the full story.

Historians have not always been clear about these nuances when explaining the meaning behind Buchanan's alleged threat. Biographer Philip Klein claims flatly that Jackson "destroyed the careers" of Rives and Tallmadge. James McPherson describes them as "two senators who had gone into political oblivion after crossing Andrew Jackson."[17] That was the impression left by the *New York Times* story from March 1858 and also from the campaign version later embellished by Douglas in October 1860, but it was not the reality. Douglas was older than Raymond but also would have been too young to know the story firsthand. He had only been a novice state legislator in his midtwenties, still serving with Lincoln in Vandalia, when the conservative Democrats had first launched their revolt against Van Buren. Ironically, the only one in this exchange who actually knew the episode well was President Buchanan, who had served as a colleague in the Senate with both Rives and Tallmadge and had even remained on good terms with the New Yorker. In fact, Tallmadge had publicly endorsed him during the 1856 presidential contest—yet another reason why it seems unlikely that Buchanan would have threatened Douglas with a reference to his friend's "fate."[18]

Still, the larger point here is that Douglas survived his presidential challenge in 1858 and did so with even greater aplomb than either Rives or Tallmadge. His rupture with the president was made final by his decision to vote against the English Bill, which passed in late spring. Despite all their efforts, there was to be no compromise between these two stubborn leaders. Instead, Buchanan began to seek wholesale retribution against Douglas by early that summer, dumping many of the senator's patronage appointees in Illinois and attempting to undermine his bid to win reelection to the Senate. In his fury Douglas even suspected Buchanan and Lincoln of conspiring against him, believing that the administration was actively helping his wily Republican opponent (designated as the "first and only choice" of Illinois Republicans in a defiant protest of their own against the machinations of opportunistic editors like

Greeley and Raymond). Yet the Little Giant ultimately beat them both, earning his third term in the Senate through a combination of closely fought legislative battles in the fall elections and holdovers from the state senate. Meanwhile, in August 1858, Kansas voters had rejected the new constitutional referendum, thoroughly repudiating the administration's Lecompton policy. It had not been an easy year for Douglas, but in the end it was a remarkable personal triumph.

Victory for Douglas was so complete that he had some reason to hope that he might be able to continue to overcome Buchanan's venom and southern bitterness in order to reunite the party for the national contest in 1860. Yet as Raymond had observed wisely in March 1858, southern Democrats were now consumed by their anger at Douglas; they had seemingly "transferred their hatred of the Republicans to him, and their chief anxiety now is, that he should not reap the reward of his 'treachery.'"[19] Douglas was able to win the Democratic presidential nomination in June 1860, though not before southern Democrats bolted from the convention in disgust and set up their own campaign. The defection of southern votes hurt the senator's chances, but in a complicated four-way race (involving Lincoln for the Republicans, John Bell for the Constitutional Unionists, and Buchanan's vice president, John C. Breckinridge, for southern Democrats), it was not necessarily a fatal blow; yet it left hardly any margin for error. Thus, when President Buchanan added to the senator's already imposing challenge by publicly signaling his unprecedented endorsement for Breckinridge and fellow party bolters in early July 1860, Douglas was truly in grave political jeopardy.[20]

Now facing his own set of crippling betrayals as the ostensible national leader of the Democratic Party, Douglas did not hesitate to lash out, and in so doing he decided for the first time in public to retell the story behind his original Lecompton confrontation with Buchanan. The senator spoke about this matter at the end of July 1860 in Concord, New Hampshire, at the start of what would soon become a grueling and unprecedented national campaign. Douglas was the first American presidential candidate to stump for the office, a decision he had made impetuously in the summer of 1860, almost out of desperation, following the breakup of the national party organization. But in doing so, he also determined to exact some personal revenge on Buchanan.

At Concord Douglas described in seemingly candid terms the pivotal conversation he had conducted with Buchanan in December 1857. "The President told me," he now claimed, "that if I did not obey him and vote to force that Lecompton Constitution on the people of Kansas against their will, that he would take off the head of every friend that I had in office."[21] There was no specific reference here to a meeting inside the White House, nor any mention of Rives and Tallmadge (nor even the late, lamented General Jackson), but as always, Douglas proved eager to impress his audience with vivid details about how he had delivered a sharp rejoinder in the moment of crisis. In this version he claimed that he had responded to the president's indelicate threat with an earnest invocation of principle: "I told him in reply, that my friends were as dear to me as those of any other man could be to him; but that if I had a friend who was not willing to lose his office rather than to degrade me into a tool of the Executive power, he did not deserve to be my friend." Then Douglas proceeded to rant at some length about the dangers of unbridled executive power and Buchanan's penchant for petty partisan leadership. He reminded the audience how the president's vendetta against him in the famous senatorial campaign against Lincoln had failed and predicted that it would be overcome yet once again.[22]

Buchanan was bitterly offended by such public indiscretion, so much so that he also decided to break political traditions. Within weeks after the Concord speech, his allies were circulating a devastating public letter to Democratic newspapers, written by the president himself, categorically denying the charges. Buchanan began by quoting Douglas's memorable line about him threatening to "take off the head of every friend" and observed coyly that there must have been some kind of "mistake." "I never held any such conversation with Judge Douglas," Buchanan informed Virginia congressman William H. Smith, his ostensible correspondent, on August 11, "nor any conversation whatever affording the least color or pretext for such a statement." He went on to add that it was simply "not in my nature to address such threatening and insulting language to any gentleman." Yet he could not help but observe that the two men had not conversed at all, on any subject, since that moment in December 1857. By the president's reckoning, the accusations about a patronage war against the Illinois senator were also wildly overblown since he had "not removed one in ten of his friends, and not one of his relatives."[23] This was a common refrain of Buchanan's. On the same day that he wrote Congressman Smith, the president had dashed off a confidential note to a journalist, claiming in this case that he had not removed "one in twenty of the Douglas office holders" and observing specifically that the senator's father-in-law and brother-in-law both still held "lucrative offices." "I do not indulge a proscriptive spirit," Buchanan boasted, conveniently ignoring his earlier well-publicized purge of prominent Douglas supporters during the 1858 campaign.[24]

Regardless of who was right about the relative vindictiveness of the Democratic administration, this public spectacle was quite unusual in American political history. Intraparty feuds were fairly common—discussing them directly in campaign speeches and through party newspapers was not. This much Buchanan acknowledged. "I have transgressed a rule," he admitted, before explaining that he had deemed "the present case a proper exception" because the candidate's extraordinary public statement "comes with such force."[25] Douglas was never one to be cowed by a rebuke, but the high-stakes nature of this intraparty spat seemed to propel him into greater discipline. In the subsequent weeks he continued to assault Breckinridge but apparently did not return to the Buchanan story, at least not until after campaign conditions changed dramatically for him in mid-October.

The next time Douglas addressed the issue in public, he was hoarse and exhausted, speaking at an outdoor rally in Milwaukee on a Saturday afternoon, October 13, 1860. The candidate was then in the midst of a period that biographer Martin Quitt describes as "a strenuous stretch of constant movement."[26] With Breckinridge and his administration allies still holding most southern Democrats and even threatening, by some accounts, to steal votes among northern conservatives in the complex race, Douglas was in dire straits. By mid-October, he had been campaigning almost without interruption since July. The Little Giant had traveled across New England, the Great Lakes region, and had even dipped into some of the border states of the upper South, powered by the nation's impressive antebellum railroad network and prodigious amounts of alcohol, at least according to persistent rumors of his inebriation.[27] Just days prior to arriving in Milwaukee, however, Douglas had received word that

Republicans had swept state elections in Indiana, Ohio, and Pennsylvania—a clear sign that his electoral slate was going to be demolished at the national polls in November despite his strenuous efforts. One can only imagine the mounting sense of frustration as the Little Giant came to realize that his campaign and the country were falling apart. From Douglas's perspective, extremists from both sides—Republicans in the North and Breckinridge Democrats in the South—had ruined him.

All of this is apparent in his recounting of the now-famous version of his showdown with Buchanan. Douglas was determined to release his venom by embarrassing the president with lurid details about his un-Jacksonian behavior. The immediate run-up to Douglas's vivid anecdote, the one he delivered in full fury at Milwaukee, is critical to understanding his mindset and yet has almost always been left out of the narrative equation. Douglas began his most colorful recounting of the events of December 1857 by announcing that an "Abolitionist newspaper" had "just been placed in my hands" that contained what he termed "ludicrous and laughable" charges from a "Breckinridge committee in Kansas," namely that he had been the secret architect of the "Lecompton swindle."[28] He was referring to an article that had appeared just the day before in the *Chicago Tribune* containing testimony from several former delegates to the 1857 Lecompton constitutional convention detailing the senator's secret role in their deliberations. This was a story that had circulated briefly in late 1857 before the Buchanan-Douglas feud had really escalated, but it had since disappeared from public discussion.[29] Now, however, these Kansas men were recalling in writing how their convention president, the late John Calhoun, a former resident of Springfield, Illinois, and one of Douglas's closest patronage friends in the territory, had shared with them a secret letter from the senator endorsing what became their controversial plan to craft a phony proslavery referendum for the territory.[30] Douglas snarled with disdain as he insisted that this idea was "false in every particular." The Milwaukee audience responded in boisterous fashion—"fictitious undoubtedly" cried one listener while hundreds of others offered "great laughter" and "immense applause." The accusation had become almost impossible to believe. It had long been understood that it was Douglas's opposition to the maneuvers of the proslavery forces at Lecompton in 1857 that had earned him Buchanan's unbridled wrath and had actually placed him in his present gloomy political fix—the losing presidential candidate of a shattered national party. Now, if this charge were true, it would seem as if he had nothing left, not even the dignity of his principles.

Nineteenth-century American campaigns were very rough affairs, full of invective, falsehoods, and often the worst kinds of bigotry or fear-mongering. Yet even by those low standards, this particular assault from the Democratic Association of Leavenworth was notably hard hitting. The charges, which first appeared in the *New Orleans Delta* on October 7, were considered highly sensational. "STARTLING DISCLOSURES" blared the headline in the *Tribune* and numerous other journals that carried the story, North and South, throughout mid-October: "Read! Read! Read!"[31] The Breckinridge forces in Kansas had pulled together ten separate, quite-detailed, and credible-sounding statements from leading Lecompton figures. Six of the men testified that, during the rump constitutional convention in the autumn of 1857, someone read to them from, or they heard about, a confidential letter by Douglas authorizing the partial submission of the proslavery constitution as a device to enable Kansas statehood. Two additional delegates also claimed to have seen the actual letter, including one old ally of Douglas's from Illinois days (a man named Green Redmon) who swore that he had even recognized the handwriting. Two others confessed that they had only heard about this mysterious document afterward, but one of them revealed that the Calhoun family now acknowledged possessing the letter and that some political agent (presumably from the Douglas camp) had recently offered them a bribe of two thousand dollars for it.

It was nearly three years since the Lecompton Constitution had been originally drafted and just over two years since it had been killed, but these painstaking references to the "partial submission" schedule still mattered in American politics. Everyone remembered how a handful of diehard Lecompton delegates had once opposed what was being called "full submission" as they met to draft a new governing document between September and November 1857. Most of those men had just wanted to craft a proslavery constitution and send it directly to Congress, where their southern allies held greater influence. The Buchanan administration was already on record favoring popular sovereignty for the territory, but southern pressure was building on the president to find a way around what had suddenly become a very inconvenient doctrine for proslavery Democrats. The solution they arrived at for Lecompton was the partial-submission process, which Surveyor General John Calhoun, the convention's president, eventually prevailed on a majority of the reluctant proslavery delegates to accept. Calhoun convinced them, perhaps using Douglas's secret endorsement, that while they could not just skip the popular vote entirely, they might submit the question of slavery—and only the question of slavery—to the people in a manner that would stack the deck in their favor. The delegates also devised what they called a "schedule" by which to implement this unusual vote. It was this initial schedule for balloting on December 21, 1857, that became the source of all subsequent controversy, mainly because it framed the slavery referendum in a devious way (by guaranteeing the continuation of at least some slavery no matter how residents voted) yet also because it stripped Governor Robert J. Walker, a leading moderate, of his powers to interfere in this process.[32]

None of the damaging affidavits that appeared near the end of the 1860 campaign mentioned this hated schedule, but they did refer more obliquely to a "plan" of "partial submission," which various delegates claimed that Douglas had either suggested or endorsed in his letter to Calhoun. Thus, it was quite revealing that, when he launched into his litany of denials in Milwaukee, Douglas began by disputing a variety of strawman claims. "I never saw the Lecompton constitution until after it had been adopted in Kansas," he declared at the outset; of course not, that would have been physically impossible. *"I never saw the schedule by which the slavery clause was submitted,"* he continued, *"until after it was forwarded to the states for publication."* On this point he was most emphatic, adding, *"I never heard, nor conceived, nor dreamed, that any man on earth ever thought of such a scheme."* Yet that was not what the Breckinridge forces were accusing him of, at least not directly. The questionnaire that the Democratic Association of Leavenworth had circulated to delegates in late 1860 did not use the word "schedule" at all but instead asked if the men had seen or heard about a letter from Douglas that "foreshadowed" the final "plan of submission" that they had adopted in 1857. This formulation was vague enough to allow a range of interpretations, but

Douglas intentionally misread these details in order to distract attention from a messier reality and to give extra force to his denials. It was a classic performance from a master debater who appreciated the benefit of staying on the offensive. In Milwaukee, Douglas explicitly tried turning the tables on his enemies. "It seems as if the disunionists of the South and the abolitionists of the North," he complained, "are determined to hunt me down by all the means that malice can invent."[33]

It was at this moment that Douglas then unleashed a four-thousand-word recollection of his "personal history" with the Lecompton swindle, providing a litany of sharp anecdotes and allegedly verbatim quotations from high-level private conversations, of which the December 3, 1857, interview with Buchanan played only a minor part. Douglas began in the spring of 1857, describing how he had helped the president convince Robert Walker to accept the position of territorial governor. He went on to detail the administration's support for popular sovereignty, or full submission, during that year by relating a series of exchanges he had with Walker that seemed to prove Buchanan's commitment to the policy. On one point, however, Douglas's memory grew noticeably fuzzy: He could not seem to remember what, if anything, he had communicated to Surveyor General Calhoun about the process of drafting and submitting the state constitution. "I may possibly have written him," Douglas conceded, though surely only for minor patronage matters. "I am not in the habit of writing political letters," claimed the Illinois senator, almost laughably.

But Douglas was perfectly clear about his reaction to the notorious referendum schedule. "I denounced it the very instant I heard of it," he declared. "I did not wait one hour or one minute when I discovered the trick by which the people were to be cheated." Yet he did wait several hours, minutes, and even days before publicly denouncing the Lecompton swindle. The convention adjourned late on Saturday night, November 7, 1857. By mid-November, reports of the so-called swindle were being circulated among the nation's newspapers. The *Chicago Tribune* offered a reasonably accurate if harsh account of the final schedule on November 12, under the headline "Astounding Disclosures," with a follow up on November 16 confirming the adjournment and the final decision for partial submission.[34] Other newspapers followed suit. Douglas made no public comment during this period, however, claiming that he needed to await the full text of the proposed constitution and all the relevant details about the schedule. He began writing private letters expressing his concern, even disgust, at the news from Lecompton, however, by Monday, November 23. "I regret the present position of things in Kansas," Douglas confessed to an ally in the territory, "and fear the consequences." He was still unsure of exactly what had happened but was becoming more critical of Calhoun's actions. "I fear he has made a fatal mistake," wrote Douglas, "and got us all into trouble."[35]

According to his recollection, Douglas was defiant from the beginning, responding to the crisis on the "very night the news arrived at Chicago." But that was just hyperbole. In reality he was deeply concerned about Lecompton by mid-November but not fully committed to any single course of action. He did not wait long to announce his position and to defy the president in public, but he did wait for a bit. This slight hesitation was only common sense because, despite some clear signals coming from the Buchanan newspapers during the second half of that month, there was no certainty about the president's final position.[36] That would not come until the annual message on December 8. This nuance matters because it helps explain an otherwise glaring inconsistency in Douglas's Milwaukee speech. He said he did not wait "one hour or minute" to denounce the swindle but then suggested how, after reaching Washington in early December and going "directly" to the White House to explain his views, the president had "begged" him "not to say anything upon the subject."

At Milwaukee, for the first time, Douglas also revealed that he had responded to Buchanan's desperate request for loyalty with a counteroffer. The senator would keep quiet until after December 21 if the president would do so as well. When Buchanan declined, explaining that his annual message would generally support the Lecompton schedule, Douglas claimed that he got angry. "I replied that if he did I would denounce it the moment his message was read." Then the senator shared with his audience all of those now-famous details about their fiery exchange regarding the threat about Tallmadge, Rives, and General Jackson, dressing up the language slightly from the way Raymond had reported it back in the spring of 1858. Now Douglas had Buchanan saying more ominously (and with the name order suddenly reversed), "Beware of the fate of

Tallmadge and Rives." More importantly, his reply to this threat was even cooler than previously described. "Mr. President," Douglas now recalled saying, "I wish you to remember that General Jackson is dead, sir."

There was no doubt about the impression that the senator intended to convey at Milwaukee. The December 1857 meeting was his moment of truth—a turning point. The president threatened to crush him. Douglas responded with courage. The battle was joined. What resulted was total triumph for the Little Giant, at least in the short term. The Lecompton Constitution was rejected in the second referendum, then the senator from Illinois won a tough reelection contest. It was a rare moment of pure vindication. As Douglas put it that day in Milwaukee, "And one thing is certain, the people of Illinois decided in 1858 that James Buchanan was not General Jackson." During the very worst moment of his 1860 campaign, it must have felt reassuring to recall the magic of his greatest political triumph.

This also helps explain why the confrontation story had grown so much in his retelling. What had worked in Concord back in July no longer seemed rousing enough by mid-October, so Douglas punched up the details. He may have done this because it was the truth or perhaps because he had since consulted the old newspaper clippings from the spring of 1858, but there can be no doubt that his story had changed and that, even within his final, most elaborate retelling, there were a host of inconsistencies and incredible claims.

Nobody really found the time to challenge Douglas directly on such points in 1860, but many of his contemporaries were skeptical of his veracity. The Washington correspondent for the *New York Herald* was particularly caustic. "The speech of Mr. Douglas at Milwaukee is regarded here as showing to what lengths a Longbow can draw his string." The *Herald* dismissed the candidate as "a first rate story teller" who "can dress up imaginary conversations equal to [Charles Walton] Sanders [a popular children's schoolbook author]." "The only thing they want," smirked the powerful Democratic newspaper, "is a seasoning of the truth."[37] The Republican newspaper in Milwaukee, edited by the well-regarded Rufus King, quoted this observation from the *Herald* approvingly just two weeks after Douglas had departed the city. "We supposed at the time, that the

MATTHEW PINSKER

'conversation' which Mr. D. related, as having occurred between President Buchanan and himself, in regard to the Lecompton Constitution, was an 'imaginary' one; and the *Herald's* correspondent confirms this belief."[38]

In fairness, the remainder of Douglas's recollected narrative at Milwaukee was somewhat more credible than what had come before it. The senator related how he had spoken out against the president's Kansas policy on December 9, 1857, immediately after the presentation of the annual message, and how he had participated in the debates that escalated in early 1858 once the returns from the Lecompton referendum were officially received. He recalled how Calhoun then came to Washington to view these debates and how the two of them met once, late at night, at the senator's home to discuss how things had fallen apart. Douglas provided a litany of details about their alleged discussion, insisting that when they were actually face to face, Calhoun "never intimated that he had any authority from me, that I approved that scheme . . . , [or] that he had received a letter from me." To support this claim, Douglas identified a witness to their conversation, US Attorney William Weer from Kansas, who was with them on that night in the senator's library. Sure enough, two weeks later at the very end of the 1860 campaign, Weer published an account in a Kansas newspaper fully backing his candidate and providing a transcript of a letter allegedly written by the senator on November 23, 1857, testifying to his concern over the Lecompton swindle and vowing to remain true to his principles.[39]

Douglas also heatedly denied the charge that his agents had tried to bribe the Calhoun family in order to recover the so-called secret letter, which had provided evidence of his involvement in the partial-submission scheme. He counterattacked aggressively on this point, bewailing what he described as a character assault on poor old widow Calhoun, whose husband had died just the year before. He also revealed his own secret information suggesting it was actually a Buchanan officeholder from Nebraska who had approached Mrs. Calhoun with the two-thousand-dollar bribe. By that point in his narrative, Douglas was reaching full throttle on his indignation. "What can you think of a body of men," he asked, "who will go around trying to bribe widow women to betray the private correspondence of their dead husbands?" Naturally, the audience answered, "They're worse than republicans." And with that rejoinder, Douglas finally concluded his lengthy diatribe. Less than a week later, in Springfield, he took notice of the charges again because they had been reprinted by the Republican newspaper in town, but he declined to go much further than referring his audience to the "full history" of the Lecompton episode, which he had recounted at Milwaukee and that had been "published" and "before the country for some days."[40]

The usual story about the end of the 1860 election is that, when Douglas first heard the disappointing results from the October state elections, he immediately changed his campaign schedule, nobly devoting the rest of his political efforts toward preventing secession. "Mr. Lincoln is the next President," he reportedly told his assistant James Sheridan. "We must try to save the Union. I will go South." This is at least what Sheridan started telling people like John W. Forney and Henry Wilson after Douglas's death in 1861 and what historians have generally relayed as fact almost ever since.[41] Yet again, just like the anecdote about Buchanan, this was not even close to the full reality. Douglas did go South, and he did argue against secession, but he spent much of October in the North, embroiled in a last-ditch effort to slander President Buchanan as a way to save his own dignity and secure some measure of personal revenge in their long-running feud over Lecompton.

It is probably unfair to conclude that everybody in this affair was lying—Buchanan, Douglas, Raymond, Sheridan, or any of the many bit players who contributed at some stage to this partisan drama. But it must be acknowledged that their stories changed frequently and often contradicted each other. There is no legitimate reason to accept anyone's version as the literal truth, and certainly no justification for putting unqualified quotation marks around the most popular lines from this legendary battle royal.

Historians who have written about this episode by presenting it almost exclusively in Douglas's terms and without any context about the evolution of the anecdote are not guilty of lying either, but they are perhaps exposing a disciplinary weakness for a good story. The paragraph that opens this essay really does belong in something like a prequel to Steven

Spielberg's movie *Lincoln* and not in a piece of serious historical writing. That paragraph, and so many others like it that have appeared elsewhere, are just too misleading. All nineteenth-century historians use recollected material, and few can afford the luxury of deconstructing every shaky memory or conflicting account. Nonetheless, this famous story has an astonishingly weak pedigree. Douglas said it, that is true, but there are just too many reasons to doubt him. Yet very few seem to doubt.

So why have historians generally reported the anecdote as delivered? Partly, the answer is that we have our own pressures to simplify. There is something powerfully appealing about the Douglas account that helps transform the complicated minutiae of Lecompton policy into a dramatic clash of egos. Yet the story behind the memory reveals so much more about the complex culture of antebellum partisanship. These were not yet the machines of Gilded Age lore or the marketing monoliths of twentieth-century campaigns. Partisan organizations still functioned throughout the 1850s as loose coalitions of what good Jacksonians always termed "men and measures." Patronage sometimes bound these men, but so did policy measures, and nothing matters more in decoding the Buchanan-Douglas confrontation than a deep understanding of Lecompton policy and its surprising, last-minute implications for the 1860 presidential contest.

It is also worth recalling just how new political parties were to the scene even in the years before the Civil War. The Democratic Party was the oldest mass political organization in the world, and yet that history translated into an existence of only about twenty-five years by the time of the Lecompton controversy. The first national Democratic convention had taken place in Baltimore in 1832. But occasional nominating conventions hardly equated to formal organization, and it would be fair to observe that Buchanan and Douglas were vying to control a national movement built on vapors. Democratic presidents from this period, even ones generally regarded as weaker figures, such as Van Buren or Buchanan, were remarkably involved in the day-to-day management of administration policy. So, too, were the few Whig executives, like Tyler or Fillmore, who struggled mightily to impose their will on balky partisan operations. Yet these often-unhappy leaders made do with hardly any staff and relied on the most indirect and inefficient communication tools. It is a wonder they accomplished anything.

That is almost certainly why they were so prone to imagine an easier past for themselves. The mythology of Jackson's strong leadership had a powerful allure that transcended party lines. Lincoln, for one, was always happy to invoke Old Hickory whenever he was communicating with fellow partisans behind the scenes. He once warned Zachary Taylor's cabinet that their president was at risk of being portrayed "as a mere man of straw" because he was not being decisive enough. According to the former Illinois militia captain, the Whig president (and renowned general) "must occasionally say, or seem to say, 'by the Eternal, I take the responsibility.'" "Those phrases," he had written in 1849, "were the 'Samson's locks' of Gen. Jackson, and we dare not disregard the lessons of experience."[42] Lincoln himself once received similar advice from none other than Nathaniel Tallmadge. "The only complaint I hear is that the Administration moves too slow," wrote the former New York senator, exactly ten days after the firing on Fort Sumter and about twenty-five years into his alleged "oblivion." "Strike terror into your country's foe— make him believe and feel that the spirit of Jackson is with you."[43] The ritual invocations about the "spirit of Jackson" and retorts that reminded people that "General Jackson is dead" were potent symbols of the era, but ultimately, they represent a political mythology that historians need to decode rather than perpetuate.

NOTES

1. Roy F. Nichols, *The Disruption of American Democracy* (New York: Free Press, 1948), 137; Allan Nevins, *The Emergence of Lincoln*, 2 vols. (New York: Charles Scribner's Sons, 1950), 1:253; James M. McPherson, *Battle Cry of Freedom: The Civil War Era* (New York: Oxford University Press, 1988), 166; Philip S. Klein, *President James Buchanan: A Biography* (University Park: Pennsylvania State University Press, 1962), 301; Robert W. Johannsen, *Stephen A. Douglas* (1973; Urbana: University of Illinois Press, 1997), 586; Kenneth M. Stampp, *America in 1857: A Nation on the Brink* (New York: Oxford University Press, 1990), 292–93; David M. Potter, *The Impending Crisis: 1848–1861*, completed and ed. Don E. Fehrenbacher (New York: Harper and Row, 1976), 316; and Jean H. Baker, *James Buchanan* (New York: Times Books, 2004), 101–2.

2. "Mr. Douglas and the Lecompton Constitution," *New York Herald*, October 20, 1860, 4; Jeriah Bonham, *Fifty Years Recollections* (Peoria, IL: J. W. Franks and Sons, 1883), 195; John G. Nicolay and John Hay, *Abraham Lincoln: A History*, 9 vols. (New York: Century, 1890), 2:120.

3. "The Position of Judge Douglas on the Kansas Question," *New York Herald*, December 4, 1857, 4.

4. "News from the National Capital," *New York Herald,* December 4, 1857, 4.

5. *New York Tribune,* December 4, 1857, 4. *Chicago Tribune,* December 4, 1857, 1.

6. "Affairs at Washington," *New York Herald,* December 5, 1857, 4.

7. James Buchanan, "First Annual Message to Congress on the State of the Union," December 8, 1857, online by Gerhard Peters and John T. Woolley, *The American Presidency Project,* http://www.presidency.ucsb.edu/ws/?pid=29498.

8. Abraham Lincoln to Lyman Trumbull, December 18, 1857, in *The Collected Works of Abraham Lincoln,* ed. Roy P. Basler, 8 vols. (New Brunswick, NJ: Rutgers University Press, 1953), 2:428.

9. Quoted in Johannsen, *Douglas,* 589.

10. Johannsen, *Douglas,* 592.

11. H[enry] J. R[aymond], "The Kansas Question; Prospect in the House; Feeling in Kansas; the Future," *New York Times,* March 26, 1858.

12. Abraham Lincoln to Lyman Trumbull, December 28, 1857, in Basler, *Collected Works of Abraham Lincoln,* 2:430.

13. See brief profiles for Rives and Tallmadge in *American National Biography,* anb.org, and *Biographical Directory of the United States Congress,* bioguide.congress.gov. Neither one has been the subject of a major modern biography, but they are discussed at some length in monographs such as James Roger Sharp, *The Jacksonians Versus the Banks: Politics in the States after the Panic of 1837* (New York: Columbia University Press, 1970); Jean E. Friedman, *The Revolt of the Conservative Democrats: An Essay on American Political Culture and Political Development, 1837–1844* (Ann Arbor, MI: UMI Research Press, 1979); and Michael F. Holt, *The Rise and Fall of the American Whig Party: Jacksonian Politics and the Onset of the Civil War* (New York: Oxford University Press, 1999).

14. Donald B. Cole, *Martin Van Buren and the American Political System* (Princeton, NJ: Princeton University Press, 1984), 306–11.

15. Tallmadge published excerpts from his communication with the late Webster in his introduction and appendix to Charles Linton, *The Healing of the Nations* (New York: Society for the Diffusion of Spiritual Knowledge, 1855), a popular spiritualist tract. Rives published the first volume of his well-received multipart biography of Madison in 1859. See Rives, *History of the Life and Times of James Madison,* 3 vols. (Boston: Little, Brown, 1859–68). In terms of the general disdain, at least for Tallmadge, James Shields, for example, apparently mocked the former New York senator for his spiritualism on the Senate floor in 1854. See "Letter from Ex-Senator Tallmadge," *Daily National Intelligencer* (Washington, DC), April 19, 1854.

16. Some examples of antebellum newspaper articles that reference the political treason of Rives and Tallmadge from the 1830s and 1840s include *Washington Daily Union,* December 16, 1854, 2; "Treason and Its Results," *Vermont Patriot & State Gazette* (Montpelier), March 2, 1855; and "The Lessons of History," *Newark (OH) Advocate,* July 13, 1860.

17. Klein, *President James Buchanan,* 301; McPherson, *Battle Cry of Freedom,* 166.

18. "Politics of the Day," *Daily National Intelligencer* (Washington, DC), September 4, 1856.

19. H[enry] J. R[aymond], "The Kansas Question; Prospect in the House; Feeling in Kansas; the Future," *New York Times*, March 26, 1858.

20. Klein, *President James Buchanan*, 347–48.

21. Speech at Concord, NH, July 31, 1860, transcribed in "Movements of Senator Douglas," *New York Times*, August 3, 1860, 2.

22. Speech at Concord, NH, July 31, 1860. See also "The President's Warfare upon Mr. Douglas," *Buffalo Daily Courier*, August 11, 1860, 2.

23. "The President and Judge Douglas," *New York Herald*, September 7, 1860, 1. See also *New York Tribune*, September 11, 1860. Congressman Smith was also known as "Extra Billy" Smith and later gained some notoriety during the Civil War as a Confederate general.

24. James Buchanan to Gerard Hallock, August 11, 1860, House Divided: The Civil War Research Engine at Dickinson College, Dickinson College Archives and Special Collections, http://hd.housedivided.dickinson.edu/node/29583.

25. Buchanan to William Smith, August 11, 1860, *New York Times*, September 8, 1860.

26. Martin H. Quitt, *Stephen A. Douglas and Antebellum Democracy* (New York: Cambridge University Press, 2012), 162.

27. Johannsen, *Douglas*, 795.

28. "Mr. Douglas and the Lecompton Constitution," *New York Herald*, October 20, 1860, 4.

29. "The Kansas Question as Between President Buchanan and Gov. Walker," *Daily Cleveland Herald*, December 3, 1857.

30. This would later become infamous as the false choice between the "Constitution with Slavery" or the "Constitution without Slavery" because even the vote for "without" would still leave the property rights of existing slaveholders in the territory unmolested.

31. "STARTLING DISCLOSURES: Douglas Responsible for the Lecompton Constitution; His Pledge to Support It; Violation of His Pledge and Treachery to His Friends; Read! Read! Read!," *Chicago Tribune*, October 12, 1860, 2.

32. One of the best accounts of these developments comes from Stampp, *America in 1857*, 144–81, 266–94. It is notable, however, that Stampp essentially ignores the 1860 charges from the Democratic Association of Leavenworth. He attributes Calhoun's successful lobbying effort at the Lecompton convention to a misunderstanding about Douglas's intentions, rooted in a strained interpretation of a *Chicago Times* editorial and not because of any secret letter. See ibid., 273.

33. "Mr. Douglas and the Lecompton Constitution," *New York Herald*, October 20, 1860, 4.

34. "ASTOUNDING DISCLOSURES," *Chicago Daily Tribune*, November 12, 1857, 2; "Adjournment of the Convention," ibid., November 16, 1857, 1.

35. Stephen A. Douglas to William Weer, November 23, 1857, quoted in Johannsen, *Douglas*, 581.

36. Stampp, *America in 1857*, 282–83.

37. *New York Herald*, October 23, 1860, quoted in "Mr. Douglas in Milwaukee," *Milwaukee Daily Sentinel*, October 26, 1860, 1.

38. *Milwaukee Daily Sentinel,* October 26, 1860.

39. *Western Argus* quoted in "Judge Douglas and the Lecompton Constitution," *National Intelligencer* (Washington, DC), October 31, 1860.

40. "Speech of the Hon. S. A. Douglas," *Springfield Illinois State Register,* October 19, 1860, 2.

41. Henry Wilson, *The Rise and Fall of the Slave Power in America,* 2 vols. (Boston: J. R. Osgood, 1872), 2:700; John W. Forney, *Eulogy upon the Hon. Stephen A. Douglas, July 3, 1861* (Philadelphia: Ringwalt, 1861), 11.

42. Abraham Lincoln to John M. Clayton, July 28, 1849, in Basler, *Collected Works of Abraham Lincoln,* 2:60.

43. Nathaniel P. Tallmadge to Abraham Lincoln, April 22, 1861, Papers of Abraham Lincoln, Library of Congress.

"BUCK ALL OVER"

James Buchanan and a Trail of Broken Relationships

WILLIAM P. MACKINNON

Messrs. Plitt and Forney think Mr. B. has behaved badly. His exceed-
ingly non-committal letters are, they say, "Buck all over, so that if Mr.
K[ane] succeeds, he may approve him, if he fails[,] disavow him."
—ELIZABETH W. KANE JOURNAL, APRIL 16, 1858

Below the surface of James Buchanan's reputation as an ineffective chief
executive presiding over the nation's slide into the bloodbath of disunion
runs a quite different image—that of a wealthy bon vivant entertaining
with Cuban cigars, jeroboams of Madeira and Old Monongahela, cro-
nyism, and the dispensation of political patronage on a scale stunning
even to the twentieth-century Watergate investigators. After four years
of social austerity and bereavement imposed on the Executive Mansion
by President Franklin Pierce and his wife, "Old Buck" the bachelor transformed the residence into one that was urbane, convivial, and even a bit
glamorous. With niece Harriet Lane as his official hostess, Buchanan's
Executive Mansion took on a patina derived from his decades as a Pennsylvania lawyer-politician, congressional insider, secretary of state, and US
minister to the imperial courts of Tsar Nicholas I and Queen Victoria.
US senator Sam Houston might sit in a corner at one of Buchanan's

receptions whittling wooden hearts for Lane, but around him jostled Washington's grandees and hopefuls, anxious to partake of the brimming presidential punch bowl as well as diplomatic favors, military appointments, postmasterships, and other largesse being dispensed by the nation's chief executive.

Normally such a persona implies an ability to forge positive, enduring relationships. Yet a close examination of Buchanan's behavior yields a mixed pattern, calling into question his ability to sustain such connections on a long-term basis. The purpose of this chapter is to explore Buchanan's capacity for friendship, especially under the political pressures of the presidency. Rather than encyclopedic, this study focuses primarily on his connection to a little-known Philadelphia lawyer important to the opening years of the administration: Thomas L. Kane, clerk of the US District Court for the Eastern District of Pennsylvania and son of its presiding judge, John K. Kane. Buchanan's relationship with the younger Kane flourished and then ended badly. At the heart of this examination is the president's problematic capacity for reciprocity, constancy, and willingness to recognize the expectations of loyal supporters who served him for years. How the president interacted with Kane, especially during the Utah War of 1857–58, provides an important indicator of whether he had the leadership skills to inspire the trust of others essential for a successful resolution of the secession crisis three years later.

This study's premise is not that Buchanan lacked any successful, enduring relationships. To the contrary, consultation of four full-length biographies as well as an examination of his surviving personal papers indicates several long-term friends, including Nahum Capen, postmaster of Boston; Robert M. Magraw of Baltimore; John Appleton of Maine; Judge and Mrs. James Roosevelt of Manhattan; and prominent Pennsylvania political figures, including Judge Jeremiah S. Black, Senator William Bigler, and Representative J. Glancy Jones.[1] As best can be determined, all of these people stood by Buchanan until their or his death, although in several cases the relationship was sorely tested. Most often, such tensions occurred when expediency drove Buchanan to sacrifice a loyalist's nomination to a prized position so that he might advance a more viable or politically useful candidate. Other disappointments arose from his inability to deliver a post as attractive as anticipated.

Perhaps the most jarring such case involved Buchanan's decision in February 1857 to bypass Representative Jones's hope to become US attorney general. Instead, the nomination fell to Judge Black so that the president-elect might use his single cabinet-level Pennsylvania patronage "card" to placate the Philadelphia faction of his home state's unruly Democratic Party. That Jones viewed Black as an unprincipled enemy aggravated the situation, as did his realization that Black had not even sought the appointment and was unaware of Buchanan's nomination until the Senate confirmed him. As consolation, Buchanan helped arrange Jones's selection as House whip and chairman of one of the chamber's key committees. Yet even this initiative was short lived when Buchanan lost control of his party and Jones his seat in Pennsylvania's midterm elections during the fall of 1858. Buchanan told his niece, "[Jones] will be a loss to the whole Country." In describing to her what had happened, the president revealed how little control he was able to exert, even in his home state, among the leaders of his own political party. It was an ineffectiveness that not all of his supporters found easy to accept or believe: "The conspirators against poor Jones have at length succeeded in hunting him down. Ever since my election [in 1856] the hounds have been in pursuit of him. I now deeply regret;—but I shall say no more. With the blessing of Providence I shall endeavor to raise him up & place him in some position where they cannot reach him." In the end Jones settled for appointment as US minister to Austria, a position that imposed hardship on his family while evoking unwelcome images of exile.[2]

In the closing days of the Buchanan administration, even a loyalist such as Attorney General Black experienced disappointment. His nomination to be an associate justice of the US Supreme Court failed in the Senate because of controversy over the administration's policies. Notwithstanding Black's years as chief justice of the Pennsylvania Supreme Court and cabinet service, the best position that Buchanan could secure for him afterward was as clerk of the US Supreme Court.

In early 1861, when Buchanan obtained Senate confirmation for friend Robert M. Magraw to be US consul in Liverpool, Magraw declined the position. His reasons are unknown, but, as a railroad president and erstwhile suitor of Harriet Lane whom Buchanan described to her in 1858 as "the good & excellent Robert . . . a man among a thousand," it is conceivable that he was unenthusiastic about the prospect of spending his time not in cosmopolitan London, as Buchanan had done, but in dealing with the personal problems of stranded American tourists and sailors in a gritty English seaport. After years of furnishing Buchanan with private railroad cars and special cigars to the point that cynics labeled him "Buchanan's baggage master," Magraw may have felt that his loyalty warranted better treatment. After all, the consulship at Liverpool was the position that an embittered John W. Forney had rejected in a huff nearly four years earlier, stating that he had no intention of going into "exile." In the aftermath of Forney's rebuff, a desperate Beverley Tucker had accepted the appointment after complaining to Buchanan's campaign manager in March 1857 that he was financially strapped and feeling ill used by the administration after his all-out support for Buchanan's presidential bid in 1856.[3]

At about the same time, Assistant Secretary of State Appleton accepted appointment as US ambassador to Russia. In doing so he must have been painfully aware that nearly thirty years earlier, President Andrew Jackson had named Buchanan to the same position while telling intimates that it was the most distant posting he could devise for the out-of-favor Pennsylvanian absent an American embassy at the North Pole. (A few years later President Abraham Lincoln also used an appointment to Saint Petersburg to purge his cabinet of the incompetent Simon Cameron.)

In addition to these loyalists, there was a large number of orphaned nieces and nephews for whom Buchanan took financial and familial responsibility long before he became president. Most, if not all, of these young dependents were undoubtedly grateful for his support. Yet there were episodic tensions with two such wards who accompanied him to the Executive Mansion: his niece Harriet and James Buchanan "Buck" Henry, who served as his confidential secretary until a breach between them drove the nephew to seek a new life in New York. "Nunc," as Harriet called the president, attended her wedding but not Buck Henry's.

Notwithstanding the existence of these and other mutually positive relationships, the papers of individuals close to Buchanan also present a quite different negative case. It is a pattern of initial friendship followed by perceived betrayal, ingratitude, enmity, and recriminations. The list below—one that is representative rather than exhaustive—includes the names of seven such individuals. Excluded from this group are three other people whose broken relationships with Buchanan have become so notorious and well studied that they need not be revisited here: Ann Coleman, Buchanan's wealthy but unstable fiancée, whose murky, self-inflicted death in 1819 drove her family to view him as her "murderer"; John W. Forney, the Pennsylvania political acolyte who so resented Buchanan's failure to arrange his election to the Senate, appointment to the editorship of the *Washington Union,* or selection for a cabinet portfolio that he established a Philadelphia newspaper dedicated to the president's political destruction; and Senator Stephen A. Douglas of Illinois, whose conflict with Buchanan over the doctrine of popular sovereignty and distribution of patronage in the Midwest created a factionalism so vicious that by 1860 it had all but destroyed the Democratic Party.[4]

These seven disaffected friends, subordinates, and political associates were:

• James C. Van Dyke, a Pennsylvania attorney whom Buchanan described to President Pierce in 1853 as a man with whom he had "been on terms of intimate friendship, for a number of years, commencing with his marriage [in the early 1840s] to a granddaughter of our glorious old Democratic Governor, Simon Snyder." At Buchanan's urging, Pierce appointed Van Dyke to be US attorney for the Eastern District of Pennsylvania; thereafter, Van Dyke became one of Buchanan's principal political advisors in Philadelphia as well as a prime guardian of his personal interests in eastern Pennsylvania, especially during Buchanan's extended absence in London as US minister. In 1858 Van Dyke became disaffected when the president failed to appoint him to the federal judgeship in Philadelphia that came open upon the death of John K. Kane. By March 1860, the Van Dyke–Buchanan relationship had so deteriorated that the president summarily removed him as US attorney. His removal prompted national political comment and provided an opportunity for a House committee to use the dismissal as a lever to pursue its investigation of corruption in the president's use of patronage and government contracts. After removal, Van Dyke struggled to build a private law practice to support his large family.

He died unsuccessful and embittered in Philadelphia six years later at age fifty-one.[5]

- Jonathan M. Foltz, US Navy surgeon and a fellow townsman of Lancaster. Notwithstanding Dr. Foltz's role in rescuing Buchanan from a near-death experience with the "National Hotel disease" during February–July 1857, perceived presidential ingratitude drove the physician to change his first-born son's middle name from Buchanan to Steinman while engaging in invective that prompted the president to consider a court-martial for disrespect to the commander in chief.[6]

- George Plitt of Pennsylvania, Democratic Party political operative, Buchanan supporter since the 1830s, and Harriet Lane's foster parent before Buchanan assumed her legal guardianship. When in 1857 Buchanan engineered Plitt's relinquishment of a long-held patronage position (clerk of the US circuit court of appeals in Philadelphia) and then failed to arrange another, he created a blow to the family finances that soured Mrs. Plitt on both politics and Buchanan while damaging George's own ardor for the president.[7]

- Sir William Gore Ouseley, senior British diplomat and decades-long Buchanan friend from postings in Washington and London, whom the president dropped after the embarrassing failure of Ouseley's attempts to resolve British-American tensions in Central America.

- Brevet Lieutenant General Winfield Scott, the army's general in chief, whom Buchanan ordered to open a second front during the Utah War from the Pacific coast without disclosing his related scheme to intervene in northern Mexico and ultimately acquire Cuba. During the Civil War, Scott dueled with Buchanan in his memoirs over the former president's prosecution of the Utah War and his handling of the secession crisis.

- Robert J. Walker of Pennsylvania and Mississippi, a Buchanan colleague in James K. Polk's cabinet, Old Buck's appointee as governor of Kansas Territory, and later a bitter critic who resigned the governorship because of inadequate political support, if not betrayal, from the Executive Mansion.

- James L. Reynolds of Lancaster, Buchanan's close friend for a half century, who stopped speaking to the former president after the death at Gettysburg of Major General John F. Reynolds, an officer Congressman Buchanan had appointed to the West Point Class of 1841. In 1863 the Reynolds family held the former president personally responsible for the war's origins and carnage, a view common enough that Buchanan's Masonic lodge brothers had to guard his Lancaster retirement mansion at night.[8]

Key to understanding the connection between Buchanan and Thomas L. Kane is their involvement in the Utah War, one of the unexpected but great challenges of the president's first years in office. How Buchanan conducted himself toward Kane during this period was a leading indicator as to whether or not he had the character and skills to inspire the trust of others in subsequent crises.[9]

What was the Utah War? In short, it was the armed confrontation over power and authority between the civil-religious hierarchy of Utah Territory, led by Governor Brigham Young, president of the Church of Jesus Christ of Latter-day Saints, and the US government. In the spring of 1857, Buchanan set out to restore federal authority in Utah by replacing Young as governor and installing a successor to be escorted west by a large army expeditionary force. It was a change that Young and his territorial militia (the Nauvoo Legion) rejected, contesting it with hit-and-run operations that morphed into a bloody guerrilla conflict. What followed brought not only casualties and atrocities like the Mountain Meadows Massacre but also treason indictments for Young and hundreds of other Mormons along with a murder indictment for the former governor. As the campaign stalemated and the army went into winter quarters at Fort Bridger, Utah, in the fall of 1857, it became the nation's most extensive and expensive military undertaking during the period between the US–Mexican War and the Civil War, pitting Young's large ter-

Thomas L. Kane (1822–83) of Philadelphia, longtime friend of the Mormons and self-appointed mediator of the Utah War. Kane is shown here early in the Civil War as lieutenant colonel of the Thirteenth Pennsylvania Reserves (the Bucktail Rifles). Courtesy Mathew Brady Collection, Library of Congress, Washington, DC.

ritorial militia against almost one-third of the US Army. In the process, the daunting costs of this armed confrontation drained the US Treasury during the worst economic recession in twenty years.

The conflict continued until two civilian peace commissioners, dispatched by Buchanan from Washington, imposed a controversial settlement in June 1858. Under this arrangement, Young accepted his removal as territorial governor, US Army forces marched unopposed into the Salt Lake Valley to garrison the territory, and the president extended a blanket pardon for Utah's entire population.[10]

As commander in chief, President Buchanan's role in this military campaign is obvious. That of Thomas L. Kane has been more difficult for historians to assess, enveloped as it was by his penchant for secrecy and nearly two centuries of Mormon folklore.

Prior to the spring of 1857, Kane was not a Buchanan intimate, but the two men became actively involved with one another because of the Utah War. At that time Kane was thirty-five years old, thirty-one years Buchanan's junior. Scion of a prominent Philadelphia family with which the president was friendly, Kane was a supporter of multiple humanitarian causes, including the antislavery and prison-reform movements. Since the mid-1840s, attracted by the Mormons' status as a persecuted minority, he had become their most prominent advocate and defender, although he was not a church member and rejected many of their religious tenets, such as polygamy. In 1846 Kane traveled to Mormon refugee camps in Iowa to assist the refugees' trek to the Salt Lake Valley and to facilitate recruitment of the Mormon Battalion for service with the US Army during the US–Mexican War. In 1850 he advised President Millard Fillmore on federal appointees for the newly established Utah Territory (including Young as governor) and delivered a major address sympathetic to Mormonism before the elite Historical Society of Pennsylvania in Philadelphia. During 1852, he helped mute eastern newspaper criticism of Young when the federal judges assigned to the territory fled Utah en mass and the church admitted to the practice of plural marriage after decades of public denial. Four years later Kane corresponded with Young to strategize about how best and when to seek statehood for the territory.

During February 1857, Kane traveled to Havana to nurse his famous Arctic explorer-brother, Dr. Elisha Kent Kane, then, upon Elisha's death, to arrange his body's return to the United States. The subsequent cross-country cortege to Philadelphia was the nation's most extensive and elaborate funeral procession during the period between the deaths of George Washington and Abraham Lincoln. When Buchanan took office the following month, Kane was clerk to the US district court in Philadelphia, over which his father, Judge John K. Kane, had long presided.[11]

In January 1857, apprehensive that Buchanan would not reappoint him as governor, Young again reached out to Kane in hopes that he might influence the president-elect. His plea reached Kane in March amid an uproar in the new administration over the latest accusations about inappropriate governance in Utah. Judge Kane and Buchanan had long been friends from their common involvement with Pennsylvania's Democratic Party, but Thomas Kane may have worked against Old Buck during the 1856 presidential campaign. Nevertheless, the son immediately swung into action on the Mormons' behalf.

On March 21 Kane wrote Buchanan advocating that he retain Young in the governorship and sought to press the case directly with the new president. Later he also wrote Attorney General Black and perhaps other influential people. As a result, on April 1 one of Young's Atlantic coast agents reported to Salt Lake City: "I had a long talk with Col. Kane yesterday; he informed me that he received a letter from you a short time since. He has written to the President and also to Judge Black Attorney General of the U.S. in relation to Utah, and the [negative] reports, urging your reappointment, how it will terminate [that is, turn out] he says he cannot at present determine, but he will do his best, and use his utmost endeavors and influence for you and the Welfare of Utah. His feelings are good." Two weeks later Mormon apostle John Taylor in New York added the news, "Col. Kane has been using all his influence with the administration; he is a true friend."

Although he was neither the party stalwart nor the Buchanan intimate that his father was, the younger Kane had good reason to assume that the president would give his letter and offer to visit Washington careful thought as the cabinet focused on Utah affairs. Buchanan never responded; months later Black and the president both claimed never to have received Kane's letters. In the meantime, interpreting their silence as a humiliating rebuff, annoyed by what he perceived as indiscreet handling of his correspondence by the administration, and beset by personal problems, Kane notified Young of his failure, withdrew from Mormon affairs, and retreated from Philadelphia to his family's timberlands in the mountains of western Pennsylvania. In a pessimistic note of March 21, Kane warned Young, "Mr. Buchanan is a timorous man, as well as just now an overworked one." Two months later, on May 21, Kane told him: "We can place no reliance upon the President: he succumbs in more respects than one to outside pressure. You can see from the [news]papers how clamorous it is for interference with Utah affairs. Now Mr. Buchanan has not heart enough to save his friends from being thrown over to stop the mouths of a pack of Yankee editors."[12]

Kane and his family returned to Philadelphia on October 3. On November 9, alarmed by a combination of urgent messages from Young, rumors of bloodshed in Utah, and army reports of Mormon determination to resist its Utah Expedition, Kane traveled to Washington to meet with the president. Whether the introduction was arranged by Judge Kane or by an intermediary such as Van Dyke is unknown. Nevertheless, this confidential meeting occurred four weeks before Congress was scheduled to reconvene, at which time Buchanan would need to speak publicly for the first time about Utah affairs.

In a memorandum Kane drafted during July 1858 for possible publication, he described this visit to the Executive Mansion. It is the only record of this first Kane-Buchanan meeting.

When I came down upon the world again [from the mountains], which was in October, and learned the true state of affairs at that time, I was inexpressibly shocked. Besides the news which the public at large were possessed of, I had a letter from Utah . . . from an individual [Brigham Young] with whom I had not corresponded for some time . . . showing me beyond question that the Mormons were determined to resist our troops and were, the most staid and reliable men among them, in an exceedingly unhappy and distempered state of mind.

An intimate friend of the President also, George Plitt Esq., had a long conversation with me upon the subject of the Utah difficulties, and took pains to state to me that he did not believe that the President did not or was not at any time prepared to attach full weight to any representations which I might be inclined to make to him. I did not inquire whether this gentleman spoke to me at the insistence of the President. I thought otherwise. But I remember his saying that he wished the President would send me [as] Commissioner to Utah, and that he urged me to go to Washington and see the President.

To be brief here, I went on to Washington[,] it was in November sometime in the 2d week of November[,] conversed with the President (A rough time I had of it at first too. He was so reluctant to admit that he had committed any error.), learned from him that the advance of the troops would be slow, that their orders and the instructions to [new] Governor [Alfred] Cumming were of a character to prevent a precipitate advance; but I do not know why I thought myself fortunate in evading a proposal on his part to appoint me to proceed to Utah—I really thought that it was too late in the season for me to force my way among the Mormons, and I will admit was sufficiently recreant a citizen to congratulate myself upon not having the responsibility put upon me of refusing the President to make an effort at that time to save the administration and the country.[13]

Within three days after Kane's return to Philadelphia on November 10, 1857, first news reached the Atlantic coast of Young's illegal proclamation of martial law, the Nauvoo Legion's destruction of more than a million dollars' worth of army materiel, and the calamitous loss of 120 civilian lives in the massacre at Mountain Meadows, thus transforming an armed confrontation into a rebellion. On December 8 Buchanan sent his first annual message to Congress. In five lawyerly paragraphs of a lengthy message dominated by Kansas affairs, he declared Utah to be in rebellion and requested authorization to expand the army by four regiments to prosecute a campaign to reassert federal authority over the territory. He discussed no strategy for ending the revolt other than the continued application of overwhelming military force. Secretary of War John B. Floyd's accompanying annual report provided more operationally oriented comments than did Buchanan's, linking Kansas and Utah and ranging into the political as well as social arenas while describing rebellious Utah's greatest threat as its strategic position astride US emigration routes to the Pacific coast.[14]

These developments led both Kane and Buchanan to consider new approaches. As Kane later put it: "My thoughts turning after this upon Utah matters and examining fully into the subject[,] the conviction gained upon me that I was perhaps leaving undone that which I ought to have done. Inquiring about among Mormons and others, I learned more than I had known of the different [travel] approaches to the [Great] Basin and learned that whatever might be the case with regard to myself, other men were able at that very date to penetrate to Salt Lake City. Let me remind you that domestic affliction came about this time to remind me that the sum of duty might not consist *in promoting the happiness* of my family &c."[15]

The day after the president sent his message to Congress, Van Dyke, Buchanan's political advisor, moved to refocus presidential attention on the possibility of resolving the Mormon problem peacefully through Thomas Kane. Van Dyke may have been motivated by his awareness that Kane's relationship with the Mormons was unique as well as his realization that a restless Congress was beginning to shift aggressively into an investigatory, partisan posture regarding the administration's Utah policy. Against this backdrop, he wrote to Buchanan on December 9 to describe Kane's current thinking about Mormon affairs and to propose a personal meeting to explore his growing desire to serve as an intermediary to resolve the Utah conflict.

> Col. Kane from his long association with that people, has much influence with the Mormons, and especially with their chief. He thinks he can do much to accomplish an amicable peace between them and the United States. He is willing to make an expedition to Salt Lake this winter, even at his own expense, if hostilities have not advanced to such a point as would render useless any efforts on his part. He has conversed with me much, on this subject, and my conclusion from all he has said has been, that it would not be an unprofitable thing if you would have a consultation with him, and hear his views. He does not wish to annoy you, unless you desire to see him. Would you have any objection in expressing in a private note to me a desire to see him, which note I might show him, but not to be used, or in writing to him. He is full of courage, and if his judgment is correct, he may be able to avert a war of extermination against a poor deluded race. He expected me to speak to you when I came to Washington, but he does not know that I have written, nor will I tell him I have done so, unless my suggestion, that you express a willingness to see him, meets your views.[16]

Van Dyke's letter produced results. On the night of December 25, he and Kane traveled to Washington from Philadelphia and the next day met with Buchanan at the Executive Mansion. Apparently they did so separately, with Van Dyke going in first. There are two accounts of how this session came about and what took place. The first, written by Kane in July 1858 for his family and perhaps publication, omitted all reference to a role by Van Dyke but was filled with self-serving posturing and convoluted phrasing not unlike his account of his November visit with Buchanan. The other narrative Van Dyke dictated in March 1859, at Kane's request, from what he characterized as his "vivid recollection."[17]

In brief, according to Kane, he spent much of this interview trying to convince the president that he intended to go to Utah and in deflecting Buchanan's arguments that the trip was too dangerous in terms of hazards from weather, Indians, and suspicious Mormons (only a few months after their murky role in the Mountain Meadows Massacre). By Kane's account, he refused Buchanan's repeated offer to commission him as some sort of official emissary and to pay his travel expenses from the government's "secret service fund," emphasizing that his safety, credibility, and effectiveness among the Mormons hinged on preserving his status as a free agent and private citizen. Based on other documents, it appears that during this session, Kane asked Buchanan for the power to recommend executive clemency in the cases of individual Mormons and indicated to the president that, when he met with Brigham Young, he intended to raise the advisability of a mass Mormon exodus from Utah and presumably the United States. With respect to Buchanan's demeanor, Kane recorded that "the expression of his face was most affectionate." In terms of his own emotions, Kane noted, "many a time after when I was hard driven, I was helped to carry myself through by remembering not merely the particular confidence to which it was a compliment that he admitted me whom he had never known except as his [political] opponent in our State, but numerous express kind and friendly words, rallying my pride of family, and convincing me that at least I would not be forgotten by him, if my life was thrown away." Apparently, the president committed to providing him with some sort of letters of introduction that would facilitate his trip but with nothing more.

Van Dyke recorded in his 1859 memorandum for Kane, "the President asked me if you were still determined upon going; and said he considered the undertaking a very hazardous one, fraught with dangers and difficulties on all sides; that he did not believe it was possible for you to reach Salt Lake at that season of the year; and that even if you should he could not help doubting whether any good would result from your visit. I told him that your mind was fully made up, that you intended to go with the sanction and approbation of the Administration if they saw fit so far to aid you; but if such prestige and aid was withheld, you would go without it; that go you would."

Kane returned home on the evening of December 29 determined to visit Utah if he could clear two hurdles: first, obtaining an appropriate understanding and related set of credentials from Buchanan, and second, negotiating the approval of his family. Back in Philadelphia, Van Dyke immediately informed the president:

Col. Kane has returned from Washington perfectly charmed with his interview with you, and satisfied that it is your determination to speed him all you can in his intended expedition to Utah. There is one subject about which he has talked to me. It is in regard to the form of the letter to be used by him amongst the Mormons. The statement that Col. "Kanes personal word would have great weight with you in your exercise of executive clemency" was intended by him to be doubly serviceable enabling him not only to reward the deserving but also to menace the refractory who should fear to forfeit his good will. Powers to declare a general amnesty would not perhaps be as desirable to him. This is his idea and I repeat it to you for consideration. He is determined to sail, and has taken passage in the Steamer [to Panama] of the 5th [of January 1858] from N. Y.

Kane's family was very much opposed to his going to Utah. Judge Kane thought that his son's mission would be a failure and worried about losing him in the face of son Elisha's death earlier in the year. Tom's wife, Elizabeth, eventually agreed to support his decision. She recognized that her husband viewed such a mission as a calling and hoped that performing it would bolster his recent acceptance of Christianity—at her urging—after a life of agnosticism. And so at year's end Kane resigned his clerkship in his father's court—his sole source of income—and, after making scant financial provision for his wife and two young children, sailed for the West on a mission of unknown duration with uncertain outcome on behalf of a reviled people whose religion he did not accept.

At the very last moment before leaving Philadelphia for New York, three letters arrived from President Buchanan. For Kane, these documents were a substantial disappointment. Given the criticism of his Utah policy then developing in Congress, what Buchanan wrote in his cautious and lawyerly fashion was a model of what, in today's presidential politics and intelligence work, would be called "plausible deniability." The letters were a means of distancing the president from Kane if his secret mission should become known, controversial, or a failure while providing signs that, on a personal basis, wished him well. There was no reference to presidential pardons for Mormons or even Kane's authority to recommend them; Buchanan essentially described him as a private, freelancing do-gooder without governmental status or backing. The letters were thin gruel and cold comfort.

From the distance of Philadelphia, George Plitt and John W. Forney—the now-jaundiced former friends of the president—and Pat Kane (Thomas's skeptical younger brother) immediately recognized the letters for what they were. Elizabeth Kane recorded their reactions in 1858 and commented: "[They] think Mr. B. has behaved badly. His exceedingly non-committal letters are, they say, 'Buck all over, so that if Mr. K[ane] succeeds, he may approve him, if he fails disavow him.'" Years later, after the Civil War, she looked back on these events with a harsh judgment, invoking the behavior of Pontius Pilate with Christ: "so Buchanan washed his hands of the blood that Kane might lose."[18]

Thus supported, Thomas L. Kane bounded up the gangway of SS *Moses Taylor* in New York Harbor, waved a handkerchief at his wife, and departed for Utah via Panama and California. He did so cloaked dramatically in the persona of "Dr. A. Osborne," a fictive scientist intent on collecting botanical specimens for a Philadelphia museum. Ironically, one of his fellow passengers was William Tecumseh Sherman, a former army captain and unemployed banker bound for California in hopes of recouping his fortunes by appointment as colonel of one of the volunteer regiments then being recruited on the Pacific coast to reinforce the Utah Expedition.[19]

This is not the place for a full description of Kane's adventures and complex maneuverings in the West before he returned to the Executive Mansion in late June 1858. Suffice it to say that his major accomplishment upon reaching Utah was to gain the trust of Young and other Mormon leaders while convincing Governor Cumming to travel to Salt Lake City from Fort Bridger without an army escort. This effort resulted in Young reluctantly ceding political authority to Cumming and publicly recognizing him as governor. It fell to the two peace commissioners named by Buchanan and who arrived in early June, not Kane (who was oblivious to their appointment), to accomplish the crucial remaining work for restoring federal authority to the territory, namely, the Utah Expedition's peaceful entrance into the Salt Lake Valley and Young's acceptance of Buchanan's blanket pardon for Utah's entire population.[20]

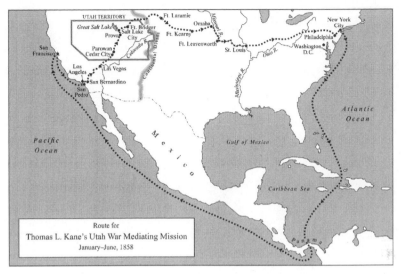

Traveling by land and sea, Thomas L. Kane journeyed approximately 6,000 miles roundtrip from Philadelphia in hopes of brokering peace between the Mormons of Utah Territory and the US government. Map by Mary Lee Eggart.

Neither Buchanan nor Young would muster the energy to meet and seek common ground, but Kane bridged the gap between the two leaders. He did so alone, in failing health, and by traveling across daunting terrain in the dead of winter by rail, ship, and wagon. The outbound leg took him from Philadelphia to Utah via New York, the Caribbean, the Isthmus of Panama, coastal California, and the Old Spanish Trail across the Mojave Desert. With his mission largely accomplished, the death of his father, and the spring opening of snow-clogged trails, Kane returned overland by crossing the Rockies and the Great Plains to the Missouri and Mississippi Rivers, then traveling by train for the Atlantic coast while on the verge of physical collapse.

Kane left Utah in mid-May to return home overland after learning that his father had died on February 21. Unwittingly, as Thomas Kane trekked eastward across the plains, Judge Kane's passing had already set in motion events that would lead to the destruction of Buchanan's relationship with the son and others. Meanwhile, Kane's skeptical family fretted that the westbound peace commissioners would upstage any credit for his herculean efforts to mediate the war and that the president might actually disavow any understandings that Kane might have forged with Young.[21]

Judge Kane had been on the US district court bench in Philadelphia since 1846. His death thus opened an important position long unavailable and for which there was no shortage of hopefuls. The judge's family thought that the president might nominate the absent Thomas to the vacant judgeship, then fell to discussing the handful of more prominent or better-connected candidates and the likely result of their appointments on the filling of the court clerkship that the younger Kane had resigned to go to Utah. The family's hope was that if Buchanan could or would not appoint the son to the judgeship, surely a grateful president would facilitate his return to the clerkship and perhaps even appoint his attorney-brother Pat to the legal reporter's position in the same court.

One of the contenders for the judgeship was John Cadwalader, whose suitability for the appointment had been brought to the president's attention by one of Pennsylvania's powerful politicians, Senator William Bigler. Cadwalader, an alumnus of the University of Pennsylvania, was a Philadelphia lawyer from a venerable and socially prominent family who had been a one-term congressman and was personally close to the president. On April 19, 1858, Buchanan sent Cadwalader's nomination as Judge Kane's successor to the Senate, where he was confirmed on April 24.

And so, Thomas Kane returned home from Utah in late June 1858 to find that Buchanan had filled his father's judgeship with Cadwalader. Kane now was unemployed and in debt for more than $2,500 for his western travel expenses. Much to his wife's dismay, he spent only one day at home upon his return, during which the couple argued over their precarious finances and unclear plans for the future. Kane then left for Washington to report to the president on his Utah mission. He spent five days with Buchanan, Secretary of War Floyd, and the rest of the cabinet in an effort to get them to adopt his recommendations for a constructive future relationship between Mormon Utah, Young, and the US government, including the recall of almost all of the president's federal appointees except Governor Cumming. Although Elizabeth later commented that "Buchanan kept his word in his sly but efficient manner," the fact was that the administration would have none of her husband's recommendations.[22]

With respect to patronage, Elizabeth Kane's recollection was that during this visit the president did broach the subject.

> It is but fair to Buchanan to say that he said to Tom that he would give him a foreign mission. It was characteristic of Buchanan that he added, "If you think there is the least possibility of your appointment passing the Senate." The power of Southern leaders crumbled away when the North took the Right into her hands, but in those days it was hopeless for a[n] Abolitionist to seek to obtain an appointment. Tom knew that Buchanan would not press his confirmation sufficiently to give him a chance with the Senate, and Tom declined his liberal offer.[23]

Kane returned home from Washington to recuperate from one of the many illnesses that had plagued him throughout his Utah mission, vowing to withdraw from Mormon affairs insofar as they involved efforts to influence the Buchanan administration. On July 15—without intervention by the president—Judge Cadwalader filled his clerkship with a stranger, not the unemployed Thomas Kane. At this point his views toward Buchanan were still ambivalent. During the summer, he reminded his brother, a skeptic about Buchanan's motives and steadfastness, that the president's flattery and kindness during their post-Christmas meeting had buoyed him during his most difficult days in Utah. In mid-July Kane's views changed, declaring to Young: "Buchanan's is certainly the most corrupt administration he has ever had to [deal] with. The old man fears [decisiveness] to[o] much to love him but this he considers a most Salutary State of mind."[24]

During his June 1858 visit to Washington, Kane had told the president that he did not intend to seek public recognition for his efforts to mediate the Utah War. As Elizabeth Kane saw it, her husband "felt as if 'glory of men' would sully the offering he had made to God. He felt, very humbly and yet very proudly that God had accepted him as a[n] instrument. He could not have done what he did through his own strength alone. Let those who wanted it have the credit—this feeling was enough for him." Buchanan took Kane at his word and all but ignored him thereafter. Elizabeth summarized the situation with a medievalism: "The page slew the bear, the peer had the gloire."[25]

Kane's friends chafed under this treatment even if he did not. On November 17 Eli K. Price, a prominent Pennsylvania Democrat and mutual friend of Buchanan and Kane, wrote the president:

> As one of the many friends of Col. Thos. L. Kane, I sympathised much in his expedition to the Mormons; and rejoiced that you were enabled to end that trouble without blood shed. Fearing the pressure of important matters might occasion [your] forgetfulness of what some of us believe it would be a pleasure to you to do, I write this note to say how much it would gratify Mr. Kane's friends to find his service noticed in your Annual Message [to Congress]. He has not felt at liberty to defend himself against misrepresentations, nor can we advise him to do so while it might prejudice any public interest.[26]

Thus pressured, the president drafted a single sentence in which he simultaneously recognized and distanced himself from Kane, telling Congress on December 6, 1858, "I cannot, in this connection, refrain from mentioning the valuable services of Colonel Thomas L. Kane, who, from motives of pure benevolence, and without any official character or pecuniary compensation, visited Utah during the last inclement winter for the purpose of contributing to the pacification of the Territory." In publishing his reminiscences ten years later, Buchanan limited discussion of Kane's Utah role to a repetition of the same sentence.[27] It was presidential appreciation of a stripe characterized by Pat Kane and Buchanan's disaffected former friends as "Buck all over."

Within a week of Buchanan's December 1858 annual message—and perhaps because of it—Kane found a way to strike back at President Buchanan's ingratitude. He shook off his vow of anonymity and disengagement from Utah affairs and stimulated an invitation to lecture at the New-York Historical Society in Manhattan, much as he had spoken at the Historical Society of Pennsylvania in 1850. He began to gather materials for an address in defense of Alfred Cumming. The Utah governor was then in serious danger of removal by Buchanan because of political criticism that, with Kane's connivance, Young had coopted and transformed Cumming into a Mormon puppet. It was nonsupport for his own appointee not unlike that leading to an embittered Governor Walker's resignation in Kansas during December 1857. Kane's was a speech designed to outmaneuver a president himself highly skilled and experienced in the manipulative art of what Young called "wire-working." Once delivered in Manhattan on March 21, 1859, and publicized nationally, with kudos for Cumming through a Mormon-engineered use of the Associated Press's telegraph facilities in New York, it was virtually impossible for Buchanan to recall the governor. Cumming remained in office until departing Utah for Georgia on the eve of the Civil War.

Buchanan left no record of his reaction to Kane's New-York Historical Society speech, but shortly afterward, George Q. Cannon, a Mormon apostle serving as Young's Atlantic-coast agent and liaison with Kane, reported to the Mormon leader,

> The lecture went off much better than would naturally be expected of one of the kind, and I was pleased in seeing the subject, which afforded but limited scope for a lecture, handled in so masterly a manner. It has had the desired effect, and firmly propped up Governor C. for the present. I understand the lecturer is very well satisfied with the result; thinks he has been quite successful in accomplishing what he desired. When it was known in Washington that a lecture had been delivered on such a subject, the Chief Magistrate [Buchanan] was quite anxious to know what had been said, and how far it agreed with or contradicted his own statements in regard to the share Governor Cumming had taken in the settlement of the [Utah War] difficulties. I presume he was afraid that his own one-sided statement, in which he so magnifies the part taken by his peace commissioners in the settlement of affairs, and almost ignores every body else, would be impugned or contradicted; but he felt much relieved when [he] heard how it was.

Years later a Mormon editor described the speech as one in which "Governor Cumming was complimented by the gallant Colonel as a clear-headed, resolute, but prudent executive, and the very man for the trying position. Because such an endorsement, sent broadcast over the Republic, coming from the lips of the gentleman who had warded off the effusion of blood, and saved the nation from the expense and horror of a domestic war, the Cabinet of Mr. Buchanan silently bowed, but they were terribly chagrined."[28]

This essay is neither a biography nor psychohistory, yet as a matter of common sense, the sources examined show James Buchanan to have been a mixed bag of behaviors. Without denigrating his many acts of generosity, Buchanan, on balance, seems to have been a "taker" rather than a "giver." As a newly inaugurated president—one in very poor health—he immersed himself and the cabinet for months in the daunting task of adjudicating thousands of competing patronage requests. Over the decades before he achieved that office, the Pennsylvanian had written hundreds of such pleas and testimonials on behalf of the party faithful, but he appears to have done so as a matter of political obligation rather than with gusto and palpable enthusiasm, especially once he entered the Executive Mansion. For example, in December 1858 he wrote a two-sentence letter of introduction to Secretary of the Navy Isaac Toucey on behalf of Henry Slaymaker Magraw, one of Robert Magraw's brothers. The note was a study in noncommittal blandness: "It affords me much pleasure to introduce to you my valued personal and political friend Henry S. Magraw Esquire, the present State Treasurer of Pennsylvania. Of this gentleman you have often heard me speak favorably."[29]

Buchanan's enthusiasm and persistence in recommending James Van Dyke for the US attorney's position in Philadelphia in March 1853 and John Appleton for posts at the American legation in London in 1853 and at the state department in Washington in 1857, was rare. In these cases he was arranging for confidants to assume roles that served his personal best interests rather than advocating for them in selfless pursuit of their independent career aspirations. For example, in 1853, even before Franklin Pierce had formally asked him to serve as US minister to the Court of Saint James, Buchanan had told Harriet Lane,

> should it be [extended and] accepted, it will be on the express condition that I shall have the liberty to choose my own Secretary of Lega-

tion. . . . I would select some able, industrious, hard-working friend, in whose integrity & prudence I could place entire reliance. In fact, I have the man [Appleton] now in my eye, from a distant state [Maine], to whom I would make the offer,—a gentleman trained by myself in the [Polk administration's] State Department. I must have a man of business, & not a carpet knight, who would go abroad to cut a dash.

Two years later, with both men ensconced in the American legation in London, Buchanan complained to her: "Mr. Appleton goes home by this steamer. . . . I resisted his importunities to go home as long as I could, but the last letter from his wife was of such a character that I could no longer resist. He is a *perfect* secretary, as well as an excellent friend."[30]

It is difficult to find a situation in which Buchanan pulled out all the stops, spent political capital, and invested his reputation to argue vigorously for a friend or supporter in need of such help. In the matter of what today's slang would call "juice," Buchanan was not a fighter of the Andrew Jackson or Sam Houston stripe.

One of the telltale signs of a friend heading for trouble with Buchanan was a request for a favor pressed directly, especially if the case was couched in emotional or confrontational tones. Faced with such situations, the president recoiled, responding with either coldness or flattering but unproductive assurances. Perhaps the multiple demands of a needy but deeply flawed John Forney and an aggressive, persistent Dr. Foltz were cases warranting rejection. Less understandable was Buchanan's unhelpful reaction to the desire of an unemployed Thomas Kane to resume his old clerkship in Philadelphia, one that he had vacated in December 1857 in order to travel more than six thousand miles at great risk and sacrifice to mediate the Utah War without public thanks or recognition.

Another likely sign of disaffection in the making was an intimate's embroilment in failure or its close cousin, controversy. Under such circumstances Buchanan's default position was to distance himself from the former friend or colleague by quietly "dropping" them. There was no helping hand or courageous, steadfast public support for such people if continued association could endanger his own image. In most such circumstances Buchanan abandoned the relationship by applying the faintly judgmental label "poor" to the unfortunate former intimate. Such was the fate of Sir William Gore Ouseley in the late 1850s when the British government recalled him after blundering diplomatically during the protracted negotiations over coastal Central America. In the fall of 1857, when Lord Clarendon assigned Ouseley to Washington temporarily, his old friend the president was delighted to have him and his American wife back in town and said so. But by April 1859, Old Buck was complaining to Clarendon that "just as I thought the work [of undoing the Clayton-Bulwer Treaty] was on the eve of being completed, Sir William Ouseley goes to Central America to give it the last finish, & although sufficiently dull & pacific in his nature, he has succeeded in raising the very D—l. . . . [T]his most important duty he has hitherto wholly neglected. He has gone off upon another scent."[31]

Similarly, when Robert Magraw's brother William disappointed Buchanan after he appointed him in the spring of 1857 to superintend the Pacific Wagon Road's Fort Kearny–South Pass–Honey Lake segment, the president remained aloof as Secretary of the Interior Jacob Thompson replaced a failed Magraw with his chief engineer. Old Buck was undoubtedly offended when word drifted back to Washington from the Great Plains that William Magraw, a heavy drinker, was telling eastbound travelers that the best introductions to the president would be a letter from himself and the smell of good liquor on the breath. After leaving the Pacific Wagon Road project, Magraw, with a Mormon bounty on his head, joined the army's Utah Expedition for nine months as a captain of volunteer troops while seeking a commission in the regular army through both Buchanan and—unknown to the president—his mortal political enemy, Senator Douglas. Both men declined to respond. In October 1858 Buchanan emphasized the sterling character of Robert Magraw to his niece but at the same time distanced himself from the unsuccessful William Magraw with the comment, "I wish I could say so much for his brother."[32]

Perhaps most troubling to those involved was Buchanan's apparent willingness to sacrifice the best interests—even livelihood—of his closest friends to advance his own political agenda with other supplicants, some of them strangers. The disposition of J. Glancy Jones's cabinet aspirations and the forced resignation of a financially strapped George Plitt fall into this category.

Beneath the surface of these cross-currents lay a deviousness in Buchanan that British diplomats labeled "too clever by half." For example, in October 1855 John F. T. Crampton, the British plenipotentiary in Washington, confided to Foreign Secretary Lord Clarendon that "the Buck is a very cunning old gentleman and a great schemer in matters of private interests."[33] In many respects this behavior took the form of a lack of forthrightness, even in dealings with intimates.

One of the most glaring such cases of furtive behavior included Buchanan's secret dispatch of Philadelphia lawyer Christopher Fallon to Madrid on December 13, 1857, to renew the president's longstanding efforts to buy Spanish Cuba. Buchanan directed him not only to sound out the Spanish royal family, with whom Fallon had extensive business connections, but also to begin discussions with European bankers on two tracks: pressuring Spain to repay its enormous foreign debt and arranging the means to finance an American purchase of Cuba. The latter was necessary since the president had sought neither congressional authorization nor an appropriation for any such acquisition. It is a telltale indication of Buchanan's deviousness that he recruited Fallon for such a mission only five days after sending his annual State of the Union address to Congress without a single reference to Spain or Cuba. In the "Private & Confidential" instructions provided to Fallon, he assured him that "both you & those with whom you converse may rely with confidence upon my silence & discretion."[34]

Within days of Fallon's dispatch, Van Dyke had, of course, arranged Kane's visit to the Executive Mansion to discuss his intended mediation of the Utah War. During this post-Christmas meeting, the president chose not to comment on Kane's intent to advise Young on a Mormon exodus from Utah, notwithstanding his own interest in seizing northern Mexico following what he hoped would be a massive, army-induced southbound flight of Mormon refugee-colonists to Sonora and Chihuahua. Thus he allowed Kane to travel west a few days later unaware of Fallon's mission and therefore oblivious to Buchanan's intent to buy Cuba or, failing that, to take the island as part of the broader Utah-Mexico-Cuba scheme the president would soon reveal to Ouseley.

Meanwhile, General Scott also prepared to travel west, equally unaware that the imminent second front for the Utah War from the Pacific coast—a campaign that he mounted under protest—was really designed by Buchanan to force Young into Mexico as part of his own secret, convoluted pursuit of Manifest Destiny through a game of presidential billiards intended to end with the United States in possession of Cuba. The president's duplicity in sending Scott on such an assignment amazed Ouseley, while Manhattan lawyer George Templeton Strong viewed the trek as a "death sentence" for the ailing general.

If Kane, Young, Scott, and perhaps Secretary of War Floyd and Secretary of State Lewis Cass were all unwitting pawns in this latest episode of the president's longstanding lust for Cuba, so too was the Congress of the United States.[35]

In summary, for more people than has been recognized, James Buchanan was not a friend and colleague who wore well over the long run. The scope and character of his broken relationships with Kane and others—combined with widespread revulsion over the carnage of the Civil War, for which many held Buchanan responsible—helps explain the absence of a monument honoring the fifteenth president in Washington until the Hoover administration, even though Harriet Lane had provided funds to erect one in a small park as early as the 1890s.[36] By the same token, when the Commonwealth of Pennsylvania decided which two native sons to honor in the Capitol's National Statuary Hall, it bypassed its only president and instead sent statues of inventor Robert Fulton and the now-obscure John Peter Gabriel Muhlenberg, a Revolutionary War general. Ironically, the State of Utah's contribution to this gallery includes a statue of Brigham Young, a man whom Buchanan removed as governor, denounced to Congress as a rebel, and saw indicted by federal grand juries for treason and murder. In 1877 Mormon apostle Wilford Woodruff directed that secret religious ordinances be performed in the St. George Temple to benefit all American presidents except for three considered enemies of his church; Old Buck was among those excluded.[37]

Small wonder that when Frederick Moore Binder wrote an article to assess the president's friendship with one of Great Britain's leading diplomats, he chose as his title "James Buchanan and the Earl of Clarendon:

An Uncertain Relationship." Even more pointed was George D. Harmon's title for his study of the dealings between Old Buck and Robert J. Walker, the colleague whom he appointed and then, in effect, abandoned: "President James Buchanan's Betrayal of Governor Robert J. Walker of Kansas."[38]

From his editorial perch in Philadelphia and with his own grudges showing, Forney poured on the invective, with presidential inconstancy and ingratitude a major theme. In early 1859 he published an editorial titled "Mr. Buchanan and his Friends." Here the newspaperman commented:

> The idea that Mr. Buchanan has ever intended to recognize friendships must be dismissed from the minds of those who have been silly enough to entertain it. It is becoming every day more apparent that he never intended to be animated by any regard for the men to whom he has been indebted for distinction, and with whom, in a great degree, he has been associated all his life. . . . No statesman in our country has ever proceeded upon the theory of sacrificing friendships and of conciliating enmities—none save Mr. Buchanan.

On the president's last day in office, Forney returned to this criticism: "Even those who envied your friends . . . were shocked at the manner in which you persecuted and hounded the men who, during many years of [Democratic Party] minority, had carried your cause upon their shoulders, until finally they placed you in the Presidential chair. No such spectacle has ever been presented in any country. You struck the most fatal blows at those who had rendered you the most devoted service."[39]

Even allowing for Forney's personal bias, it is fair to ask whether this was a president with the personal qualities, strength of character, political skills, warmth, and capacity to maintain relationships essential to leading a troubled nation on the brink of disunion. Buchanan was a clever but scheming chief executive, not one who reciprocated the loyalty or earned the trust necessary to lead others (or their nation) away from the "Valley of the Shadow."

At the beginning of the Utah War, Kane took Buchanan's measure and told Young, "we can place no reliance upon the President: he succumbs in more respects than one to outside pressure. . . . Now Mr. Buchanan has not heart enough to save his friends."[40] It is emblematic that during the Civil War that followed the Utah conflict, Buchanan's sole communication with President Lincoln was his request for a borrowed book inadvertently left behind in the Executive Mansion.[41]

❧❧

Anticipating death in 1868, Buchanan specified that his marble sarcophagus was to bear a single sentence setting forth his name, dates, and identity as fifteenth president of the United States. If Charles Dickens's Ghost of Christmas Past were to visit Lancaster's Woodward Hill Cemetery, the shade might pause to consider an addendum to this inscription derived from the lamentation of Sophie Plitt, the beneficiary of what she and others viewed as rank ingratitude. From the shelter of the Cratchit-like Philadelphia cottage the Plitts dubbed "Shantee," Mrs. Plitt surveyed the wreckage of the family finances after the forced resignation of her husband, George, as a federal court clerk in 1857. Worried yet proud, she wrote Buchanan's niece and her former ward: "I don't care who is Prest. I worked for one nearly all my life—my husband was removed from office, & we have been ever since *counting every dollar to keep our home.* I despise politics. . . . There is too much ingratitude in political men & I *am not a spaniel.*"[42]

James Buchanan once commented with self-satisfaction that the only woman who could stand her ground with him was his faithful housekeeper Hettie Parker. In so believing, he underestimated Sophie Plitt and the men who shared her resentment while plotting vengeance. The latter included Thomas L. Kane and the three former friends who, with high hopes and misplaced admiration, had named sons after their one-time hero—James C. Van Dyke, John W. Forney, and Dr. Jonathan M. Foltz.

NOTES

Epigraph: Elizabeth W. Kane Diary, April 16, 1858, Thomas L. and Elizabeth W. Kane Papers, L. Tom Perry Special Collections, Harold B. Lee Library, Brigham Young University, Provo, UT (hereafter BYU).

1. See George Ticknor Curtis, *Life of James Buchanan, Fifteenth President of the United States,* 2 vols. (New York: Harper and Brothers, 1883); Philip S. Klein, *President James Bu-*

chanan: A Biography (University Park: Pennsylvania State University Press, 1962); Elbert B. Smith, *The Presidency of James Buchanan* (Lawrence: University Press of Kansas, 1975); and Jean H. Baker, *James Buchanan* (New York: Times Books, 2004). A useful bibliography of the other monographs, articles, and conference records dealing with various aspects of Buchanan's life, presidential administration, and surroundings is contained in the notes to "Introduction: Bum Rap or Bad Leadership," *James Buchanan and the Coming of the Civil War*, ed. John W. Quist and Michael J. Birkner (Gainesville: University Press of Florida, 2013), 15–19.

2. Michael Todd Landis, "Old Buck's Lieutenant: Glancy Jones, James Buchanan, and the Antebellum Northern Democracy," *Pennsylvania Magazine of History and Biography* 140 (April 2016): 183–210; Buchanan to Harriet Lane, October 15, 1858, in *The Works of James Buchanan, Comprising His Speeches, State Papers, and Private Correspondence*, ed. John Bassett Moore, 12 vols. (Philadelphia: J. B. Lippincott, 1910), 10:229. For context, see Sister Frances L. Conlin, "The Democratic Party of Pennsylvania from 1856 to 1865," *American Catholic Historical Society Records* 47 (June 1936): 132–83.

3. Buchanan to Harriet Lane, October 15, 1858, in Moore, *Works of James Buchanan*, 10:230; Beverley Tucker to John Slidell, March 7, 1857, Special Collections, Swem Library, College of William and Mary, Williamsburg, VA. For Robert Magraw's role as a presidential friend and its benefits to his younger brother William, see William P. MacKinnon, "The Buchanan Spoils System and the Utah Expedition: Careers of W. M. F. Magraw and John M. Hockaday," *Utah Historical Quarterly* 31 (Spring 1963): 127–50.

4. Klein, *President James Buchanan;* Robert W. Johannsen, *Stephen A. Douglas* (New York: Oxford University Press, 1973). See also David E. Meerse, "Origins of the Buchanan-Douglas Feud Reconsidered," *Journal of the Illinois State Historical Society* 67 (April 1974): 154–74.

5. Buchanan to Pierce, March 8, 1853, James Buchanan Papers, Waidner-Spahr Library, Dickinson College, Carlisle, PA. Van Dyke has no biographer and virtually nothing has been written about him except a few brief references to his dealings with President Buchanan and service as US attorney in Philadelphia. See John Hill Martin, ed., *Martin's Bench and Bar of Philadelphia* (Philadelphia: Rees Welsh, 1883), 10, 319. The most substantial known collection of material about the Van Dyke–Buchanan relationship is in the author's research files.

6. Charles S. Foltz, *Surgeon of the Seas: The Adventurous Life of Jonathan M. Foltz in the Days of Wooden Ships* (Indianapolis: Bobbs-Merrill, 1931), 183–86, 189–90, 339.

7. Ethan Greenberg argues that the clerkship held by Plitt since 1846 was used as a bargaining chip by President-elect Buchanan in late February 1857 to influence the vote of Associate Justice Robert Grier of Pennsylvania to support the majority in the US Supreme Court's then-undecided case of *Dred Scott v. Sandford.* Grier wanted Plitt's clerkship to go to his son-in-law. Buchanan refused but then, after securing Plitt's resignation, placed in the position Benjamin Patton, Justice Grier's fishing companion and the man who earlier had been instrumental in arranging President James Polk's nomination of Grier to the Supreme Court. That Buchanan and Grier had corresponded improperly about the *Dred*

Scott case just before the inauguration has long been known, but the assertion that Plitt's clerkship was somehow involved is not well understood. Greenberg, *Dred Scott and the Dangers of a Political Court* (Lanham, MD: Lexington Books, 2009), 175–77.

8. Klein, *President James Buchanan*, 426.

9. This segment is adapted from William P. MacKinnon, "Thomas Kane's 1858 Utah War Mission: A Study in Presidential Ingratitude and Manipulation," *Utah Historical Quarterly* 86 (Fall 2018).

10. For the most recent scholarship on the war, from which this summary is derived, see William P. MacKinnon, ed., *At Sword's Point: A Documentary History of the Utah War, Part 1, to 1858;* and *Part 2, 1858–1859* (Norman, OK: Arthur H. Clark, 2008; 2016); David L. Bigler and Will Bagley, *The Mormon Rebellion: America's First Civil War, 1857–1858* (Norman: University of Oklahoma Press, 2011); Ronald W. Walker, Richard E. Turley Jr., and Glen M. Leonard, *Massacre at Mountain Meadows* (New York: Oxford University Press, 2008); and Norman F. Furniss, *The Mormon Conflict, 1850–1859* (New Haven, CT: Yale University Press, 1960).

11. Matthew J. Grow, *"Liberty to the Downtrodden": Thomas L. Kane, Romantic Reformer* (New Haven, CT: Yale University Press, 2009); Albert L. Zobell, *Sentinel in the East: A Biography of Thomas L. Kane* (Salt Lake City: Nicholas G. Morgan, 1965).

12. MacKinnon, *At Sword's Point, Part 1*, 73–77, 111–20, 135; Grow, *"Liberty to the Downtrodden,"* 154–61. Kane used the military title "colonel" after his appointment during the US–Mexican War by the governor of Pennsylvania to the honorific militia rank of lieutenant colonel on his staff. He saw no active service until his 1861 appointment as a lieutenant colonel of volunteer troops in the Union army. Kane resigned in 1863 as a brevet major general of US Volunteers.

13. MacKinnon, *At Sword's Point, Part 1*, 405–11; Kane, Memorandum, July 1858, Thomas L. Kane Collection, American Philosophical Society, Philadelphia.

14. "First Annual Message to Congress," December 8, 1857, in Moore, *Works of James Buchanan*, 10:129–63; Floyd, "Report of the Secretary of War," *Message of the President of the United States*, 35th Cong., 1st Sess., S. Exec. Doc. 11, serial 920, 6–9.

15. See note 12.

16. Van Dyke to Buchanan, December 9, 1857, James Buchanan Papers, Historical Society of Pennsylvania, Philadelphia (hereafter HSP).

17. These documents, the most complete record of what transpired in the Executive Mansion immediately after Christmas 1857 between Buchanan, Kane, and Van Dyke, may be found in MacKinnon, *At Sword's Point, Part 1*, 485–87, 494–99, 501–3.

18. MacKinnon, *At Sword's Point, Part 1*, 500–12; Van Dyke to Buchanan, December 29, 1857, Buchanan Papers, HSP; Kane Diary, April 16, 1858, BYU; Elizabeth W. Kane, "The Story of the Mother of the Regiment," vol. 2, chap. 3, ibid.

19. For Sherman's attempts during 1857–58 to reenter the army for the Utah campaign, see MacKinnon, *At Sword's Point, Part 2*, 261–62.

20. MacKinnon, *At Sword's Point, Part 2*, 187–243, 275–308, 347–81, 419–66, 505–54. See also William P. MacKinnon, *Across the Desert in 1858: Thomas L. Kane's Mediating Mission*

and the Mormon Women Who Made it Possible, 35th Annual Juanita Brooks Lecture (St. George, UT: Dixie State University Library, 2018).

21. Kane Diary, April–June 1858, BYU.

22. Kane, "Story of the Mother of the Regiment," vol. 2, chap. 3.

23. Kane, "Story of the Mother of the Regiment," vol. 2, chap. 3.

24. Memorandum accompanying Kane to Young, July 18, 1858, Church of Jesus Christ of Latter-day Saints History Library, Salt Lake City, UT (hereafter LDS History Library).

25. Kane, "Story of the Mother of the Regiment," vol. 2, chap. 3.

26. Price to Buchanan, November 17, 1858, Lot 1139 (detail), Nate D. Sanders Auctions, http://natedsanders/lot-13885.aspx, accessed April 17, 2014 (and LDS History Library).

27. "Second Annual Message of the President," December 6, 1858, in Moore, *Works of James Buchanan,* 10:245; James Buchanan, *Mr. Buchanan's Administration on the Eve of the Rebellion* (New York: D. Appleton, 1866), 238.

28. Cannon to Young, April 6, 14, 1859, LDS History Library; Edward W. Tullidge, *History of Salt Lake City and Its Founders* (Salt Lake City: Star Printing, 1886), 232–33; William P. MacKinnon, *"The Executive of Utah": Selected Utah War Documents and Commentary Relating to Thomas L. Kane's Lost Lecture in Defense of Governor Alfred Cumming, New-York Historical Society, 21 March 1859* (Norman, OK: Arthur H. Clark, 2016).

29. Buchanan to Toucey, December 22, 1858, Raab Collection, https://www.raabcollection.com/james-buchanan-autograph/james-buchanan-signed-was-president-james-buchanan-financially-corrupt, accessed September 3, 2016. In 1855, while W. M. F. Magraw was transporting US mail across the plains on the Independence, Missouri–Salt Lake City route, Henry S. Magraw and a partner were in California seeking a contract to operate a semimonthly mail from San Francisco to Olympia, Washington Territory, by coastal steamer. Clarence B. Bagley, *History of Seattle from the Earliest Settlement to the Present Time,* 2 vols. (Chicago: S. J. Clarke, 1916), 1:44–45. The issue of patronage and its abuse would, of course, dog the character of Buchanan's administration on a long-term basis. During the Watergate hearings of the early 1970s, a congressionally sponsored study of presidential misconduct conducted by historians concluded that such corruption "culminated and flourished most luxuriantly under Buchanan. . . . His administration marked the low point before the Civil War and somewhat approached later levels of corruption." C. Vann Woodward, ed., *Responses of the Presidents to Charges of Misconduct* (New York: Dell, 1974), xvi. See also two studies by David E. Meerse, "James Buchanan, the Patronage, and the Northern Democratic Party, 1857–1858" (PhD diss., University of Illinois, 1969), and "Buchanan's Patronage Policy: An Attempt to Achieve Political Strength," *Pennsylvania History* 40 (January 1973): 37–52.

30. Buchanan to Harriet Lane, March 19, 1853, November 16, 1855, in Moore, *Works of James Buchanan,* 8:503, 9:465; Curtis, *Life of James Buchanan,* 2:155–56.

31. Buchanan to Clarendon, April 8, 1859, in Moore, *Works of James Buchanan,* 10:315–16.

32. W. Turrentine Jackson, *Wagon Roads West: A Study of Federal Road Surveys and Construction in the Trans-Mississippi West 1846–1869* (Berkeley: University of California Press, 1952), 360n22; Magraw to Buchanan, January 2, 1858, Buchanan Papers, HSP; Magraw

to Douglas, January 22, 1858, Stephen A. Douglas Papers, Special Collections Research Center, University of Chicago Library; Buchanan to Harriet Lane, October 15, 1858, in Moore, *Works of James Buchanan*, 10:230.

33. Crampton to Clarendon, October 2, 1855, in *Private and Confidential: Letters from British Ministers in Washington to the Foreign Secretaries in London, 1844–67*, ed. James J. Barnes and Patience P. Barnes (Selinsgrove, PA: Susquehanna University Press, 1993), 138–39.

34. Buchanan to Fallon, December 13, 1857, Buchanan Papers, HSP.

35. William P. MacKinnon, "Hammering Utah, Squeezing Mexico, and Coveting Cuba: James Buchanan's White House Intrigues," *Utah Historical Quarterly* 80 (Spring 2012): 132–51; MacKinnon, *At Sword's Point, Part 2*, 174–86.

36. Homer T. Rosenberger, "Two Monuments for the Fifteenth President of the United States," *Journal of the Lancaster County Historical Society* 78 (1974): 29–48. For unsuccessful attempts to rehabilitate Buchanan's presidential standing over the decades, see Stephen Patrick O'Hara, "'The Verdict of History': Defining and Defending James Buchanan through Public Memorialization" (MA thesis, Virginia Polytechnic Institute and State University, 2012).

37. Brian H. Stuy, "Wilford Woodruff's Vision of the Signers of the Declaration of Independence," *Journal of Mormon History* 26 (Spring 2000): 64–90. Notwithstanding Apostle Woodruff's selectivity, in 1932 some forgiving but unknown Latter-day Saint performed vicarious ordinances of baptism and endowment on Buchanan's behalf in the Salt Lake Temple.

38. Frederick Moore Binder, "James Buchanan and the Earl of Clarendon: An Uncertain Relationship," *Diplomacy and Statecraft* 6 (July 1995): 323–41; George D. Harmon, "President James Buchanan's Betrayal of Governor Robert J. Walker of Kansas," *Pennsylvania Magazine of History and Biography* 53 (1929): 51–91. See also Pearl T. Ponce, "Pledges and Principles: Buchanan, Walker, and Kansas in 1857," *Kansas History: A Journal of the Central Plains* 27 (Spring–Summer 2004): 87–99.

39. John W. Forney, editorials, *Philadelphia Press*, February 10, 1859, March 4, 1861.

40. See note 18.

41. Buchanan to Lincoln, October 21, 1861, Papers of Abraham Lincoln, Manuscript Division, Library of Congress.

42. Sophie Plitt to Harriet Lane, September 5, 1860, quoted in Klein, *President James Buchanan*, 283.

SLAVERY AND THE BREAKUP OF THE DEMOCRATIC PARTY IN THE NORTH

A Battle of Ideas and Organization

FRANK TOWERS

Given its importance in dividing the opposition to Abraham Lincoln in the 1860 presidential contest, the breakup of the Democratic Party in the run-up to the election has been the subject of extensive research. This essay seeks to further that scholarship by exploring the surprisingly strong showing of southern Democrat John C. Breckinridge in parts of the border South and the North, regions where slavery had little to no presence and where most Democrats supported rival Stephen A. Douglas. These anomalies hold a clue to a practice of partisan organizing that had held Democrats together in support of slaveholders' rights for thirty years but had begun to falter by the late 1850s, especially in the more populous states of the North. To understand those connections, it will help first to review the prevailing explanation of the 1860 election returns.

That election's four candidates offered voters clear choices on the status of slavery in federal territories, the crucial question of the day. Kentuckian John C. Breckinridge, sitting vice president and nominee of a mostly southern faction of the Democratic Party, represented the proslavery extreme with his call for a federal slave code to enforce slaveholders' property rights in the territories, a policy that pushed President

James Buchanan's support for the *Dred Scott* decision (1857) and slavery in Kansas to its logical conclusion. Senator John C. Bell of Tennessee, standard-bearer of the Constitutional Union Party, also a new organization, pledged to maintain the "Constitution, the Union, and the Enforcement of the Laws" and to "restore peace, with justice to both sections of the Union—not to perpetuate strife," a policy that implied another round of compromise to secure some of the territories for slavery.[1]

Shorn of many southern supporters who went to Breckinridge, the mostly northern faction of the Democratic Party backed Illinois senator Stephen A. Douglas and his doctrine of popular sovereignty, which devolved the decision on slavery's status in new states to their settlers. Douglas's adherence to popular sovereignty, the basis for his Kansas-Nebraska Act of 1854, had forced a breach with Buchanan, who endorsed the fraudulently ratified Lecompton Constitution that would have imposed slavery on Kansas despite abundant evidence that a majority of its voters opposed the measure. Although theoretically possible for slavery to spread, Douglas argued that the institution had reached its natural limits. (He and many others believed that it profited only through cultivating staple crops, which could not survive in the West's arid soils.) At the other end of this spectrum stood Douglas's fellow Illinoisan Abraham Lincoln, nominee of the six-year-old Republican Party. He promised to ban slavery in the territories and argued against "groping for some middle ground between the question of right and wrong."[2]

State-by-state 1860 vote totals show a clear correlation between voter preference and the density of slaves and slaveowners. Breckinridge swept the seven lower South states, the subregion with the highest concentration of slaves and the most capital invested in human property and plantation crops. Bell won Kentucky, a border South slave state that in choosing him rejected its native son, Breckinridge. Bell also carried two of the four upper South states, a subregion where slaves composed roughly one-quarter of the total population and where plantation crops competed with other commodities and industries. Douglas's sole victory came in border-state Missouri, where slaves made up only 10 percent of the population. He also won three of the seven Electoral College votes in New Jersey, a free state near the sectional border that, through a technicality of its gradual-emancipation law, still contained eighteen "apprentices for life" in 1860.[3] The rest of the North went for Lincoln, giving him an Electoral College majority and the presidency.

In this broad overview the most proslavery candidate won where slavery was most entrenched, compromise candidates fared best near the sectional border, and the most antislavery candidate won where slavery was illegal. It would be logical, therefore, to infer that voters in the 1860 presidential election cast ballots for the candidate whose views best matched the social and economic dynamics of their region.

As noted above, some anomalies related to the Breckinridge vote complicate this interpretation. A closer look at the map reveals that he won Delaware and Maryland, two border South states that should have rejected his hard line on slavery. In 1860, Delaware, at 2 percent, had the lowest proportion of slaves in its population of any southern state, while Maryland, at 13 percent, came in third just behind Missouri. Tobacco farmers in southern Maryland and a handful of plantations in southern Delaware continued to use slave labor, but the institution had long been in decline in both states.[4] Moreover, opponents of lower South Democrats had considerable power in these places. Even as they voted for Breckinridge, Delawareans elected a Republican to their only seat in the US House. In Maryland the anti-immigrant party and antisectionalist American Party (called "Know-Nothings" by critics) still held important offices, including the governorship and a US Senate seat.[5]

Zoom in beneath the statewide winners and more anomalies appear. Breckinridge staked an equal claim to Pennsylvania's 179,000 Democratic fusion ballots (two-fifths of the state's total vote) and polled 21 percent of Connecticut's vote, placing him in third just one point behind Douglas. These were free states that had completed the process of gradual emancipation by 1800. Each had strong Republican Party organizations and influential Douglas Democrats; a southern rights candidate should have barely registered in their election returns. Furthermore, these four states accounted for 31 percent of Breckinridge's nationwide vote, with Pennsylvania and Connecticut providing 70 percent of the Breckinridge ballots cast in the free states.[6]

Because these findings fly in the face of common sense, some explanation is required. For Connecticut, Delaware, and Maryland, few dispute that a ballot for Breckinridge was a ballot for Breckinridge. His supporters fielded a ticket separate from the other candidates, and their tallies were their own. Pennsylvania, however, was more complicated. It was one of four northern states that tried some form of fusion among Lincoln's opponents, a strategy endorsed by Breckinridge but strongly opposed by Douglas.[7] Pennsylvania's fusion differed from three other statewide efforts to unite against Lincoln. In May 1860, a month after the Democratic Party divided at its convention in Charleston, South Carolina, Pennsylvania's state party committee announced that if successful, its slate of presidential electors would vote for whichever Democrat stood the best chance of defeating Lincoln in the Electoral College. Although most Douglas supporters accepted the deal, a diehard minority fielded their own slate, giving anti-Breckinridge Democrats a clear protest vehicle. The other fusion states differed. Rhode Island's Breckinridge faction capitulated by endorsing a slate of Douglas electors. In New York fusionists divided their thirty-five electors into three blocks: seventeen for Douglas, ten for Bell, and eight for Breckinridge. New Jersey's Douglas Democrats refused to join a combined Bell-Breckinridge ticket. Unlike the other fusion tickets, then, Pennsylvania's was the only one that offered Breckinridge a chance at winning the state's entire electoral vote.[8]

This essay argues that the enduring strength of a few state and local political networks within the Democratic Party explains the anomaly of Breckinridge's strong showing in Connecticut and the middle Atlantic states but nowhere else outside of slavery's core areas. In a year when the party split over slavery, a few pieces of its cross-sectional proslavery alliance held together, bringing about some election results that defy the logic of a North united in opposition to slaveholder aggression. To understand the power of these networks, this essay also explores alternative theories of voter motivation in the mid-nineteenth century.

Accounts of Breckinridge's northern campaign are rare. Instead, the prevailing interpretations of the 1860 election highlight sectional divisions within and between parties that made for "a two-party campaign in each section," one in the South between Bell and Breckinridge, the other in the North between Lincoln and Douglas. According to one prominent study, "on the election's crucial issue, the expansion of slavery, the nation was split in two. If northerners disagreed about the efficacy of Douglas's popular sovereignty idea, the returns showed them thoroughly

Storming the Castle: "Old Abe" on Guard. Currier and Ives, 1860. This print depicts presidential candidate Abraham Lincoln as a sentinel of the people stopping his opponents as they try to break into the Executive Mansion. Lincoln is dressed as a member of the Wide Awakes, a pro-Lincoln political club. Meanwhile, John Breckinridge (aided by his patron James Buchanan), Stephen Douglas, and John Bell are attired as conventional politicians. The cartoon bolstered the Republican message that Lincoln was a nontraditional candidate who would restore honest government to Washington.

united about the necessity to halt slavery's spread." Another history of the contest says, "the number of northerners for Breckinridge was minuscule." Similarly, a recent study of the secession crisis calls the election "a bizarre contest that . . . developed into two separate campaigns." Even when noted by scholars, Breckinridge's support outside the lower South passes by with little analysis.[9]

Notwithstanding these broad assessments, in 1860 Breckinridge Democrats had a few reasons to hope for their candidate's success beyond the lower South. John Cabell Breckinridge hardly fit the prototype of a fire-eating disunionist. He hailed from the border slave state of Kentucky, and his family included several prominent unionists and Whigs. Moreover, his ascent within the Democratic Party had little to do with pushing a hard line on slavery. By most accounts, in 1856 Buchanan chose Breckinridge as his running mate to make peace with supporters of Douglas, who had contended for the nomination and counted the Kentuckian as an ally in the passage of the Kansas-Nebraska Act. Moreover, in his only public speech of the campaign, Breckinridge denied charges that he favored disunion.[10]

Working with these details, a few scholars have examined Breckinridge's northern campaign. One biographer has argued that the Kentuckian epitomized "the spirit of moderation and conciliation. . . . The vice-president's vote, especially in the North and in the border states, manifested a willingness to grant the South its protection of property, and thereby avoid disunion." This perspective drew on Seymour Martin Lipset's influential study of the 1860 vote distribution in the South, which found that "most voters in that year voted along traditional lines": that is, party loyalty retained its hold on the electorate notwithstanding the tumult of the prior four years. In the lower South, Lipset argued, Breckinridge did best in Democratic-leaning counties that had few slaveholders, a surprise given Breckinridge's platform and his support from proslavery disunionists. Moreover, in legislative elections and referendums held after the presidential election, counties that supported Breckinridge opposed immediate secession. Although Lipset looked only at the South, others could infer that Breckinridge may have benefited from long-held partisan allegiance in the free states. As an earlier study put it, "So closely did the vote . . . follow Whig or Democratic tradition that one wonders how strongly Southern rights, fear of secession or love of Union—the issues stressed by speakers and editors—figured in how the voters acted."[11]

Yet subsequent quantitative studies of the election have revised Lipset's work to show that Breckinridge actually performed well among slaveholders and that his supporters often went on to back secession. This pattern held in the upper South as well as the cotton states.[12]

In light of these findings, some recent studies of the 1860 election include Breckinridge's northern campaign but portray it as a pyrrhic act of defiance against Douglas by supporters of the reviled Buchanan wing of the party. These historians agree that Breckinridge lacked an effective organization in the North, and despite his claims to be a Union saver, "his candidacy aided the cause of Southern separatism by offering proslavery voters an ultra platform, by further inflaming the already overheated national discourse on the territories, and by perpetuating a crippling division within what had been the majority party." Furthermore, Breckinridge's association with fire-eating disunionists such as Alabama's William Lowndes Yancey, who campaigned for him in the North, and South Carolina's Robert Barnwell Rhett, both Jr. and Sr., reinforced northerners' perception that he stood for proslavery extremism. As a contribution to the larger interpretation of the presidential contest, these recent studies of Breckinridge's efforts in the North reaffirm the "two elections" view that he had little chance there and performed poorly as a result.[13]

Unlike these assessments, Michael Holt's 2017 study of the election rejects the "two elections" framework to argue for the importance of Breckinridge's northern campaign. Holt finds it a vigorous effort in the free states that took aim at Douglas and defended the unpopular *Dred Scott* ruling on slavery in the territories, thereby dividing northern Democrats and decisively lowering their voter turnout. His findings comport with those of Michael Robinson's recent book on the border South in 1860–61. My essay agrees with Holt's points but is more interested in those border South and free-state Democrats who came out to vote for Breckinridge than in the ones who stayed home, and it is more focused on the influence of political networks on voter mobilization.[14]

Despite its close fit with the Electoral College map of state-by-state winners, the "two elections" interpretation of 1860 oversimplifies the geographic distribution of proslavery and antislavery voters and reinforces an essentialist perspective on slavery as a sectional institution as opposed to a national one. Recently, the case for slavery's national reach has been made from a range of scholarly perspectives. Steven Hahn argues for the salience of fugitive-slave recapture and racial discrimination in the North as a necessary complement to chattel slavery in the South.[15] Social and economic histories interested in slavery's place in American capitalism emphasize northern complicity in the late-antebellum slave economy, reviving the arguments of the period's abolitionists that the North's "lords of the loom" colluded with the South's "lords of the lash."[16]

Meanwhile, political historians have renewed interest in the "slave power" arguments advanced by Lincoln's Republicans to assess whether or not northern politicians, mostly Democrats, fit the free-soiler description of them as "dough-faced" servants of southern planters. Some recent studies agree that Democrats were indeed "northern men with southern loyalties"—allies of the South who acted primarily out of support for slavery and white supremacy—whereas others identify doughfaces as true moderates who put preserving the Union above all other concerns and thus "were not merely racists or tools of the Slave Power."[17] This debate relates to a similar one over the balance of wartime northern political support for slavery and preservation of the Union.[18]

The Breckinridge campaign's surprising showing beyond the lower South offers a different angle of vision for considering the intent of northern and border South voters in 1860. Although it would be Lincoln and the Republicans who led the war against the slaveholders' rebellion, they could not have succeeded without support from the almost two million men who voted against Lincoln in the North and the loyal border South states. What those anti-Republican but pro-Union men voted for in 1860 shapes conclusions about the purpose of the northern effort during the Civil War and the challenges faced by supporters of emancipation and equal rights.

Viewed in its totality, the Breckinridge campaign supports the case that most northern Democrats rejected the proslavery, southern-accommodating wing of their party. Although the free states gave Breckinridge a surprising share of his nationwide total, he nonetheless won only 8 percent of all ballots cast outside the South, compared to 41 percent for Douglas. What remains, then, is the anomaly of Breckinridge dramatically outperforming expectations in four states where he should have suffered the same crushing defeat he experienced everywhere else outside the soon-to-be Confederacy. To explain this strange aspect of the electoral outcome, historians will do well to supplement studies of voters' ideological motivation with an analysis of voter mobilization.

The failure of the regional concentration of slaves to fully predict the Breckinridge vote pattern suggests a problem for standard ways of explaining voter turnout. Although historians now rarely use the statistical methods pioneered by "new political history," which rose to prominence in the 1960s, its basic assumptions about voting continue to inform explanations of past elections. Like other subjects of behaviorist social theory, the new political history treated voting as a product of individual rational choice. According to Lee Benson, a founder of the school, "in American history the act of voting is the best single test of opinion. Under the American political system, even with nonsecret ballots, voting *ordinarily* does not entail a heavy risk, nor are extremely heavy external pressures (government or social) brought to bear upon men to vote a given ticket. Some social pressures undoubtedly are brought to bear upon voters almost everywhere and at all times; but those pressures usually do not prevent some reasonable degree of 'free choice.'"[19]

In making this argument for individual decision making, new-political historians wanted to look beyond a narrow focus on leaders and events in order to understand mass behavior. Benson went on to argue that free choice was not readily visible in a single election. In order to make reliable inferences about voters' intentions, historians needed to consider long runs of election returns and measure them against partisan messages, on the one hand, and the social characteristics of the electorate, on the other.[20] This model assumed that vote totals signified voluntary preferences by individuals that could then be aggregated to reveal the influence of public opinion on politics and, in turn, the effect on voter preference of social identities, such as religion, ethnicity, and occupation. Seeking to shift historians' "focus from the episodic and the formal to the underlying uniform patterns of political life," the new political history combined computerized data analysis with the insights of mid-twentieth-century structural-functionalist social theory, which regarded the formal objectives of institutions, such as political parties, as often less important than their "latent functions" as foundations of the social order.[21]

In the past twenty years, such voter studies have become rarer as historians have opened new lines of inquiry into culture, civil society, gender, and institutions as well as reviving grand narratives of leaders and pivotal events.[22] Nevertheless, when it comes to explaining election outcomes, scholars continue to rely on the new political history's premise that election returns reflected choices made by voters based on the fit between their own interests and values and the message of a particular candidate or party.

As an alternative to the rational-choice model, some political historians advocate a community-based explanation of voting that emphasizes the influence of social organization and geography on determining who voted and how they did so.[23] These studies have relied on poll books that recorded the names of individual voters. In the few states that required a voter to verbally announce his preference to an election official, poll books also show how a person voted. Three examples illustrate the problem such data poses for a rational-choice theory of voting.

First, the demographic characteristics of the electorate differed substantially from the demographics of actual voters. In his study of poll-book returns for Clinton, Ohio, Kenneth Winkle found that four-fifths of voters participated in five or fewer of the thirty-seven elections held between 1822 and 1860, with half of them only voting in one. These single-election voters accounted for only two-fifths of all votes cast during these years, whereas persistent voters, a minority of the electorate, cast a majority of the ballots. Persisters were a unique group. They not only tended to be long-term residents but also richer than other eligible voters. In 1850s Baltimore, white-collar professionals made up 5 percent of the city's population, 12 percent of its eligible voters, and 30 percent of its actual voters. In Congress, Ohio, the median persistent voter was ten years older than a new one and owned twice as much property. Rather than turning out a cross-section of the electorate, candidates did better by winning over the local elites, who predominated at the polls.[24]

Second, Americans voted in groups, not as individuals, and they did so under the leadership of active partisans. For example, in the 1843 federal congressional election held in Russell Precinct in Virginia's Frederick County, 101 voters split their preferences comparatively evenly between the Whig and Democratic candidates (the Democrat won). Yet only 9 voters approached the election judge without another supporter of their candidate behind them.[25] The majority of voters approached the ballot box in a pack of at least four, and almost two-fifths (38 percent) did so in a line of seven or more likeminded men. For Washington County, Oregon, Paul Bourke and Donald DeBats found a similar "platoon" voting pattern in which the first man to approach the voting window was usually a well-known party activist, followed by several supporters. Platoon voting suggests that without being organized to march to the polls, potential voters were less likely to turn out no matter their individual views on the candidates.[26]

Third, the prevailing partisan organization of particular neighborhoods could override class and ethnic identifications in shaping voter allegiance. In a study of 1850s Newport, Kentucky, DeBats found that Prussian immigrants who lived in established Democratic neighborhoods voted for Democrats, but those who settled in neighborhoods dominated by Know-Nothings voted for those candidates.[27]

These brief examples from community-based election studies highlight the importance of voter mobilization. Rather than a voluntary, individual choice, voting in antebellum America better resembled a communal event orchestrated by partisan activists who used personal networks to bring supporters to the polls.[28] Although voters certainly made choices about candidates and whether or not to vote, those decisions occurred in a campaign environment in which partisan activists drew on local family and associational networks to bring supporters to the polls.

This alternative model of voter mobilization helps explain Breckinridge's strong showing in a few places in the North and border South. Echoing Lipset's finding that Breckinridge's southern support came from districts that had traditionally voted Democratic, in Connecticut, Delaware, Maryland, and Pennsylvania, Breckinridge polled best in counties that Democrats had consistently won. Conversely, with the exception of Baltimore, he did poorly in opposition-dominated districts and areas that had switched back and forth between the parties.

In Pennsylvania, which Buchanan carried four years earlier, the fusion ticket won only twelve of the state's sixty-four counties. Those twelve counties were Democratic bastions that had gone for the party nominee in every presidential election since Andrew Jackson's first run in 1824.[29] Unlike Pennsylvania, Connecticut went to Republican John C. Frémont in 1856. In 1860 Republicans increased their Connecticut margin by 4 percentage points and won all eight of its counties. Among the anti-Lincoln voters, Breckinridge outpolled Douglas in four counties, each of them one of the Democrats' top four in 1856 and all of which had voted Democratic in 1852.[30] Delaware, which ended its long allegiance to Whigs in 1852, gave Breckinridge 46 percent of its votes and victories in each of its three counties. Within this pattern, the vice president did best in Kent, which was also Buchanan's lead county in 1856.[31] In these states Breckinridge's support was concentrated in areas of longtime party strength, suggesting that he won the votes of those most loyal to the Democratic banner.

Maryland differed slightly in that Breckinridge not only won the core Democratic counties in the tobacco-growing south and Eastern Shore but also a narrow majority in Baltimore, a city that had been controlled by the Know-Nothing Party until the October 1860 municipal election, when they were defeated by the City Reform Association, an officially nonpartisan organization that was led by Democrats and allied with them at the state level. A month later those same voters cast ballots for Breckinridge rather than Bell, who had the support of their local Know-Nothing enemies.[32]

This pattern of Breckinridge doing best in areas of traditional Democratic strength did not prevail region-wide, however. Elsewhere, he lost Democratic core counties to Douglas and Lincoln. For example, in Vermont Breckinridge outpolled Douglas in only one county, Windham, which Republicans had won by a landslide of 83 percent in 1856; none of the strong Buchanan counties put him ahead of Douglas four years later. In Ohio, a Frémont state in 1856, only four counties gave Breckinridge more than 10 percent of the vote (he finished fourth statewide with 2.6 percent), and none of them had been longtime bases of Democratic support.[33] Meanwhile, in the other border slave states, he placed well behind Bell, who beat him by ten points in Kentucky and sixteen in Missouri, where Breckinridge ended up in third. Had Lipset's thesis about party loyalty held throughout the North and border South, Breckinridge would have done much better. The fact that it mattered only in a few states suggests that there was something unique about Democratic party solidarity in these places.

What distinguished Breckinridge's campaign in Connecticut and the three middle Atlantic states were influential Democratic leaders who favored him over Douglas and who retained the loyalty of lower-level activists capable of turning out the vote. These powerbrokers had remained loyal to President Buchanan and southern Democrats in their battles with Douglas over slavery in the territories. Breckinridge had influential backers in other states, too, but they could not hold their midlevel followers together in sufficient numbers to stage a credible campaign.

In Pennsylvania Breckinridge's most important supporter was Buchanan himself, a native of the state who commanded substantial patronage powers as president and held personal debts accumulated over a lifetime in politics. Buchanan had already brought these powers to bear against Douglas after their break in 1857, and he continued to do so during the 1860 campaign. For example, when the president learned that some Pennsylvania Douglas supporters were running a separate ticket, he ordered Philadelphia's customs chief to obtain from "every Democratic candidate in every county a pledge to support the Cresson arrangement," a reference to an August meeting in which the terms of fusion were reaffirmed by the party.[34] Breckinridge had other prominent Keystone State allies, including Henry Foster, Democratic 1860 gubernatorial candidate and Breckinridge's cousin; William Bigler, a longtime Buchanan ally who had served as governor and US senator; and George Mifflin Dallas, a former US senator and vice president and currently minister to Russia.[35]

Thomas H. Seymour, an ex-governor and Dallas's predecessor in Saint Petersburg, headed the Connecticut Breckinridge campaign and made a failed return run for governor in April 1860. Seymour's long career in state politics built on a family dynasty that stretched back to the colonial era. He was joined by Ralph Ingersoll, former New Haven mayor and US congressman, and Isaac Toucey, former governor, US senator, and US attorney general then serving as Buchanan's secretary of the navy.[36]

Breckinridge's most important Delaware supporter was James A. Bayard Jr., a US senator and a member of the state's most powerful political dynasty (his father and brother had also served in the Senate as would his own son in the late 1800s). Bayard had opposed Douglas since the passage of the Kansas-Nebraska Act and had worked to stop his bid for the 1856 Democratic nomination.[37] Four years later at the Charleston convention, Bayard again led the charge against the Illinois senator.[38] Within Delaware, Bayard used his friendship with Buchanan to control the customs house, the state's most lucrative source of patronage.[39] Along with Bayard, Breckinridge had the support of William G. Whiteley, the state's lone congressman, and most of the lower-level operatives in New Castle County, home of Wilmington and nearly half of the state's voters.

In Maryland the state's Democratic leadership uniformly backed Breckinridge and ignored Douglas, which helps explain the latter's meager 6-percent share of the vote, comparable to his single-digit showing across much of the border and upper South. More significant for Breckinridge's victory was the refusal of Democratic leaders to switch to Bell, the choice of moderate southern Democrats elsewhere.[40]

Reinforcing their loyalty to Buchanan, a surprising number of pro-Breckinridge leaders in these four states had family ties to prominent southern Democrats known for their outspoken defense of slavery. James Mason Campbell, son-in-law of Supreme Court Chief Justice Roger B. Taney, author of the majority opinion in the *Dred Scott* case and an ardent Buchanan ally and Breckinridge supporter, helped organize the Baltimore Breckinridge campaign. Pennsylvania senator Richard Brodhead, a Buchanan loyalist, had married Jefferson Davis's niece, naming his son Jefferson Davis Brodhead, and in the mid-1850s used their friendship to enlist Davis's aid as secretary of war in placing a government foundry on land owned by his brother.[41]

Another set of connections ran through the Chew family dynasty, headquartered in Philadelphia. The Chews counted among their close friends and associates Bayard, Dallas, and James Murray Mason, a Virginia US senator who had authored the Fugitive Slave Law and had married into the family. These three politicians traded speeches in each other's states, exchanged family visits, and shared legal work, handling the Chew estate's many land and inheritance cases. That business relationship extended to E. Wyatt Blanchard, a Baltimore lawyer who was active in his state's Breckinridge campaign.[42]

The Chews also served as the conduit for friendships to prominent Maryland Democrats through the descendants of Margaret Oswald Chew, married to John Eager Howard, an early governor of the state. Dallas was a lifelong friend of their son Benjamin Chew Howard, a Democratic congressman in the 1830s and later reporter for the Supreme Court who made a failed bid for governor in 1861. Several members of the Howard family took part in the City Reform Association that overthrew the Baltimore Know-Nothings and helped swing the city's vote to Breckinridge. In turn, the Baltimore network reached to Connecticut, where Seymour maintained a long friendship with Samuel K. George, a vice president of the City Reform Association.[43]

Within their states, these leaders commanded networks of lesser officials who performed invaluable work, stifling Douglas challengers at Democratic meetings, spreading Breckinridge's message, and turning out voters on election day. A few examples of these activities illustrate their scope. To get the message out, local Breckinridge activists relied on party leaders to provide the needed materials. "If convenient will you be so kind as to forward me some Breckinridge documents," a Democrat in Duck

Landing asked Delaware's Thomas Bayard, Senator Bayard's son and de facto campaign manager, "I want them to circulate."[44] Baltimore's Gustav Lurman, a German-born merchant known as "strongly pro-southern," worked with South Carolina's fire-eating US senator James Chesnut to translate Breckinridge speeches into German for urban immigrants.[45] In Connecticut Seymour's allies begged him to counteract Republican rallies. "We think that in Hartford you should not let the republicans hold large meetings addressed by distinguished speakers from abroad and do nothing to counteract this effect."[46] Speakers and pamphlets mattered as much for showing party energy as they did for their intrinsic persuasive value.

Equally important were party ballots. In the mid-nineteenth century, parties, not the state, printed and distributed ballots. Printing duties usually fell to partisan editors like Connecticut's Alfred Burr, owner of the *Hartford Times,* who pressed his allies for information on ballots. "Have arrangements been made for supplying *every Town* in your *County* with Breckinridge Electoral votes?," he asked a Middlesex County Democrat. "If not, there should be no delay. . . . I am supplying 30,000 of the specimen I enclose to Hartford, Litchfield, Tolland and Windham Co[untie]s. . . . I look upon this matter of *sending* votes into every town as of considerable importance."[47] Beyond the usual work of distributing ballots, Burr noted that in the wake of the Buchanan-Douglas feud: "Town Committees are disarranged this year and in many cases will not send for votes. They should have enough in season." Simply having sufficient Breckinridge ballots on hand helped his supporters defeat opponents who may have lacked their own printed tickets and thus been forced to ask voters to laboriously write out their choices.

Mobilizing supporters for local party meetings was another critical campaign task. Intractably opposed to Douglas, Delaware's Breckinridge Democrats fought efforts to have the state party endorse a fusion ticket. Stopping this required constant vigilance at state and county meetings, where Douglas backers tried to pass resolutions favoring a united front. Typical of these efforts, a Sussex County Breckinridge activist told Thomas Bayard, "I thought it was understood that we are to make an effort to appoint our own men, and I sent a man out to get our men in town to attend the meeting. . . . [T]he day however was so unfavourable that there were but five here," a number barely sufficient to carry the meeting's nominations.[48] Commenting on their tactical victories over Douglas supporters, Thomas Bayard told his father: "There is no use in attempting conciliation with such suckers. We beat them to death."[49]

Networks also served as conduits for political intelligence on the opposition. In the absence of modern polling operations, campaigns depended on local activists to report on voter opinion. These reports often discussed "divisions" or the relationship between local powerbrokers and the voters they could deliver. For example, Edwin Stearns, a Middletown resident and former chairman of the Connecticut Democratic Party, told Isaac Toucey, who as a member of Buchanan's cabinet helped with the national Breckinridge campaign, "I wish that I could say that we were in every respect harmonious in this town, but the course of Walter S. Carter has been such as to create many serious divisions." Stearns worried that Carter, a local editor who antagonized fellow Democrats but nonetheless sought the area party's nomination for state legislature, would disincline his Democratic opponents to vote for nominees higher on the ticket, including Breckinridge.[50] Indicating the value placed on these insider accounts, James Bayard worried about Breckinridge's chances in Virginia but could not be sure: "I have no other information from there than the newspapers give."[51] This kind of political intelligence mattered in the same way modern polls do for campaigns—they informed decisions about messaging and resources. The better the intelligence, the more effective the campaign.

Although hard to trace in archival records, money also played an important role in nineteenth-century campaigns. In the 1856 presidential campaign, Buchanan's campaign manager, John Weiss Forney, asked a Pennsylvania activist to "please draw on me at three days sight, for $150 which must be put into circulation at once so as to increase your vote. I need not invoke [sic] you to see that this fund is properly distributed according to your best judgment."[52] Notwithstanding allegations of vote buying, receipts from party activists indicate that campaigns spent on legitimate activities, such as supplies for rallies, travel for speakers, and printing of partisan literature. Perhaps because Seymour worried that Republicans "will spend money freely at the last moment," his Connecticut supporters promised to find speakers and "send money to the Towns named by you."[53]

In all these ways Breckinridge's ability to utilize a standard-issue campaign apparatus in a few states helps explain his strong showing in them, especially when compared to his abysmal performance where these networks were absent. But to emphasize the role of organization does not preclude real ideological affinity between his partisans and their candidate's proslavery policies. In fact, when discussing their candidate, Breckinridge allies typically blended organizational questions about personal loyalty and party strength with shorthand references to policy. A Bristol, Connecticut, Breckinridge supporter described the town elections as a contest for proslavery ideas. "I am not bound up with the religious people of the present day at the North," the writer told Seymour, "but go in for Southern views and [the] principles of our Democratic Party."[54] Similarly, Stearns said, "One year more in my opinion, the party will be purged of its pollution, when Douglas will have found his proper element in the ranks of the B[lac]k Republicans."[55] Chief Justice Taney's insider observations contained the same assumptions about what Breckinridge stood for in the North. Commenting on the shift by many Virginia Democrats to Bell, he said: "I am satisfied that there are true men enough in the free states to have elected Breckinridge. But how could they be expected to quarrel with their neighbors for southern rights while the South was everywhere quarrelling among themselves[?]"[56] Casual references to partisan identities in these discussions of network organization show the entanglement of personal loyalty with ideological commitment to Breckinridge's platform.

This mixture of political belief and personal obligation found expression in the formal messages that Breckinridge activists sent to prospective voters. Along with attacks on Douglas as a party apostate, Breckinridge's northern and border South supporters advocated for slavery's westward expansion and federal protections for it in the territories, the same proslavery positions that characterized the campaign in the South. A brief survey provides some examples.

A fusion pamphlet directed at Pennsylvania voters prior to the October 9 gubernatorial election, which was widely understood as a test of Lincoln's statewide strength, warned that a vote for the Republicans was a vote for "the compulsory restriction of slavery within its present limits . . . and the exclusion from the common territories of our southern brethren, whose money has been used and whose blood has been shed in their acquisition."[57] That argument built on speeches made at an August 21 Philadelphia rally for Breckinridge and Oregon senator Joseph Lane, Breckinridge's running mate. There, former Oregon governor Isaac Stevens said: "The Dred Scott decision declares that the South has a right to bring its property into a Territory, and they demand protection. That is true Democratic doctrine, that is the doctrine of our standard bearers, Breckinridge and Lane. The object of all government is to protect persons and property and nothing else."[58]

In Connecticut H. H. Barbour, a prominent Hartford attorney and Democratic activist, told an audience at a September Breckinridge and Lane rally: "In the Constitution we have entered into a compact to concede to the people of all the States equal rights in the territories and we cannot deprive them of that right or of their slave possessions in any portion of the territorial property, without violating the compact. . . . It will not do to say that slave property, recognized by the Constitution, is not entitled under that compact to as much protection as any other species of property."[59] Although using the measured language of law and institutions, Barbour clearly argued for the right of slaveholders to hold humans as property throughout federally administered lands.

In Wilmington, Delaware, a Democratic audience heard Alabama's less-measured fire-eater William Lowndes Yancey call "Black Republicans" the "negro party, or mixed negro and white party, making it the mulatto party. While the Breckinridge party was essentially the white man's party." Yancey made a blunt case for the candidate's proslavery policies. "We stand upon the dark platform of southern slavery, and all we ask is to be allowed to keep it ourselves." Like other Breckinridge Democrats, Yancey issued the veiled threat that should a free-soil northerner win, secession would follow.[60]

These examples, all from prominent campaign events that were widely reported in the press, show Breckinridge surrogates making the same arguments about slavery's expansion and disunion that characterized his campaign in the lower South.[61] As recent studies of the Breckinridge campaign in the North argue, his surrogates took a defiant stand against regional opinion on slavery. Yet as shown above, this appeal fell flat except in those places that maintained strong pro-Buchanan networks.

Given the failure of the Breckinridge platform to win outside of states where he benefited from strong patron-client networks, it would be tempting to conclude that ideas did not matter that much to his supporters, an argument that echoes that Lipset thesis about long-term loyalties blinding voters to immediate issues. But the foregoing evidence indicates that belief and organization were hard to separate, suggesting that when voters cast ballots for Breckinridge, they did so with an awareness of the policies they voted for. The case of one Pennsylvania Democratic activist, William Watts Hart Davis of Bucks County, a Democratic stronghold that fell to Lincoln in 1860, indicates the tight bond between the medium (political organization) and the message (political ideas).

In Davis's case, support for Democratic doctrine went hand in hand with personal advancement. William Davis learned about politics from his father, John, a grocer and militia officer who campaigned for Jackson and the Democrats from 1824 onward. In 1838 John Davis won election to the US House of Representatives but lost his reelection bid in 1840 and failed again two years later. He had more success winning elections to serve as a militia commander, giving him influence over an important group of eligible voters predisposed to civic engagement. John Davis also spoke out for Democratic positions on flashpoint issues of his time, such as keeping the mails open on Sunday, supporting President Martin Van Buren's independent treasury, and in 1838 being, what his son described as, "one of the most active promoters" of an amendment to the state constitution that formally restricted voting to whites only.

Democratic administrations rewarded John Davis's loyalty with several patronage plums. They designated his store as a federal post office—a boon for business—and named him state appraiser of public works and later surveyor of the Port of Philadelphia. At the port Davis hired John Forney as one his clerks, furthering a friendship with a powerful editor and an influential Buchanan ally. Forney helped convince Davis to back Buchanan in his struggle for ascendancy within the state Democratic Party. Place and position clearly influenced this decision. Recounting Buchanan's 1848 bid for the presidency, Elizabeth Davis (William's sister) said: "Forney had a meeting the other night at his house and had more than fifty there. He is very warm and says Buchanan is the boy and should he get elected we can all have the run of the White House kitchen."

Along with the example provided by his own career, the elder Davis advised his son on the importance of combining self-interest with public service, saying that young men "never can rise in public esteem while they remain poor. There is nothing which tends to advance a young man so much as industry and economy which makes him prosperous. The public soon discover this and conclude that he is fit for public trust."[62]

William Davis took these lessons to heart. In 1843 he moved to Portsmouth, Virginia, to teach at a military academy, a job that built on his family experience in the militia system. Three years later he left for Harvard, then served in the army during the US–Mexican War. In 1849 he returned to Bucks County to practice law and write for the *Doylestown Democrat,* the party's local newspaper. Each move occurred with helpful endorsements from his father and his political friends. Such favors implied reciprocity. During these years, William periodically returned home to promote his father's political fortunes at militia encampments and public conventions. Along the way he built his own alliances with men like Forney and established his speaking credentials by stumping for Democratic candidates.[63]

In 1854 William Davis left Bucks County for patronage posts in New Mexico Territory, where he served first as US attorney and then territorial secretary. When he first heard of Buchanan's election to the presidency, Davis was delighted. Disenchantment set in quickly, however, when he failed to secure a federal appointment. "I do not believe that Buchanan would appoint me constable," he complained to Lewis Coryell, a wealthy lumber merchant and longtime powerbroker in the Bucks County Democratic Party. "He already shows a disposition to turn the cold shoulder on those who have served him the longest," a reference to Buchanan's surprising refusal to keep Forney in place as the editor of the *Washington Union,* the national organ of the Democratic Party. Forney had run afoul of southern Democrats in earlier party battles, and they drove him out as the price of their support for Buchanan.

Shortly thereafter Forney came out against Buchanan's Kansas policy and turned his efforts to promoting Douglas. His attacks on the president focused on both the folly of Lecompton and the denial of patronage to Douglas supporters. His fury was particularly intense toward J. Glancy Jones, a US congressman from south-central Pennsylvania and one of

Buchanan's trusted lieutenants. Forney argued that Jones's success owed to "convincing the Southern men that he controls his own state. . . . He is an essential toady, too, and courts power to the uttermost, flattering the weakness of the President, and crawling under the lash, instead of resisting it like a man. In this way he gets places for a few men, which he takes good care to 'divide. . . ,'and in making Lecompton a test, he is a huge hero." In 1860 Forney rejected the fusion ticket, urging his readers to vote only for Douglas.[64]

On the outs in New Mexico and in Washington, in 1857 Davis returned to Bucks County, where he persuaded Coryell, who had earlier invested several thousand dollars with him in a mining company, to fund his purchase of the *Doylestown Democrat*.[65] The move was risky because Coryell backed Buchanan and wanted Davis to do the same. "Buchanan must be supported right or wrong for he is the President of our choice," he told him. "I am with him to the hilt, and Douglas is now contributing to the Black Republican strength."[66] This edict put Davis in a difficult spot. On the one hand, he valued Coryell's patronage and wanted to preserve harmony within the Bucks County branch of the party. On the other, his family was closely allied with Forney, who now led the anti-Buchanan fight.

Forced to choose, the Davises picked Forney and Douglas.[67] Their reasons inevitably mixed organizational loyalty with public policy. For William Davis, Buchanan's original sin was betrayal of a friend. "The promise [Buchanan] made [Forney] was not redeemed, and that was at the bottom of their estrangement." Policy also mattered. John Davis asked Coryell, "Do you think the Democrats in the free states can sustain themselves by advocating the principle (entirely new) that Slavery or the *property* in slaves is higher and above all constituency and therefore out of the reach of the people?" William Davis told him: "I am in favor of the whole [Lecompton] Constitution being submitted to the people. . . . This is the only way to carry out the Kansas Nebraska bill in full faith." He knew this stand risked Buchanan's wrath, but he felt that he now had little to lose. "I suppose this is treason . . . and I ought to be read out of the party. So be it."[68]

An indignant Coryell threatened to start a rival Democratic paper and use his influence to deny the Davises patronage, telling William that he had hoped "to prevent your indulgence of your feelings at the expense of not only your interests but also your reason."[69] The family went on to support Douglas in 1860, while Coryell organized the county for Breckinridge, winning praise from Buchanan for "your indefatigable energy in the good cause."[70] Neither man switched to Lincoln, but the loss of the party newspaper and the disaffection of the Davises contributed to Republican victory in Bucks County, which Democrats had won consistently since 1840. As William Davis said of election day, "Up this way the Republicans did all the voting, and we looked on."[71]

The Davis-Coryell split was part of a larger fracture among northern Democrats that tilted their support to Douglas but overall aided the Republicans. It also left a few islands of Breckinridge support created by strong patron-client networks that remained loyal to Buchanan and the southern wing of the Democratic Party. In an election that marked the death of national support for slavery's continued expansion, Breckinridge's strong showing in a few northern and border slave states, as well as the enduring networks that mobilized his voters, resemble the skeletal remains of a once-mighty animal. Given the importance of patron-client networks to winning elections, it should come as little surprise that the families enriched by slaves, America's earliest and most profitable source of wealth, invested in these long-term relationships that connected pro-slavery politicians, at the top, with communities of voters, at the grassroots. But the country was changing, and older methods for bringing out the vote were under pressure. The declining power of local patronage networks to maintain national party unity, and with it the defense slavery, is perhaps best revealed by Delaware, where Breckinridge did best among the four states in question.

That success reflected the fact that patron-client networks were most effective in states with small electorates. In 1860, Pennsylvanians cast 476,442 ballots compared to only 16,115 by Delawareans, 1/29th of their neighboring state's total. In Delaware James Bayard Jr. had effectively inherited his father's senate seat and strengthened existing relationships with loyal supporters in key posts throughout the small state. Insurgents tried to defeat him and Breckinridge, but they were shut down in a state party convention controlled by the Bayard network. Pennsylvania was more riven by faction. Despite his ascendancy in state politics, Buchanan never fully vanquished his intraparty rivals. Some, like Forney, opted for Douglas, whereas another contingent, headed by future Lincoln cabinet member Simon Cameron, joined the Republican Party. Ideas mattered in these partisan switches, but Forney's decision to bolt his patron also involved the denial of what he viewed as a deserved reward. Similarly, Cameron, a notorious wheeler-dealer, left in part because of a broken promise regarding a senatorial nomination.[72]

The kinds of personal loyalties that helped Bayard control Delaware were harder to replicate in larger states, where more people and more territory diversified the electorate and weakened the power of personal networks. America in the 1850s was not Delaware, and the power of patronage networks to sustain the political order was fast weakening in rapidly growing, socially diverse states.

Significantly, Breckinridge won not only the states with the highest concentrations of slaves (excepting Delaware and Maryland) but also those with the smallest electorates. Because of the three-fifths rule for apportionment in the House of Representatives, in 1860 the median number of eligible voters per district in the South (20,603) was roughly one-fifth smaller than in the North (25,184), and, measured by the 1860 presidential elections, the median number of actual ballots cast in a southern congressional district (15,201) was fully one-third less than that of a free-state election (22,877). Of the eleven states Breckinridge carried, ten were in the bottom half of the nation's thirty-three states in terms of total-vote size. Georgia, the only Breckinridge state in the top half of this category, ranked sixteenth.[73]

Each state was different, but those that voted for Breckinridge shared in common smaller electorates that could be better controlled by influential local leaders and their allied operatives, a way of conducting campaigns that came in for criticism during the 1850s. The realignment of major political parties in that decade gave rise to intensely sectionalized politics that culminated in Lincoln's election and southern secession. Along with conflict over slavery, immigration, and moral reform, realignment occurred because of a popular critique of party politics in and of itself.[74] Antiparty critics cited the corruption of patronage and the dominance of insider cliques as evils that could only be fixed by a clean sweep of old officeholders and organizations.[75] Among the factors that brought the nation to civil war was a method of political mobilization that proved both too effective in perpetuating entrenched interests and too obvious a target for the growing number of voters opposed to politics as usual and the interests it protected. In their dual roles as obstacles to change and the focus of criticism of the political establishment, the linkages between slavery's federal supporters and grassroots voters made an undeniable contribution to the coming of the Civil War.

NOTES

1. National Executive Committee of the Constitutional Union Party, *John Bell's Record* (Washington, DC: William H. Moore, 1860), 30.

2. Cooper Union Address, February 27, 1860, in *The Collected Works of Abraham Lincoln*, ed. Roy P. Basler, 8 vols. (New Brunswick, NJ: Rutgers University Press, 1953), 3:55. Recent histories of the election of 1860 include A. James Fuller, ed., *The Election of 1860 Reconsidered* (Kent, OH: Kent State University Press, 2013); Michael S. Green, *Lincoln and the Election of 1860* (Carbondale: Southern Illinois University Press, 2011); and Douglas R. Egerton, *Year of Meteors: Stephen A. Douglas, Abraham Lincoln, and the Election That Brought on the Civil War* (New York: Bloomsbury, 2010). For older works that continue to shape scholarship, see James M. McPherson, *Battle Cry of Freedom: The Civil War Era* (New York: Oxford University Press, 1988); David M. Potter, *The Impending Crisis, 1848–1861*, completed and ed. Don E. Fehrenbacher (New York: Harper and Row, 1976); and Allan Nevins, *Ordeal of the Union*, vol. 4, *Prologue to Civil War, 1859–1861* (New York: Scribner's 1950).

3. James J. Gigantino II, *The Ragged Road to Abolition: Slavery and Freedom in New Jersey, 1775–1865* (Philadelphia: University of Pennsylvania Press, 2015), esp. 240.

4. Patience Essah, *A House Divided: Slavery and Emancipation in Delaware, 1638–1865* (Charlottesville: University Press of Virginia, 1996); Barbara Jeanne Fields, *Slavery and Freedom on the Middle Ground: Maryland in the Nineteenth Century* (New Haven, CT: Yale University Press, 1985).

5. William J. Evitts, *A Matter of Allegiances: Maryland from 1850 to 1861* (Baltimore: Johns Hopkins University Press, 1974); Jean A. Baker, *The Politics of Continuity: Maryland Political Parties from 1858 to 1870* (Baltimore: Johns Hopkins University Press, 1973).

6. Federal election data found in David Leip, *David Leip's Atlas of U.S. Presidential Elections. 1860*, https://uselectionatlas.org.

7. James L. Huston, *Stephen A. Douglas and the Dilemmas of Democratic Equality* (Lanham, MD: Rowman and Littlefield, 2007), 170.

8. Roy F. Nichols, *The Disruption of American Democracy* (1948; repr. New York: Collier, 1962), 339; John F. Coleman, *The Disruption of the Pennsylvania Democracy, 1840–1860* (Harrisburg: Pennsylvania Historical and Museum Commission, 1975), 126–27, 140–41.

9. James McPherson and James K. Hogue, *Ordeal by Fire: The Civil War and Reconstruction*, 4th ed. (New York: McGraw-Hill, 2010), 132–33; Sean Wilentz, *The Rise of*

American Democracy: From Jefferson to Lincoln (New York: W. W. Norton, 2005), 765; Green, *Lincoln and the Election of 1860*, 106; Russell McClintock, *Lincoln and the Decision for War: The Northern Response to Secession* (Chapel Hill: University of North Carolina Press, 2008), 28.

10. William C. Davis, *Breckinridge: Statesman, Soldier, Symbol* (Baton Rouge: Louisiana State University Press, 1974), 139; Frank H. Heck, *John C. Breckinridge, 1821–1875* (Lexington: University Press of Kentucky, 1976), 59; Shearer Davis Bowman, *At the Precipice: Americans North and South during the Secession Crisis* (Chapel Hill: University of North Carolina Press, 2010), 157.

11. Davis, *Breckinridge*, 246; Seymour Martin Lipset, "The Emergence of the One Party South," in *Political Man: The Social Bases of Politics* (New York: Doubleday, 1960), 347; Frank H. Heck, "John C. Breckinridge in the Crisis of 1860–1861," *Journal of Southern History* 21 (August 1955): 330–31.

12. Thomas B. Alexander et al., "The Basis of Alabama's Antebellum Two-Party System," *Alabama Review* 19 (October 1966): 243–76; William L. Barney, *The Secessionist Impulse: Alabama and Mississippi in 1860* (Princeton, NJ: Princeton University Press, 1976); Peyton McCrary, Clark Miller, and Dale Baum, "Class and Party in the Secession Crisis: Voting Behavior in the Deep South, 1856–1861," *Journal of Interdisciplinary History* 8 (Winter 1978): 429–57; Robert E. Baker and Dale Baum, "The Texas Voter and the Crisis of the Union, 1859–1861," *Journal of Southern History* 53 (August 1987): 395–420; Daniel W. Crofts, *Reluctant Confederates: Upper South Unionists in the Secession Crisis* (Chapel Hill: University of North Carolina Press, 1989), 133, 378.

13. A. James Fuller, "A Forlorn Hope: Interpreting the Breckinridge Campaign as a Matter of Honor," in Fuller, *Election of 1860 Reconsidered*, 77; Michael Todd Landis, *Northern Men with Southern Loyalties: The Democratic Party and the Sectional Crisis* (Ithaca, NY: Cornell University Press, 2014), 238; Egerton, *Year of Meteors*, 195 (quotation).

14. Michael F. Holt, *The Election of 1860: "A Campaign Fraught with Consequences"* (Lawrence: University Press of Kansas, 2017), esp. chap. 7; Michael D. Robinson, *A Union Indivisible: Secession and the Politics of Slavery in the Border South* (Chapel Hill: University of North Carolina Press, 2017), chap. 3.

15. Steven Hahn, *The Political Worlds of Slavery and Freedom* (Cambridge, MA: Harvard University Press, 2009), 43–44.

16. Sven Beckert, *Empire of Cotton: A Global History* (New York: Vintage Books 2014), esp. chap. 5; Calvin Schermerhorn, *The Business of Slavery and the Rise of American Capitalism, 1815–1860* (New Haven, CT: Yale University Press, 2015); Sven Beckert and Seth Rockman, eds., *Slavery's Capitalism: A New History of American Economic Development* (Philadelphia: University of Pennsylvania Press, 2016).

17. Leonard L. Richards, *The Slave Power: The Free North and Southern Domination, 1780–1860* (Baton Rouge: Louisiana State University Press, 2000); James Oakes, *Freedom National: The Destruction of Slavery in the United States, 1861–1865* (New York: W. W. Norton, 2013); Paul Finkelman, "James Buchanan, Dred Scott, and the Whisper of Conspiracy," in *James Buchanan and the Coming of the Civil War*, ed. John W. Quist and Michael J.

Birkner (Gainesville: University Press of Florida, 2013), 38–42; Landis, *Northern Men with Southern Loyalties*. For doughfaces as unionists, see Matthew Mason, *Apostle of Union: A Political Biography of Edward Everett* (Chapel Hill: University of North Carolina Press, 2016); Nicholas Wood, "'A Sacrifice on the Altar of Slavery': Doughface Politics and Black Disenfranchisement in Pennsylvania, 1837–1838," *Journal of the Early Republic* 31 (Spring 2011): 81 (quotation).

18. For this question's influence on interpretations of the Union war effort, compare Gary W. Gallagher, *The Union War* (Cambridge, MA: Harvard University Press, 2011), with Oakes, *Freedom National*.

19. Lee Benson, "An Approach to the Scientific Study of Past Public Opinion," *Public Opinion Quarterly* 31 (Winter 1967–68): 565.

20. Leading examples of the new political history include Lee Benson, *The Concept of Jacksonian Democracy: New York as a Test Case* (Princeton, NJ: Princeton University Press, 1961); Paul Kleppner, *The Cross of Culture: A Social Analysis of Midwestern Politics, 1850–1900* (New York: Macmillan, 1970); Ronald P. Formisano, *The Birth of Mass Political Parties: Michigan, 1827–1861* (Princeton, NJ: Princeton University Press, 1971); and William G. Shade, *Banks or No Banks: The Money Issue in Western Politics, 1832–1865* (Detroit: Wayne State University Press, 1972).

21. Samuel P. Hays, "The Social Analysis of America Political History, 1880–1920," *Political Science Quarterly* 80 (September 1965): 373 (quotation); Donald A. DeBats, "Political Consequences of Spatial Organization: Contrasting Patterns in Two Nineteenth-Century Small Cities," *Social Science History* 35 (Winter 2011), 533.

22. A fuller discussion of this scholarship can be found in Frank Towers, "Party Politics and the Sectional Crisis: A Twenty-Year Renaissance in the Study of Antebellum Political History," in *The Routledge History of Nineteenth-Century America*, ed. Jonathan D. Wells (New York: Routledge, 2017), 109–30.

23. Important examples are Kenneth J. Winkle, *The Politics of Community: Migration and Politics in Antebellum Ohio* (New York: Cambridge University Press, 1988); Paul Bourke and Donald A. DeBats, *Washington County: Politics and Community in Antebellum America* (Baltimore: Johns Hopkins University Press, 1995); Christopher J. Olsen, *Political Culture and Secession in Mississippi: Masculinity, Honor, and the Antiparty Tradition, 1830–1860* (New York: Oxford University Press, 2000); and Lori D. Ginzburg, *Untidy Origins: A Story of Woman's Rights in Antebellum New York* (Chapel Hill: University of North Carolina Press, 2005).

24. For Baltimore, see Frank Towers, *The Urban South and the Coming of the Civil War* (Charlottesville: University of Virginia Press, 2004), 56n40. Ohio data are in Winkle, *Politics of Community*, 105–7, 149.

25. Russell, poll book, April 27, 1843, in Frederick County, Election Records/Census Records, Viva Voce Election Polls, 1840 Census, 1917–20 voting lists, box 2, Library of Virginia, State Records Center, Richmond.

26. Bourke and DeBats, *Washington County*, 292.

27. DeBats, "Political Consequences of Spatial Organization," 530–31.

28. Glenn C. Altschuler and Stuart M. Blumin, *Rude Republic: Americans and their Politics in the Nineteenth Century* (Princeton, NJ: Princeton University Press, 2000), 79. Also see Richard Frank Bensel, *The American Ballot Box in the Mid-Nineteenth Century: Law, Identity and the Polling Place* (New York: Cambridge University Press, 2004), chap. 2.

29. Wilkes University Election Statistics Project, *Pennsylvania Election Statistics: 1682–2006,* http://staffweb.wilkes.edu/harold.cox/, accessed October 8, 2012.

30. *Connecticut Courant* (Hartford), November 8, 1856, November 11, 1860. Know Nothings had not been a factor in 1856, winning only 3 percent of the vote.

31. Michael J. Dubin, *United States Presidential Elections, 1788–1860: The Official Results by County and State* (Jefferson, NC: McFarland, 2002), 117, 137, 161.

32. These events are detailed in Towers, *Urban South and the Coming of the Civil War,* chap. 5.

33. Dubin, *United States Presidential Elections.*

34. Buchanan quoted in Nichols, *Disruption of American Democracy,* 340.

35. On Bigler, see *Washington (PA) Reporter,* July 12, 1860.

36. Joanna D. Cowden, "The Politics of Dissent: Civil War Democrats in Connecticut," *New England Quarterly* 56 (December 1983): 541; John E. Talmadge, "A Peace Movement in Civil War Connecticut," *New England Quarterly* 37 (September 1964): 307.

37. Brion T. McClanahan, "A Lonely Opposition: James A. Bayard, Jr. and the American Civil War," (PhD diss., University of South Carolina, 2006), 23.

38. Landis, *Northern Men with Southern Loyalties,* 229.

39. Bruce Bendler, "'The Old Democratic Principles': Samuel Townsend and the Democratic Party, 1836–1881," *Delaware History* 33 (Spring/Summer 2010): 34.

40. Crofts, *Reluctant Confederates.*

41. Marriage Notice, Richard Brodhead Genealogical Files, Jane Moyer Library, Northampton Historical and Genealogical Society, Easton, PA; Joseph Mortimer Levering, *A History of Bethlehem Pennsylvania, 1741–1892* (Bethlehem, PA: Times Publishing, 1903), 724.

42. J. P. Montgomery to George M. Dallas, January 29, 1849, George Mifflin Dallas Papers, Historical Society of Pennsylvania, Philadelphia (hereafter HSP); James A. Bayard Jr. to George M. Dallas, February 7, 1854, ibid.; James M. Mason to Anna Sophia Penn Chew, May 8, 1861, Anna Sophia Penn Chew Correspondence, Chew Family Papers, HSP; Robert W. Young, *James Murray Mason: Defender of the Old South* (Knoxville: University of Tennessee Press, 1998), 21–22. For Blanchard, see E. Wyatt Blanchard to Thomas F. Bayard, February 24, October 15, 1860, Thomas Bayard Papers, Library of Congress, Washington, DC; and *Daily Exchange* (Baltimore), October 11, 1860. For speeches, see J. W. Pratt, Chester Co., PA, to James A. Bayard, September 4, 1860, Bayard Papers; and Young Men's Breckinridge Club of Philadelphia to James A. Bayard, October 2, 1860, ibid.

43. Correspondence from George Mifflin Dallas to Benjamin Chew Howard, various dates, John Eager Howard Papers, box 32, Maryland Historical Society, Baltimore; Samuel K. George to Thomas H. Seymour, October 13, 1859, Thomas H. Seymour Papers, Connecticut Historical Society, Hartford. For George and the City Reform Association, see *Baltimore American,* November 1, 1859.

44. James A. George to Thomas Bayard, Aug. 23, 1860, Bayard Papers.

45. Gustav W. Lurman to James Chesnut, July 2, 1860, James Chesnut Papers, box 37, South Carolina Historical Society, Charleston; Dieter Cunz, *The Maryland Germans: A History* (Princeton, NJ: Princeton University Press, 1948), 312.

46. Henry A, Mitchell to Thomas H. Seymour, March 7, 1860, Seymour Papers.

47. Alfred E. Burr to Edwin Stearns, October 29, 1860, Stearns Family Papers, Connecticut Historical Society, Hartford.

48. Edward Wootten to James A. Bayard, March 21, 1860, Bayard Papers.

49. Thomas F. Bayard to James A. Bayard Jr., August 11, 1860, Bayard Papers.

50. Edwin Stearns to Isaac Toucey, n.d., [1860], Stearns Family Papers.

51. James A. Bayard to Thomas Bayard, September 1, 1860, Bayard Papers.

52. John W. Forney to Henry Chapman, October 24, 1856, Henry Chapman Papers, Bucks County Historical Society, Doylestown, PA.

53. Receipts, Democratic Party to Edwin Stearns, 1834–64, Stearns Family Papers, folder A, box 7; A. E. Burr to Edwin Stearns, March 10, 1860, ibid., box 6; Thomas Seymour to Edwin Stearns, March 25, 1860, ibid., box 6.

54. John Danforth to Thomas Seymour, October 2, 1860, Seymour Papers.

55. Edwin Stearns to Issac Toucey, [n.d.] 1860, Stearns Family Papers.

56. Roger B. Taney to James Mason Campbell, October 19, 1860, Howard Papers.

57. Anon., *The Last Appeal* (n.p., [1860]), 2, copy at the Library Company of Philadelphia.

58. *Philadelphia Inquirer,* August 21, 1860.

59. *Columbian Register* (New Haven, CT), September 22, 1860.

60. Eric H. Walther, *William Lowndes Yancey and the Coming of the Civil War* (Chapel Hill: University of North Carolina Press, 2006), 260 (quotation).

61. Olinger Crenshaw, *The Slave States in the Presidential Election of 1860* (1945; repr., Gloucester, MA: Peter Smith, 1969), 244.

62. For this paragraph and the preceding two, see William W. H. Davis, *The Life of John Davis* (Doylestown, PA: "for private circulation," 1886), 32, 45, 85, 94–97, 103, 107, 115, 130–32; Robert A. Suhler, "A Territorial Imperative: W. W. H. Davis Investigates New Mexico," *Password* 30, no. 4 (December 1985): 188; W. S. Lee to William W. H. Davis, November 19, 1843, William Watts Hart Davis Papers, HSP; John Davis to William W. H. Davis, June 3, 1843, ibid.; and John Davis to Martin Van Buren, February 20, 1839, Dreer Collection, HSP. For the Davises and Forney, see Elizabeth Davis to William W. H. Davis, November 30, 1847, Davis Papers, HSP; and John W. Forney to William W. H. Davis, November 10, 1852, W. W. H. Davis Papers, Beinecke Rare Book and Manuscript Depository, Yale University, New Haven, CT.

63. Elizabeth Davis to William Davis, June 18, 1843, Davis Papers, HSP; John W. Forney to William W. Davis, November 4, 1845, ibid.; Elizabeth Davis to William W. H. Davis, December 27, 1846, Davis Papers, Yale; Charles H. Mann to William W. H. Davis, December 28, 1846, ibid.

64. For the wider rift between Forney and Buchanan, see Coleman, *Disruption of the Pennsylvania Democracy,* 103–5, 128. "Occasional" [John W. Forney], May 14, 1858, The

Letters of Occasional, 1857–1861, Special Collections, Morris Library, University of Delaware, Newark.

65. William W. H. Davis to John Davis, May 25, 1855, Davis Papers, Yale.

66. Lewis Coryell to William Davis, December 25, 1857, Davis Papers, HSP.

67. Coleman, *Disruption of the Pennsylvania Democracy,* 103, 112–13.

68. Davis, *Life of John Davis,* 157; John Davis to Lewis Coryell, June 6, 1858, Lewis C. Coryell Papers, HSP; William W. H. Davis to Lewis Coryell, December 25, 1857, ibid.

69. Lewis Coryell to William W. H. Davis, May 31, 1858, Davis Papers, HSP.

70. James Buchanan to Coryell, September 26, 1860, Coryell Papers.

71. William Watts Davis to Anna Davis, November 7, 1860, Davis Papers, HSP.

72. Erwin Stanley Bradley, *Simon Cameron, Lincoln's Secretary of War: A Political Biography* (Philadelphia: University of Pennsylvania Press, 1966), 106.

73. These calculations are based on Joseph C. G. Kennedy, *Population of the United States in 1860* (Washington, DC: Government Printing Office, 1864). Method takes the estimate of white men over twenty-one minus non-naturalized residents as the electorate. Slaveholders constituted 22 percent of the eligible voters in the South—an inflated figure as female slaveholders were ineligible to vote. Additionally, South Carolina did not select its presidential electors by popular vote.

74. The leading work on this topic is William Gienapp, *The Origins of the Republican Party, 1852–1856* (New York: Oxford University Press, 1987). See also Michael Holt, *The Rise and Fall of the American Whig Party: Jacksonian Politics and the Onset of the Civil War* (New York: Oxford University Press, 1999). Additional sources are listed in Holt's bibliography.

75. Mark Voss-Hubbard, "The 'Third Party Tradition' Reconsidered: Third Parties and American Public Life, 1830–1900," *Journal of American History* 86 (June 1999): 121–50; Voss-Hubbard, *Beyond Party: Cultures of Antipartisanship in Northern Politics before the Civil War* (Baltimore: Johns Hopkins University Press, 2002); Adam I. P. Smith, *No Party Now: Politics in the Civil War North* (New York: Oxford University Press, 2006).

FRIENDS AND OUTLIERS

Varina Davis, James Buchanan, and Gender
Relations in Antebellum Washington

JOAN E. CASHIN

In the Old South the gender system was built upon the bedrock assumption that the sexes were profoundly different, and one gender was inferior to the other. That would be the female gender, and those assumptions held true for all races, classes, ethnic backgrounds, and religious affiliations. Almost all social relations were organized around this fact. The law, the church, the university, politics, the family—everything operated according to this premise. This meant that even white women led very constricted lives. They were not allowed to practice law or medicine or join the clergy, attend universities, teach at universities, vote, or run for public office. Instead, they were expected to marry, have many children, and devote themselves to the household. In their marriages they were expected to conform to their husbands' wishes.[1]

White women from prosperous families led more privileged lives than other women, of course, being spared the hard physical labor that yeomen farmers' wives or slaves performed. They had more material comforts than other women, and they became literate, as many women did not. But they were still women, and gender mattered in their lives, whether they were the daughters of merchants, planters, doctors, or lawyers. These women were not supposed to be too literary or too well educated, and they were not supposed to show any interest in politics. They were not allowed to travel from home without an escort, usually a family member. They had few rights under the legal system pertaining to marriage, dowry, or property holding. Yet they too were expected to marry young, devote themselves to the family, and defer to their spouses. So much depended on whom a woman married since her husband exercised considerable authority in every aspect of her life.[2]

By the standards of the Old South, Jefferson Davis was considered an attractive man. He was tall and handsome, with the smooth manners of a Mississippi gentleman. He excelled at the traditional male pastimes of riding, hunting, and shooting. But he also had the large ego of a plantation owner. He was wealthier than most planters, the owner of over seventy slaves in the 1840s, and he was used to giving orders to people. He graduated from West Point Military Academy, which underscored his sense that he was in charge, and he was the indulged youngest son of a large family. In adulthood he had an overweening sense of entitlement. In his private life he took it for granted that men were superior to women and that husbands should make the decisions for their wives. His first wife, Sarah Knox Taylor, had died after a brief illness, and in 1843 he met Varina Howell, the teenaged daughter of a merchant. She was well read and high spirited, and although she was not classically beautiful, she had glossy hair and large dark eyes. They fell in love and married in 1845.[3]

Born in 1826, Varina Howell grew up in Natchez, Mississippi, where she received many of the conventional messages about gender as her contemporaries did. But her parents did not fulfill traditional gender roles, that is, the powerful, capable man and the meek, dependent woman. Her father, William Howell, went bankrupt in 1837 and never recovered financially; her mother, Margaret Kempe Howell, who was quiet and capable, managed the household. Varina, the oldest daughter, often helped her, and she absorbed her mother's values: competence, hard work, and the love of books, for Margaret Howell was an avid reader. Varina adored her mother but saw that Mrs. Howell's devotion to the family did not protect them from embarrassment or financial struggle since the Howells survived largely because of help from their relatives. As a young woman, Varina was highly literate, sociable, and "outspoken" by her own descrip-

Varina Howell Davis. Carte-de-visite, ca. 1860.
Courtesy Virginia Historical Society, Richmond.

tion. She hoped to marry, but she wanted a companionate marriage, a partnership. She seems to have been attracted to Davis's good looks, but it is somewhat mysterious how these different personalities fell in love.[4]

After Miss Howell wed Jefferson Davis, she discovered that life with this attractive older man could be very difficult. His ideas about gender often made her unhappy, beginning with a dispute over the will of Jefferson's older brother Joseph. A planter who was even richer than Jefferson, Joseph often gave plantations to his siblings, but he kept the land deeds so that he could control disposition of the properties. He, too, had traditional ideas about gender, and he took a strong dislike to his sister-in-law; after he announced that he would exclude Varina from his will, she naturally objected. Jefferson nonetheless sided with his brother. He then punished her by leaving her in Mississippi when he went to Washington in 1847–48 to serve in the US Senate; she wanted to move to the district, which she had visited in 1845, but he insisted that she submit to his wishes. Eventually, she gave in, and he permitted her to go to the capital with him. Future marital disputes would occur over money, the in-laws, and other issues, which all involved the raw assertion of Jefferson's will: he did not want a companionate marriage, and he believed that he should make important decisions himself. Yet divorce was not a realistic option for mismatched couples since it still had a terrible stigma, and the legal system made it hard for couples to part. Mississippi law permitted divorce only on a few grounds, such as bigamy, none of which applied to the Davises.[5]

So Mrs. Davis realized that she would have to turn elsewhere for emotional fulfillment. Beginning in the 1840s, she cultivated a series of close, long-lasting friendships; indeed, she turned out to have a talent for friendship. As her husband served in public office in Washington, DC, she lived there most of the time until 1861. There, she made friends, both male and female, from all over the United States, and many of those ties endured for years, such as her friendships with Jane Pierce, wife of President Franklin Pierce; John Garrett, the railroad magnate; and members of the Blair family, including Frank Preston Blair Sr., who had been Andrew Jackson's confidant, his son Montgomery, the legal counsel for Dred Scott, and his daughter-in-law Mary Woodbury Blair, Montgomery's wife. In her friendships with men, she sought out highly verbal men who had unconventional, relatively egalitarian views toward women.[6]

Friendship has been celebrated since ancient times by such writers as Homer, Plato, Montaigne, and Christine de Pizan because it is dedicated to the mutual benefit of both parties, providing them with comfort and stimulation. The relationship is voluntary, and most friends relate to each other as equals. Friendships have taken a great variety of forms over the centuries, but the theme of equality persists in many cultures. Same-sex friendships have been common since the ancient Greeks, while the idea of platonic friendship between women and men is a relatively new development in the modern world. One of the best known of the latter dates from the early American republic, that of Abigail Adams and Thomas Jefferson, which other scholars have already explored. In nineteenth-century America only certain men would be more receptive to these kinds of relationships.[7]

James Buchanan was one such man. Born in Pennsylvania in 1791, the son of a merchant, he became a successful attorney while still a young man. His legal practice in the commonwealth provided an easy segue into politics, as he served as a congressman, cabinet officer, and diplomat before being elected president in 1856. His engaging personality facilitated his rise in the political world. Buchanan was an excellent conversationalist, a superb dinner companion, and a good mixer, at ease in many social settings. He, too, had many friends of both sexes in Pennsylvania, Washington, and at his diplomatic posts overseas. Buchanan grew up in a large family with many sisters and developed the ability to listen when a woman was talking, an uncommon skill among male politicians of his generation. He particularly enjoyed sophisticated, vivacious women.[8]

Buchanan never married, however, and his single status became the topic of some controversy. After Ann Coleman of Pennsylvania broke their engagement in 1819, he had a longtime friendship with Alabama politician William Rufus King. The two men often lived together as roommates in Washington, and the evidence on the nature of the relationship is thin; from this distance in time, it is impossible to know the interplay of emotional, romantic, or physical elements between them. But some of Buchanan's remarks, such as his description of their bond as a "communion," go beyond the typical language of same-sex friendship of his era. After King died in 1853, Buchanan kept his likeness at his home, proclaiming that, in three decades of "intimate acquaintance," King had never committed a selfish act. That too is unusual. But openly declaring a gay relationship—if that is what it was—would have been political suicide for Buchanan. Same-sex friendships were acceptable so long as they were not too affectionate; homosexuality was perceived as the ultimate violation of contemporary notions of masculinity. Such a man would have been considered unqualified for any public office, regardless of class, ethnic background, or party membership, in every part of the United States.[9]

Whether or not Buchanan and King were lovers, some of their Washington acquaintances privately ridiculed Buchanan's demeanor and unmarried status. The national press sometimes questioned his masculinity in sexualized language, both before and during his presidency, as journalists called him "yielding," "submissive," a "milksop," and a coward who lacked "manhood." As if the message was not clear, one writer added that "nary" a "woman" would miss him when he left office. Even in an age of harsh political invective, this kind of language in the national press was rare. Varina Davis heard a lot of gossip in Washington, a hothouse of rumor and speculation, and she read the newspapers. She undoubtedly heard the rumors about Buchanan and King, but she either chose to disbelieve the gossip or did not care if it was true.[10]

In fact, Buchanan accepted many of his generation's assumptions about women. He thought that all women should marry and that they should practice their religious faith. He wanted his niece Harriet Lane to marry and advised her to choose a man she loved, a man of sound morals, and a man who made a good living. Yet he made some interesting departures from conventional attitudes about gender. He pitied American women who wed British aristocrats and led empty lives of self-indulgence. He confided in a woman, Harriet Lane—and only in her—his thoughts on his presidential prospects in the 1850s and his opinions of diplomatic matters, then on political questions after he became president. Buchanan made occasional unorthodox remarks about gender identity. When he closed one missive to Lane with advice about marriage, he observed that his comments resembled those a woman might write. Small departures, perhaps, but it is hard to imagine Jefferson Davis using such language about himself, or for that matter any of the other powerhouses in national politics of the era, such as Henry Clay, Franklin Pierce, or Stephen Douglas.[11]

Varina Davis, who became one of Buchanan's good friends, also abided by most of the gender conventions of the day. She gradually learned to accede to her husband's wishes on family decisions, with occasional fiery rebellions, and she did what was expected as a Washington hostess. In the 1840s and 1850s, the Davises rented several houses in downtown Washington for entertaining, and when Jefferson served as Pierce's secretary of war, she hosted many receptions and dinner parties. This high-wire social life continued into Jefferson's term in the US Senate in the late 1850s. The Davises moved in the top political circles. After Varina recovered from an illness in the spring of 1857, the outgoing President Pierce and the incoming President Buchanan both paid calls on her. David Dixon Porter, who became a Yankee naval hero during the Civil War, described her as a "magnificent" lady who shone in the sky like the planet Venus, brighter than all other women in antebellum Washington. She was witty, a brilliant conversationalist, and generous with her friends. She was better read than most people in town, of either sex.[12]

Moreover, the Davises and Buchanan resided in a city that fostered close friendships. The district was home to about thirty thousand people, but most of the public buildings were clustered together in the space of a few miles. During their residence in town, the Davises rented houses that stood within walking distance of the Executive Mansion, Lafayette Square, the Capitol, and other landmarks as well as the boardinghouses where numerous congressmen lived. The town featured an exuberant social life of parties, dinners, and receptions attended by many personalities who shared a genuine liking for people. That is one reason many politicians entered politics, and many of their wives shared that quality. Buchanan liked people, as did Varina Davis. She did not display the sectional hatreds that had begun to fester in mid-nineteenth-century politics, and thus she did not mind one bit that he hailed from Pennsylvania.[13]

A warm friendship with a lifelong bachelor such as Buchanan provided Davis with some relief from her difficult marriage. He was some thirty years older than she was, a Democrat, generally in agreement with states' rights advocates like her husband, and, for all those reasons, safe. Yet they were both outliers to some extent, departing in subtle fashion from the rigid gender roles that prevailed for both sexes during their lifetimes. Aside from that, she liked him immensely and seemed genuinely concerned for his well-being. Varina met Buchanan in Washington when he began serving as secretary of state in the 1840s—the exact circumstances are unknown—and the friendship, which seems to have blossomed quickly, lasted until 1861. Some of Buchanan's peers found him cold, but Davis called him one of the most charming men she had ever known. He was meticulously groomed, with striking blue eyes, and while she noticed his nervous twitch (probably the result of a minor stroke), his personality made that easy to overlook. She admired his quick wit, which he displayed at one Washington party. When a rival joked that he was too ambitious, Buchanan immediately quoted Shakespeare's *Henry the Sixth:* "Fearless minds climb soonest unto crowns."[14]

Henry the Sixth, one of the Bard's early works, portrays the conflicts between English aristocrats during the Wars of the Roses. The principal theme in the three-part play is the fierce combat between the House of York and the House of Lancaster for the crown. In Act Four, Scene Seven, Richard, Duke of Gloucester and a member of the House of York, utters the remark on "fearless minds" as he urges his brother, Edward, to seize power and proclaim his authority throughout the country. Edward agrees and takes the throne. The implication in Buchanan's quote is that determined personalities should seek power eagerly, openly. Not all nineteenth-century women would have been familiar with the play, one of Shakespeare's less-popular works, but Davis instantly recognized the quote.[15]

Their shared knowledge of literature constituted another strong link in the Davis-Buchanan friendship. This has been true for writers of many backgrounds, and both Varina Davis and James Buchanan would go on to write their memoirs. The same has been true for dedicated readers of both genders and all sexual orientations. Ideas embedded in books came to life in conversation with other readers, when people found insights that pertained to their own experiences and aspirations, as Buchanan did in *Henry the Sixth.* These friendships required a questing intelligence, a good memory, and the capacity for spontaneous communication. Varina Davis cherished such relationships, recalling the exchange with Buchanan vividly years afterward.[16]

While James Buchanan served in the White House, the friendship continued, rooted in years of lively conversation about politics and books. He still relished conversation with educated women, and Varina and her husband dined often with the president. Mr. and Mrs. Davis were both states' rights Democrats, although she favored compromise in politics as a general principle, as he did not. Buchanan sought out what a nephew called noble women, and for that reason, his nephew believed, Buchanan never became cynical about women, as did many men of his age. Varina Davis was one of those women, but the friendship shifted because of the status differential between them. He was the chief executive of the country, after all, and she was not so noble that she neglected the benefits of having such a powerful friend. She sometimes asked the president for political favors, such as his help in getting her brother appointed to the US Marine Corps, and he agreed. She seemed blind to Buchanan's shortcomings, such as his discomfort with confrontation, probably because she was so fond of him.[17]

Buchanan's single term as president was not very successful, as we know. His time in office was filled with conflicts—the *Dred Scott* decision, the Lecompton Constitution, John Brown's raid—which soon overwhelmed him. He allied himself with the dominant proslavery wing of his party, including Jefferson Davis, but the president realized that he could not meet the challenges before him. He obtained his crown, one might say, but found it hard to wield power effectively. Buchanan said repeatedly, once in Varina Davis's presence, that a sectional crisis was coming and hoped it would not occur on his watch. After the national election in November 1860, Varina could tell that the president dreaded what might happen next. Jefferson Davis voted for southern Democrat John C. Breckinridge, as did most voters in Mississippi and the Deep South. If his wife could have exercised the suffrage, she would have voted for the southern unionist, the former Whig John Bell of Tennessee.[18]

After the election, the town's vibrant social life shut down, and that holiday season was drab. President Buchanan shared in the atmosphere of increasing suspicion and fear. He confided in Mrs. Davis his anxiety that he might be physically harmed before he left office, and she sympathized with him even as South Carolina seceded and other states began to consider leaving the Union. On Christmas Day 1860 Varina sent the president a gift, a pair of slippers she had made for him herself, and she wrote him a letter conveying her "sincere affection" and "great regard." She signed it "faithfully your friend" and stayed on good terms with him after her husband broke off contact with Buchanan that winter. (By contrast, Jefferson thought that the president's statements during the secession winter were too strongly pro-Union). Many of Buchanan's female friends from the South turned against him, but as the Davises prepared to leave Washington in the new year, Varina went alone to the Executive Mansion to bid him what she called an "affectionate" farewell. The president responded in kind, saying that he wished her well wherever her lot might be cast.[19]

Varina Davis was a conservative unionist, both pro-Union and proslavery, like thousands of white southerners. She felt distinctly ambivalent about secession. Later she observed that South Carolina precipitated the secession crisis by its "hasty action" in December 1860. She enjoyed living in Washington, where she had so many friends, and did not want to leave. But her husband made the major decisions for both of them, so when he decided to leave town in early 1861, she had to go with him. That was the unavoidable truth of the Davis marriage. Varina said that departing Washington felt like death, and she later portrayed her residence there as the happiest time in her life. After her husband became the Confederate president, she reluctantly journeyed to the South with him. In March 1861, while she was in Montgomery, Alabama, she composed a last letter to Buchanan, saying that she still thought of him with pleasure.[20]

This letter of March 1861 was both a final goodbye and a masterpiece of carefully worded reassurance. Davis told Buchanan that the public respected him both for what he had accomplished and for what he had tried to accomplish. She thought that war was coming and said that he might be the last president in a long distinguished line; trying to comfort him, she observed that republics treated their presidents as badly as stepchildren treat their stepmothers. In her new role as Confederate First Lady, she would try to play the "lady civil" and be a good politician, as he had once described her. Varina closed by saying that she would remain his "attached friend" always, in all circumstances. No reply survives from Buchanan, although she secretly exchanged letters with other northern friends during the war. In any case, she never saw him again. He did not mention her in his memoir of 1866. When he died in 1868, she was in England and said nothing in writing about his death. But when she published her own memoir of 1890, Davis praised his elegant dress, his rapier wit, and his charisma.[21]

Judah P. Benjamin. Courtesy Virginia Historical Society, Richmond.

During Davis's tenure as Confederate First Lady, she forged a similar friendship with Judah P. Benjamin, another politician with an unorthodox private life. He lived apart from his wife, Natalie, for most of their marriage as he served first in the US Senate, representing Louisiana, and then in Richmond, where he held several posts in the rebel government. In terms of his personality, he was the Confederate version of Buchanan: verbal, fluent, and emotionally open, as Varina's husband was not. Furthermore, Jefferson Davis was often absorbed in his duties as Confederate president, so his wife had to renew or create friendships in a new environment. In Washington Varina had known Benjamin, who easily made friends with women. He was a nonobservant Jew, which sometimes made him the target of bigotry, but she was remarkably free from the anti-Semitism common in her generation. These two outliers became good friends, thrown together in the Confederate capital. And they had something else in common—they both loved books.[22]

Her friendship with Benjamin was one of the most enjoyable of her tenure in Richmond, where she was not very happy. The city was about the same size as Washington, with thirty thousand residents, but it was much older, dating from the seventeenth century. Local society was run by a small, tightly knit elite that did not warm to newcomers, no matter who they might be. The Confederate First Lady did not fit in very well, and not just because she was a new face with no ties to the city. She made literary allusions in conversation that people did not always understand, and she sometimes declared that she missed her Washington friends. Even worse, she occasionally blurted out her opinion that the South did not have the resources to win the war, which her peers duly noted. She felt relieved when the war ended in 1865.[23]

During the postwar years, the Davis marriage continued much as it always had, with Jefferson making most of the decisions about their money, their place of residence, and other subjects. Varina maintained many of her longtime friendships with such people as the Blairs, but if they ever discussed James Buchanan, there is no reference in the surviving correspondence. The Davises moved around, living in Montreal, London, Memphis, and rural Mississippi—the destinations chosen by Jefferson in his search for a new occupation—and she made new friends in those places too. When her husband died in 1889, Varina moved to New York City, where she supported herself as a journalist. She never remarried. During her widowhood, she cultivated additional friendships with both men and women, some of them quite surprising, including Julia Dent Grant, a widow living in Gotham. When Davis died in 1906, she was buried in Richmond next to her husband.[24]

Varina Davis's biography reminds us that the inflexible gender norms of her generation could be hard on individual human beings, including public figures. Those who deviated in ways large or small had to find some way to cope, and her method, her great consolation, was friendship with such outliers as James Buchanan. Neither Davis nor Buchanan were entirely comfortable with the gender regime of the mid-nineteenth century, and they did not fully conform to convention in their behavior. Their friendship, and the history of other friendships in political context, can offer new perspectives on gender in nineteenth-century America.

NOTES

1. Margaret Ripley Wolfe, *Daughters of Canaan: A Saga of Southern Women* (Lexington: University Press of Kentucky, 1995), 58–80; Joan E. Cashin, ed., *Our Common Affairs: Texts from Women in the Old South* (Baltimore: Johns Hopkins University Press, 1996), 1–26; Anya Jabour, *Scarlett's Sisters: Young Women in the Old South* (Chapel Hill: University of North Carolina Press, 2007); Loren Schweninger, *Families in Crisis in the Old South: Divorce, Slavery, and the Law* (Chapel Hill: University of North Carolina Press, 2012).

2. Cashin, *Our Common Affairs*, 1–41; Joan E. Cashin, *The First Lady of the Confederacy: Varina Davis's Civil War* (Cambridge, MA: Harvard University Press, 2006), 26; Marli F. Weiner, *Mistresses and Slaves: Plantation Women in South Carolina, 1830–80* (Urbana: University of Illinois Press, 1998), 28–49.

3. Cashin, *First Lady*, 5, 16–38; William C. Davis, *Jefferson Davis: The Man and His Hour* (New York: HarperCollins, 1991).

4. Cashin, *First Lady*, 14–30, 45.

5. Cashin, 44–45, 49–53, 59, 71–73, 83–87.

6. Cashin, 43, 64, 73, 75, 89, 167–68, 178–79.

7. David Konstan, *Friendship in the Classical World* (Cambridge: Cambridge University Press, 1997); Christine de Pizan, *The Book of the City of Ladies*, ed. Rosaline Brown-Grant (New York: Penguin Books, 1999); Sandra Lynch, *Philosophy and Friendship* (Edinburgh: Edinburgh University Press, 2005), x, 3; Barbara Caine, ed., *Friendship: A History* (New York: Routledge, 2014); Cassandra A. Good, *Founding Friendships: Friendships between Men and Women in the Early American Republic* (New York: Oxford University Press, 2015), 1–8, 14–18.

8. Jean H. Baker, *James Buchanan* (New York: Times Books, 2004), 10–12, 15–18; Philip Gerald Auchampaugh, *James Buchanan and His Cabinet on the Eve of Secession* (Lancaster, PA: Privately printed, 1926), 11; R. G. Horton, *Life and Public Services of James Buchanan* (New York: Derby and Jackson, 1856), 420; Rachel A. Shelden, *Washington Brotherhood: Politics, Social Life, and the Coming of the Civil War* (Chapel Hill: University of North Carolina Press, 2013), 88, 161; George Ticknor Curtis, *Life of James Buchanan, Fifteenth President of the United States*, 2 vols. (New York: Harper and Brothers, 1883), 2:103, 110, 115; Philip S. Klein, *President James Buchanan: A Biography* (University Park: Pennsylvania State University Press, 1962), 3–4; Cashin, *First Lady*, 43.

9. Klein, *President James Buchanan*, 29–32, 111, 149; Baker, *James Buchanan*, 26, 28, 58; Horton, *Life and Public Services of James Buchanan*, 424; John D'Emilio and Estelle B. Freedman, *Intimate Matters: A History of Sexuality in America*, 2nd ed. (Chicago: University of Chicago Press, 1997), 121; Herbert Sussman, *Masculine Identities: The History and Meanings of Manliness* (Santa Barbara, CA: Praeger, 2012), 133–38. Jean Baker argues that

there is slim evidence for a romance with King, while Philip Klein ignores the possibility of a relationship and portrays Buchanan's broken engagement to Coleman as the key romance of his life. Baker, *James Buchanan*, 25–26; Klein, *President James Buchanan*, 27–34. In the second chapter of this book, Thomas J. Balcerski depicts the relationship in the 1830s as a friendship.

10. Carl Sferrazza Anthony, *First Ladies: The Saga of the Presidents' Wives and Their Power, 1789–1961* (New York: Quill William Morrow, 1990), 162; "Conservatism and the Disunionists," *National Era* (Washington, DC), October 9, 1856, 162; "Notes from the Capitol," *The Independent* (Washington, DC), December 27, 1860, 1; "Gone to His Doom," *The Liberator*, March 15, 1861, 42; "The Old Granney," *Wisconsin Daily Patriot* (Madison), January 19, 1861, 1; Cashin, *First Lady*, 67.

11. Curtis, *Life of James Buchanan*, 2:19, 20, 102, 114, 152, 153, 160, 164–65; Anthony, *First Ladies*, 161. On whether gay culture subverts sexism in the culture at large, see R. W. Connell, *Masculinities* (Cambridge, UK: Polity, 2005), 144.

12. Cashin, *First Lady*, 54, 64–69, 71–72, 73, 77, 80–83, 94.

13. *Map of Washington, D.C.,* 1851, David Rumsey Historical Map Collection, Rumsey. geogarage.com/maps/gct0007456b.html, accessed November 16, 2016 (link no longer valid); Cashin, *First Lady*, 42, 54, 64–69, 73, 80–83.

14. Michael Todd Landis, *Northern Men with Southern Loyalties: The Democratic Party and the Sectional Crisis* (Ithaca, NY: Cornell University Press, 2014), 168–225; Lawrence A. Blum, *Friendship, Altruism, and Morality* (New York: Routledge, 2010), 31; William Seale, *The President's House*, 2 vols. (New York: White House Historical Association with the cooperation of the National Geographic Society, Washington, DC, and Harry N. Abrams, 1986), 1:333; Varina Howell Davis, *Jefferson Davis, Ex-President of the Confederate States of America: A Memoir*, 2 vols. (New York: Belford, 1890), 1:223–24.

15. *The Complete Works of William Shakespeare, Illustrated* (New York: Avenel Books, 1975), 619; Alden T. Vaughan and Virginia Mason Vaughan, *Shakespeare in America* (Oxford: Oxford University Press, 2012), 61; Cashin, *First Lady*, 18, 43, 75–76.

16. David Laskin, *A Common Life: Four Generations of American Literary Friendship and Influence* (New York: Simon and Schuster, 1994), 17–94, 400–401; Rosemary M. Magee, ed., *Friendship and Sympathy: Communities of Southern Women Writers* (Jackson: University Press of Mississippi, 1992), xx–xxi; Cashin, *Our Common Affairs*, 85, 93, 103; Caleb Crain, *American Sympathy: Men, Friendship, and Literature in the New Nation* (New Haven, CT: Yale University Press, 2001), 2, 16–53; Davis, *Memoir*, 1:223–24.

17. Seale, *President's House*, 1:357; Curtis, *Life of James Buchanan*, 2:240; Rosemary Blieszner and Rebecca G. Adams, *Adult Friendship* (Newbury Park, CA: Sage, 1992), 29; Cashin, *First Lady*, 57, 76, 81–83, 267.

18. Cashin, *First Lady*, 76, 92, 98.

19. Cashin, 92–93, 100; James Buchanan, *Mr. Buchanan's Administration on the Eve of the Rebellion* (New York: D. Appleton, 1866), 133; Anthony, *First Ladies*, 167.

20. Cashin, *First Lady*, 97–99, 102, 104, 105, 167; Daniel W. Crofts, *Reluctant Confederates: Upper South Unionists in the Secession Crisis* (Chapel Hill: University of North

Carolina Press, 1989); Margaret M. Storey, *Loyalty and Loss: Alabama's Unionists in the Civil War and Reconstruction* (Baton Rouge: Louisiana State University Press, 2004).

21. Cashin, *First Lady*, 105–6, 114–15, 119, 153, 184–85; Buchanan, *Mr. Buchanan's Administration;* Davis, *Memoir,* 1:222–23.

22. Eli N. Evans, *Judah P. Benjamin, the Jewish Confederate* (New York: Free Press, 1988), 33, 103–5, 215–16; C. Vann Woodward, ed., *Mary Chesnut's Civil War* (New Haven, CT: Yale University Press, 1981), 288–89, 550, 561; Cashin, *First Lady,* 121–22.

23. Emory M. Thomas, *The Confederate State of Richmond: A Biography of the Capital* (Austin: University of Texas Press, 1971), 3, 6, 24–25; Cashin, *First Lady,* 111–13, 121, 131, 133, 143–44, 155, 294.

24. Cashin, *First Lady,* 166–67, 180–83, 189–91, 199, 208, 218–19, 264–82, 283–305, 306–8.

"LIKE THE BASELESS FABRIC OF A VISION"

Thaddeus Stevens and Confiscation Reconsidered

JOHN DAVID SMITH

Lore in Lancaster, Pennsylvania, has it that one day the pro-southern, anti-emancipation local historian Alexander Harris met Thaddeus Stevens on a narrow path. Harris detested Stevens and refused to give way, remarking, "*I never stand aside for a skunk.*" Stevens, quick on his feet and sharp tongued, moved aside and quipped, "*I always do.*"[1] Many decades later another historian, Alabamian Walter Lynwood Fleming, denounced Stevens as the archetypical Radical Republican of Reconstruction. "The more I work on Recon.," Fleming informed a fellow southern scholar, "the more firmly I believe in hell for Thad. Stevens & co. It will be hard for them to get their just des[s]erts, no matter how hot it may be."[2]

During his long legal and political career, Stevens rarely yielded to anyone and frequently provoked his enemies' ire. In fact, in terms of his firm commitment to equality and republicanism, he positioned himself one step ahead of everyone—figuratively, at least, if not literally.[3] According to historian Harold M. Hyman, "a self-appointed scourge, Stevens relentlessly illuminated many dark corners of contemporary life in Pennsylvania as well as in the slaveholding states, while tenaciously nudging constituents toward brighter alternatives."[4] Another scholar, Charles A. Jellison, has described the congressman as "intensely partisan, brilliant, and unforgiving." In his opinion, "this leonine old Radical had long led where others had followed."[5] Damned by critics as "an agent of the devil out of hell" and worshipped by friends as "an avenging angel of the Lord," Stevens's strong personality elicited sharp commentary. "When Thad Stevens shall die," the Reverend Henry Ward Beecher sermonized in April 1867, "his virtues will be better appreciated and his name will be more highly honored than now. . . . For he is one of those valuable men who are very inconvenient when alive, and very valuable when dead."[6] When, a year later, Stevens passed away, his body lay in state in the Capitol rotunda, guarded by black troops from Massachusetts, men whose cause he had worked tirelessly to serve during the Civil War. The *New York Times* dubbed the dead Pennsylvanian the "Evil Genius of the Republican Party." "Publicly, he was an evil, but a necessary evil," asserted the *New York Herald.*[7] No Civil War–era politician combined a commitment to both idealism and pragmatism more than the "Commoner."[8]

In antebellum Pennsylvania politics Stevens vigorously attacked the Masons, promoted free public education, championed free speech, campaigned for the separation of church and state, advanced debtor relief, and fought for homesteads and the cause of free labor. An early proponent of the repatriation of blacks to Africa, after 1836 he began to espouse antislavery, then abolition, as a political movement, combining "substantial calculations of political advantage as well as . . . stirring principle." Like other antislavery lawyers and political abolitionists, his ideological and political opposition to slavery became more radical during the 1850s.[9] To be sure, Stevens was a consummate politician, historian Eric Foner explains, but the Pennsylvanian was "certainly as much an abolitionist as anybody, and more of a racial egalitarian than a lot of people on the Left then."[10]

For example, in February 1850, during his first term in the House of Representatives, Stevens delivered a speech, "The Slave Question," pronouncing his "unchangeable hostility to slavery in every form, and in every place," labeling America's "peculiar institution" "the most absolute and grinding despotism that the world ever saw." Unlike other antislavery Whigs, however, Stevens did more than simply criticize slavery in speeches; he also defended slave runaways in court in south-central Pennsylvania. Recent archeological evidence further suggests that he practiced what he preached, concealing fugitive slaves in a cistern in the courtyard of his Lancaster home. As the sectional crisis of the late 1850s reached its climax, Stevens ranked as one of America's fiercest proponents of abolition and racial equality. According to Daniel W. Crofts, "Stevens was anathema in the South. His hatred of slavery was irrepressible, and his readiness to affirm the equal capabilities and worth of all people was a century or more ahead of his time." The Confederate attack on Fort Sumter in April 1861 provided him the opportunity to help free the South's slaves and to begin overturning racial proscription and discrimination in American life.[11]

Early in the Civil War, Stevens lobbied for full-scale emancipation, the recruitment of black troops, the confiscation of rebel property, increased tariffs, and paper currency—in short, according to historian Hans L. Trefousse, "he was truly a radical of radicals." About two weeks before President Abraham Lincoln issued his Preliminary Emancipation Proclamation on September 22, 1862, Stevens complained to his law partner in Lancaster that the nation required a leader "with a sufficient grasp of mind, and sufficient moral courage, to treat this as a radical revolution, and remodel our institutions. . . . It would involve the desolation of the South as well as emancipation; and a re-peopling of half the Continent. This ought to be done but it startles most men."[12]

As the war's end neared, Stevens grasped that emancipation would never become complete, that the freedpeople would never be truly free, without direct action by the federal government. He believed that Confederate defeat opened the door for truly revolutionary steps that would eliminate slavery forever, remake the South along democratic lines, institutionalize racial equality, and establish citizenship and civil rights for all Americans. Only then would people of color have equal protection under the law. Stevens was the most rabid of Radical Republicans and the leading architect of Reconstruction, a complex period of national "debates about federal authority, citizenship, and race."[13] He stood determined to render impotent the power of the old slaveholding class and transform southern society by confiscating prominent rebels' land and distributing it to the freedpeople and white unionists.

During Reconstruction, Stevens radiated contempt for the South, urging a cotton tax, lobbying to keep white southerners ineligible for West

Point, and opposing appropriations for the repair of dikes in Mississippi, Alabama, and Louisiana. As for the levies, these states lacked representation in Congress, he said, and consequently, if they needed repairs, they could fund their own internal improvements. Regarding the former rebels, Stevens quipped, "I will not be in favor of hanging them but I do not think I should interfere if the Lord should choose to drown them out."[14]

Stevens played a major role in crafting the Thirteenth, Fourteenth, and Fifteenth Amendments. He also led the Jacobins' efforts to decapitate President Andrew Johnson for his encouragement of former rebels to regain political power during Presidential Reconstruction and then his obstructionism after 1867, when the Radicals assumed control of restoring the Union. Self-interested and focused, sardonic and vindictive, Stevens was both an idealistic egalitarian committed to expanding freedom and a skilled political pragmatist. "His great genius, indomitable will, and his great passions, inflamed into an intensity of hate . . . made him burn and flame like an electric light, so intense and fierce that lesser lights were dim," noted political opponent James R. Doolittle, a senator from Wisconsin.[15] As historian David Brion Davis has put it, Stevens's insatiable "drive for power was harnessed to an overwhelming need to combat evil and abolish injustice."[16]

Following the lead of Ohio radical abolitionist and congressman James M. Ashley, Stevens believed that, in order to reconstruct the South, the federal government needed to restrict the power of the antebellum large planters, to protect the freedpeople, and to transform the former Confederacy into a society with republican institutions.[17] Confiscation would help accomplish all three goals as well as serving to compensate the former slaves for their two centuries of unrequited toil.[18] Land reform signified the centerpiece of Stevens's Reconstruction program. As Foner has explained, Stevens believed that the destruction of the planter class held the key to remaking the agricultural South. "Take their land and they're gone, and that would have changed the whole political configuration of the South."[19]

Most Radical Republicans, however, envisioned black suffrage, not land confiscation and redistribution to the freedpeople, as the means to accomplishing these objectives. Stevens, doubtful that without economic independence the ex-slaves could instantly become independent voters, underscored the importance of land confiscation as a prerequisite to black voting and political organization. Unlike former slave and women's rights activist Sojourner Truth, who in the 1870s petitioned Congress to confiscate southern plantations as the nation's way of paying its debt to the ex-slaves, Stevens defined confiscation as an investment in the blacks' economic future. Their economic survival and a reordering of southern society depended on land ownership.[20]

Stevens argued further that confiscation would help create a new biracial yeomanry that would function as the bedrock of future southern political and social power, one that would ally with northern middle-class Republicans. Convinced that slavery and the racism that it bred—not inherent racial characteristics—held blacks back, Stevens believed that providing them land would set the freedpeople on a course to becoming market-driven middle-class yeomen like those of the North he idealized. He also maintained that land confiscation would serve other purposes— punishing former Confederate leaders, deterring them from performing other disloyal acts, providing millions of acres of land to be sold to defray the national debt, funding pensions, lowering taxes, and compensating loyalists for war damages.[21]

According to Stevens, breaking up the aristocrats' large estates would transform the South by decentralizing economic power and strengthening the economic and political power of small landholders. He considered this essential in order to refashion the fabric of southern society, transforming it from a hierarchical, undemocratic order into a democratic society premised on republican liberty. Stevens also maintained that confiscation would reconstitute the South's social and political institutions. Otherwise, he explained, "all our blood and treasure have been spent in vain."[22]

As early as 1861, in debates over the largely ineffectual First Confiscation Act (passed August 6), Stevens, then the powerful chair of the House Ways and Means Committee, determined that secession had abrogated the Confederates' rights under the Constitution and federal laws. The rebels had established a belligerent state, and, accordingly, President Lincoln's government must use any powers to conquer it and render it into a defeated province or territory. Secession, Stevens argued, removed the rebels from constitutional protections, leaving them under international law as belligerent enemies at war vulnerable to emancipation, mobilization of their slaves as soldiers, and war indemnities, including confiscation to defray the costs of the conflict.[23] He believed that reconstructing the South was a special, constitutional case and favored keeping the region as a "subject province" until a new generation could be reeducated to republican values. While Stevens insisted that "the government could not try rebels for treason any more than it could enemy combatants of any other foreign power," he nevertheless was convinced that "Congress could confiscate property—say, from 70,000 planters—redraw boundaries, mandate school systems, or hold the South under military rule for as long as it chose."[24]

As congressmen debated the First Confiscation Act, Stevens passionately favored seizing white southerners' estates. "If their whole country must be laid waste, and made a desert, to save this Union from destruction, so let it be." He added, "I would rather . . . reduce them to a condition where their whole country must be repeopled by a band of freemen than to see them perpetrate the destruction of this people through our agency."[25] Later, outraged that Lincoln had failed to enforce the Second Confiscation Act (passed July 17, 1862), which in fact limited the forfeiture of the right to the property to the life of the guilty party and would permit the return of any confiscated land to the heirs, Stevens formulated a more radical vision and a comprehensive confiscation program, revising it repeatedly during the war and Reconstruction. He premised this project on the principle of belligerency, the accordant right to seize enemy property, and its appropriation to pay expenses and damages of war.

In July 1862 Stevens espoused his most extreme position on confiscation to date.

> I would seize every foot of land, and every dollar of their property as our armies go along, and put it to the uses of the war and to the pay-[ment] of our debts. I would plant the South with a military colony if I could not make them submit otherwise. I would sell their lands to the soldiers of independence; I would send those soldiers there with arms in their hands to occupy the heritage of traitors, and build up there a land of free men and of freedom, which, fifty years hence, would swarm with its hundreds of millions without a slave upon its soil.[26]

Responding to such rhetoric of treating the Confederates as traitors and defeated belligerents whose land should be confiscated, in January 1863 fellow Republican congressman Owen Lovejoy of Illinois criticized Stevens in Congress as "an ocean of wisdom with a little island of folly."[27]

Undeterred, in April 1863 Stevens proposed to the Union League of Lancaster that military tribunals accompany federal forces into the South, selling rebel territory to the highest bidder. In occupied Virginia, for example, the army should

> sell every acre . . . belonging to traitors to bold and loyal settlers. How much better to have a friendly population, than the present hostile one, who are constantly betraying our troops and giving information to the enemy. The land might sell low; but in the aggregate the sum would be large; and when all our conquests were thus disposed of, the national debt would be paid. Brave settlers and adventurers will always be ready for such speculations, even if they had to carry arms to the field like our frontiers-men against the Indians.[28]

For his part, during the war, Lincoln allowed the sale of some estates on the South Carolina sea islands for the payment of back taxes, but he rejected confiscation as a policy, thereby blocking a revolutionary movement that could "have had incalculable political and economic consequences." At best, by 1865, freedmen on the sea islands had purchased several thousand acres of land at tax sales, while others in Georgia and Florida acquired possessory titles to thousands more. As the war drew to a close, abolitionists and Radical Republicans looked to the US Congress to guarantee these titles and to allocate more land for the former slaves. They considered confiscation and land redistribution—awarding land to those who had worked under compulsion for generations—a mere act of simple justice and retributive compensation. Abolitionists believed that land, along with education and the vote, ultimately held the key to a successful reconstruction of the former Confederacy.[29]

Stevens and likeminded abolitionists, including George Washington Julian, Charles Sumner, Wendell Phillips, Benjamin Butler, Wendell P. Garrison, William Goodell, Thomas Wentworth Higginson, Carl Schurz, and Charles K. Whipple, believed that confiscation could transform "the Republican revolution into channels traditionally followed by revolutions of the past, with the thorough-going economic destruction of a privileged class."[30] Like citizens of the rebellious German states following the failed Märzrevolution (1848), Indians after the Sepoy Mutiny (1857–58), Austrians following the Austro-Prussian War (1866), and the French after the Franco-Prussian War (1870–71), the Confederates would be punished by having to pay war indemnities.[31] Addressing the Fortieth Congress, Stevens noted that, unlike the former rebel states, the defeated German states had accepted their fate under the laws of war, recognizing that they must concede to the wishes of their conqueror. He asked, "Where is our statesmanship that we suffer the enemy to escape from the payment of the cost and damages of the war?"[32]

As the war progressed, Stevens continually refined the details of his confiscation plan. In May 1864, while Lincoln worked to build unionist coalitions in Louisiana, Arkansas, and other Confederate states and Senator Benjamin Wade and Representative Henry Winter Davis hammered out their famous bill, Stevens explained what he considered the sine qua non of Reconstruction policy. First, upon seceding and committing armed insurrection against the Union, the rebel states forfeited all rights under the US Constitution and, upon being conquered, they became territories. Second, under "the laws of war the conqueror had the right to seize the property, real and personal, of the enemy and appropriate it to the payment of the expenses and damages of the war, and make provision for our wounded soldiers and for the families of the slain." Put another way, Stevens declared "that the property of the morally and politically guilty should be taken for public use." He introduced an unsuccessful substitute to the Wade-Davis Bill declaring the former Confederate states as federal territories and confiscating all rebel land in excess of one hundred acres and all property worth three thousand dollars and above.[33] Although revising his confiscation proposals over time, Stevens never softened his determination to remake the South by carving out homesteads for the freedpeople from the estates of their former masters.

Stevens's confiscation plans, of course, also appeared in context. Major General William T. Sherman's Special Field Order No. 15 (January 16, 1865) awarded possessory, not fee-simple, titles to 40,000 freedmen on

485,000 acres of abandoned lands in South Carolina and Georgia that had fallen to federal forces. The grants, dispensed within an area from the Atlantic coast to thirty miles inland and from Charleston to Jacksonville, consisted "of no more than forty acres of land per family until Congress shall regulate their title."[34] By July 1865, more than 40,000 freedpeople had settled on approximately 400,000 acres in the so-called Sherman Reserve. In October 1865 President Johnson, by executive order, forced Major General O. O. Howard, commissioner of the Freedmen's Bureau, to compel the freedpeople to surrender their plots of land (except for homesteads previously sold under court-order decrees) to planters that the president had pardoned under his amnesty proclamation of May 29, 1865, and subsequent special pardons.[35] Despite the blacks' protests and the refusal of Major General Rufus Saxton, assistant commissioner of the Freedmen's Bureau for South Carolina, Georgia, and Florida, to dispossess the properties (in January 1866 Johnson cashiered Saxton), the government forced most of the freedpeople off these lands. In June 1866 Johnson declared the Second Confiscation Act to be a war measure and hence not in effect during peacetime. His actions effectively halted land confiscations.[36]

Another piece of federal legislation, the Freedmen's Bureau Bill of March 3, 1865, included a provision awarding ex-slaves and white refugees 40 acres of confiscated or abandoned land to be leased for three years—but with no promise of permanent ownership—during which the freedpeople could purchase the property at its 1860 appraised value.[37] In 1865 the bureau controlled more than 850,000 acres of abandoned lands; at best this constituted only 0.2 percent of southern territory.[38] These shaky precedents established the persistent myth, then and now, that the government intended to grant "forty acres and a mule" to the freedpeople. In fact, the pardoning of almost 13,000 former rebels by President Johnson and then restoring their property ownership essentially squashed confiscation by early 1866, forcing all but about 4,000 families off the small landholdings they had occupied since the war. By mid-1866, one-half of the land previously controlled by the bureau had been restored to its former owners.[39]

Several months following passage of the Freedmen's Bureau Bill, in early September 1865, Stevens launched his formal land-confiscation campaign, addressing the Pennsylvania Republican State Convention in Lancaster. He couched confiscation as a means of empowering the freed-people to become independent and productive citizens and as a vehicle toward remaking the South by weakening its planter class. Additionally, land redistribution would serve as a way to recoup the costs of the war and to punish the rebels for their political crimes.

Imploring his Lancaster audience to support his proposal, Stevens waved "the bloody shirt." He reminded them of their neighbors who had returned from the war as amputees or with wounds resulting from what he termed "rebel perfidy." Beyond this, Stevens argued that contemporary Americans must protect future generations from the roughly $4-billion war debt accrued in defeating the Confederates. It was imperative, he declared, "to compel the wicked enemy to pay the expense of this unjust war. In ordinary transaction he who raises a false clamor, and prosecutes an unfounded suit, is adjudged to pay the costs on his defeat." He added, "by the law of nations, the vanquished in an unjust war must pay the expense."[40]

Stevens judged confiscation the best means of punishing leading rebels—"nabobs" he called them—"the few rich about Charleston whose millions has been earned by running the blockade, and whose heads reached the stars while their feet were trampling upon freemen and freedom." Loss of their land would diminish the nabobs' economic and social power, Stevens said, which was appropriate because they, not rank-and-file white southerners, had sparked secession. Beyond this, confiscation would serve to begin the refashioning of the South. Nothing less, according to Stevens, than the "reformation" of the rebel states "*must* be effected; the foundation of their institutions, both political, municipal and social, *must* be broken up and *relaid,* or all our blood and treasure have been spent in vain."[41]

Specifically, Stevens proposed confiscating the property of the top 10 percent of the largest former slaveholders, about 70,000 southerners. These were former rebels whose estates were valued over $10,000 or those who held over 200 acres of land. The redistribution would amount to 40 million acres and would allot 40-acre plots to each adult male freed-man. The remaining land, totaling 354 million acres, would be sold to the highest bidder. Stevens predicted that it would sell for approximately $10 per acre; the proceeds would yield the US government $3.54 billion for veterans' pensions, for payment of damages suffered by unionists, and for reduction of the national debt. He informed critics of his plan that only the richest ex-Confederates would have their land confiscated, leaving the real property of nine-tenths of the South's white population untouched.[42]

Stevens acknowledged that confiscation was a radical step, what he termed "remodeling the institutions, and reforming the rooted habits of a proud aristocracy." But together with land redistribution, it would increase the number of small proprietors in the South, thereby ridding the region of its aristocracy—what he caustically termed "70,000 proud, bloated and defiant rebels." Stevens explained further: "If the South is ever to be made a safe republic, let her lands be cultivated by the toil of the owners or the free labor of intelligent citizens. This must be done though it drive her nobility into exile. If they go, all the better." This, Stevens reasoned, was preferable to colonizing four million freedpeople to Africa. He further predicted that loyal, independent yeomen would produce more cotton per acre than slaveholders had, and beyond that, "he who produced it will own it and *feel himself a man.*"[43]

Despite his impassioned plea, Stevens's land-redistribution proposal generally fell on deaf ears. For example, *New York Tribune* editor Horace Greeley preferred empowering the freedmen with political rights, not confiscating rebel land. "We protest against any warfare against Southern property," Greeley wrote, "because the wealthier class of Southerners, being more enlightened than the ignorant and vulgar, are less inimical to the blacks." Lacking popular support, Stevens never brought the topic of confiscation before the Joint Committee of Fifteen on Reconstruction, the influential congressional body of which he was a member. That said, Stevens nonetheless continued to advocate for land reform before the House.[44]

For example, when addressing Congress in December 1865, Stevens returned to the topic of providing homesteads for the former slaves. He explained paternalistically: "We have turned, or are about to turn, loose four million slaves without a hut to shelter them or a cent in their pockets. The infernal laws of slavery have prevented them from acquiring an education, understanding the common laws of contract, or of managing the ordinary business of life." Stevens reminded his congressional colleagues that the United States was not a "white man's Government," but rather a "man's Government; the Government of all men alike; not that all men will have equal power and sway within it." He acknowledged that differences between men existed, the understandable result of "accidental circumstances, natural and acquired endowment and ability"—factors that influenced individual fortunes. Accordingly, Stevens continued: "This Congress is bound to provide for . . . [the freedpeople] until they can take care of themselves. If we do not furnish them with homesteads, and hedge them around with protective laws; if we leave them to the legislation of their late masters, we had better have left them in bondage." He predicted that without direct federal aid the emancipated men and women would fare worse than Union prisoners had at Andersonville. "If we fail in this great duty now, when we have the power," Stevens warned, "we shall deserve and receive the execration of history and of all future ages."[45]

Between 1866 and 1868 (until his death in August of that year), Stevens continued to promote confiscation. For example, during debates over continuation of the Freedmen's Bureau in February 1866, he introduced a substitute bill authorizing the president to reserve for the use of the freedmen and loyal white refugees three million acres of land taken "from forfeited estates of the enemy" in Florida, Mississippi, Alabama, Louisiana, and Arkansas. Stevens proposed dividing it into parcels not exceeding forty acres and leasing them for not more than ten cents per acre per year; after a set term the renters could acquire title for a sum not to exceed two dollars per acre. To bolster his argument, Stevens cited the example of Russian tsar Alexander II, who, when he emancipated 22 million serfs in 1861, "compelled their masters to give them homesteads upon the very soil which they had tilled; homesteads not at a full price, but at a nominal price; 'for,' said he in his noble words, 'they have earned this, they have worked upon the land for ages, and they are entitled to it.'"[46]

Stevens also moved to protect the freedpeople (the more than 40,000 blacks residing on 485,000 acres and holding possessory titles) who Johnson had ordered dispossessed of their homesteads in the Sherman Reserve. Stevens noted that they resided on land "ordered to be confiscated as enemy's property" and upon which the freedpeople had created villages and erected schools and churches. The freed settlers on the Sherman Reserve "have the right to retain those lands forever; . . . it is a burning cruelty . . . to allow them to be turned off in three years."[47] Objecting to confiscating rebel land, the House soundly defeated Stevens's substitute bill 126 to 37. According to historian Ralph Korngold, by doing so Republicans "overlooked an excellent opportunity to create a following of small property owners in the South upon whose support it would be able to rely for generations to come."[48]

In March 1867 Stevens, determined to add confiscation to the terms outlined in the First Military Reconstruction Act, offered a bill in the House that modern champions of awarding reparations to the descendants of American slaves often consider the first major attempt to fund slave-reparations legislation in US history.[49] The Pennsylvania congressman stated emphatically that land confiscation "was an indispensable part of Reconstruction without which neither the civil nor the political rights of the freedmen could be maintained." His "ideas were born in an earlier century's concept that liberty came from the soil and that land ownership brought self-sufficiency, voting rights, and political power." In other words, Stevens envisioned transforming the freedpeople into a free-black yeomanry committed to economic autonomy and imbued with neo-Jeffersonian republicanism.[50]

Stevens couched in biblical terms his famous "Damages to Loyal Men" speech, the oration that became his fullest and most comprehensive argument for land reform. Confiscation of rebel estates and redistribution of their lands, he said, would provide homesteads for the freedpeople, pay damages to loyalists who had lost their property at the hands of Confederates, and fund the pensions of wounded Union veterans. Stevens's speech retained the gist of his September 1865, Lancaster Reconstruction address except that he now proposed also seizing the estates of white southerners worth more than $5,000 (not $10,000) who could not take the loyalty oath specified by the Second Confiscation Act (July 17, 1862). This thus enlarged the amount of land to be appropriated by the federal government. As Hans Trefousse has explained, "as there was no conquered government to pay reparations, individuals would have to be held liable."[51]

Stevens argued that land confiscation would bring many benefits to the freedpeople, including elevating their character and offering them retributive compensation for two hundred years of slavery. "Nothing is so likely to make a man a good citizen as to make him a freeholder," he declared. "Nothing will so multiply the production of the South as to divide it into small farms. Nothing will make men so industrious and moral as to let them feel they are above want and are the owners of the soil which they till." And if one framed confiscation in what Stevens termed "the mere score of lawful earnings," America's slaves had "toiled, not for years, but for ages, without one farthing of recompense. They have earned for their masters this very land and much more. Will not he who denies them compensation now be accursed, for he is an unjust man?" He continued: "If we refuse to this down-trodden and oppressed race the rights which Heaven decreed them, and the remuneration which they have earned through long years of hopeless oppression, how can we hope to escape still further punishment if God is just and omnipotent?"[52]

The congressman implored the federal government to expropriate land from former Confederates, specifically 70,000 leading rebels, and distribute it to the former bondsmen, granting the head of every former slave family (male or female) forty acres of land and a cash payment of fifty dollars to build a structure. Trustees would hold the property for the freedpeople for ten years "during their pupilage." Land confiscation, Stevens argued, would compensate the "injured, oppressed, and helpless men, whose ancestors for two centuries have been held in bondage and compelled to earn the very property[,] a small portion of what we propose to restore to them." He added: "No people will ever be republican in spirit and practice where a few own immense manors and the masses are landless. Small independent landholders are the support and guardians of republican liberty." In short, forty-acre homesteads would transform the freedpeople into economically independent agriculturists and dethrone the southern oligarchy. Stevens envisioned confiscation as overcoming the economic control of white elites by joining the freedmen and poor whites in a common economic laboring class.[53]

Maintaining that the Second Confiscation Act (which remained on the books), specifically the bill's fifth section, already authorized the seizure of rebel "estates and property, money, stocks, credits, and effects," Stevens implored his fellow congressmen simply to enforce an existing law. Beyond this, he averred that only Congress was authorized to determine the fate of the defeated former Confederate states; their treatment in fact was to be governed by international law, not the US Constitution.

By seceding from the Union, the vanquished southern states had lost their constitutional protections and were instead "subject to the conqueror's will." Unlike Stevens, who defined the vanquished South as a "conquered province," Lincoln had maintained that secession was an illegal act, denying that the Confederacy was an established independent republic. Nevertheless, Stevens justified confiscation by quoting Swiss philosopher Emer de Vattel's *The Laws of Nations* (1758). According to Vattel, when "a conqueror who has taken up arms not only against the sovereign, but against the nation herself, and whose intention it was to subdue a fierce and savage people, and once for all to reduce an obstinate enemy, such a conqueror may with justice lay burdens on the conquered nation, both as a compensation for the expenses of the war and as a punishment." Confiscating property of the defeated, Stevens explained, served as "remuncration" for the expenses and damages of the injured party. "Where the subdued belligerent is composed of traitors," he continued, "their personal crimes aggravate their belligerent offense and justify their severer treatment, just as a tribe of savages are treated with more rigor than civilized foes."[54]

Stevens considered the homestead feature of his bill its most essential element—even more necessary than suffrage—for the future success of the South's ex-slaves. "Four million persons have just been freed from a condition of dependence," he argued, "wholly unacquainted with business transactions, kept systemically in ignorance of all their rights and of the common elements of education." With few skilled mechanics or tradesmen among them, the freedmen had to become economically self-sufficient in order to avoid being exploited by the "dethroned tyrants of the luxury of despotism." Stevens begged Congress to implement his bill to help the destitute freedpeople. "Make them independent of their old masters, so that they may not be compelled to work for them upon unfair terms, which can only be done by giving them a small tract of land to cultivate for themselves."[55]

Stevens also underscored the vital nexus between slavery, which he judged to be a heinous and barbaric institution, and confiscation. "The cause of the war was slavery. We have liberated the slaves. It is our duty to protect them, and provide for them while they are unable to provide for themselves." Stevens next asked, again quoting Vattel, "Have we not a right . . . 'to do ourselves justice respecting the object which has caused the war,' by taking lands for homesteads for these 'objects' of the war?" Unquestionably, he argued, the federal government had the right "to indemnify ourselves for the expenses and damages" resulting from the war.[56]

By his calculation, the rebels owed as much as $5,000,000,000 for federal wartime expenditures and damages sustained by unionists combined. If Congress followed Vattel to the letter of international law, Stevens declared, it could inflict harsh penalties on the former Confederates both as "'a fierce and savage people'" and as an "'obstinate enemy,' whom it is our duty to tame and punish." He ominously added: "Our future safety requires stern justice."[57]

Stevens next cataloged a long list of war crimes allegedly committed by the rebels that justified their categorization as a "savage or fierce people." The Confederates reportedly starved thousands of prisoners of war, executed or enslaved captured members of the US Colored Troops, employed secret agents who plotted to burn northern cities, shipped "infected materials" to populated areas to spread contagious diseases among noncombatants, and assassinated the US president. Such barbaric behavior entitled Congress "to reduce to absolute submission and dependence" the former rebel states. Speaking three months following the Battle of the Hundred Slain (December 21, 1866), where Lakota, Cheyenne, and Arapaho Indians massacred US cavalrymen in Wyoming, Stevens noted sarcastically that it "would do great injustice to those mild savages"—the Confederates—to be treated differently from "the wild Indians of the West," who the federal government expelled from their territory and seized their lands.[58]

To support his confiscation plan, Stevens again invoked the example of Alexander II. "When that wisest of monarchs, the Czar of Russia, compelled the liberation of twenty-five million serfs, he did not for a moment entertain the foolish idea of depriving his empire of their labor or of robbing them of their rights. He ordered their former owners to make some compensation for their unrequited toil by conveying to them the very houses in which they lived and a portion of the land which they had tilled as serfs. The experiment has been a perfect success."[59]

America's former slaves, Stevens continued, had a similar right to land. "I do not speak of their fidelity and services in this bloody war." Instead,

he believed that the country owed the freedpeople their "lawful earnings."
Stevens asked, "Have we not upon this subject the recorded decision of
a Judge who never erred?" He went on to assert that the ancient enslave-
ment of millions of Jewish persons in Egypt "was mild compared with
the slavery inflicted by Christians." Throughout world history, Stevens
continued, for all of recorded slavery, Christian slavery was more "cruel
and heartless" than that of "Pagan, heathen, or Mohammedan" slaveholders. And, he insisted, of all "Christian slavery American slavery has been
the worst." In Stevens's opinion, "God, through no pretended, but a true
Moses," had led America's bondsmen

> out of bondage, as in our case, through a Red sea, at the cost, as in
> our case, of the first born of every household of the oppressor. Did
> He advise them to take no remuneration for their years of labor? No!
> He understood too well what was due to justice. He commanded the
> men and women to borrow from their confiding neighbors "jewels of
> silver and jewels of gold and raiment." They obeyed him amply, and
> spoiled the Egyptians, and went forth full-handed. There was no blas-
> phemer then to question God's decree of confiscation. This doctrine
> then was not "satanic." He who questions it now will be a blasphemer,
> whom God will bring to judgment. If we refuse to this down-trodden
> and oppressed race the rights which Heaven decreed them, and the
> remuneration which they have earned through long years of hopeless
> oppression, how can we hope to escape still further punishment if God
> is just and omnipotent?

Stevens went on to predict that the divine punishment could come in the
form "of plagues or of intestine wars—race against race, the oppressed
against the oppressor. But come it will." He then firmly cautioned: "Seek
not to divert our attention from justice by a puerile cry about fatted
calves!"[60]

Despite Stevens's dire warnings, his confiscation and land-
redistribution program never gained traction, and, as Congressional
Reconstruction unfolded, few of his colleagues advanced such a radical
policy, a fact he acknowledged at the start of his "Damages to Loyal Men"
speech.[61] At best confiscation received "limited popular support." New

York's *Independent* endorsed the idea, linking it to enfranchising black males. According to its editor, "Given two things the negro question solves itself—the easiest of all difficult problems: Land and the Ballot—land, that he may support his family; the ballot, that he may support the state. Grant these to the negro, and . . . he will trouble the nation no more." *Harper's Weekly* also endorsed Stevens's proposal, reporting, "it is very foolish to speak of Mr. Stevens's desire of confiscation as a frantic act of vengeance. His philosophy is very far from ridiculous." Whenever possible, southern politicians would exploit and manipulate the votes of freedmen who remained landless, and "without land they lack a vital element of substantial citizenship." The editor interpreted Stevens's "mild confiscation" plan as a means of punishing those disloyal southerners who had robbed loyal citizens and enabling the freedmen to acquire land. "It may be an inexpedient measure under the circumstances, but to call it vindictive or to suppose that it has no defensible reason is absurd." Other supporters of the confiscation bill underscored its value in lowering the national debt and thus reducing taxes. One correspondent, A. G. Bemon, wrote Stevens that once northerners understood that confiscation would remove their own taxes, "there will be but one solid vote for the [Republican] party."[62]

Despite the persistence of Stevens's calls for confiscation, most people either dismissed it as unrealistic or judged it negatively. In May 1867, for example, Benjamin F. Perry, the former unionist provisional governor of South Carolina, fearful of a possible uprising by the freedmen, identified "a great deal more danger of 'Cuffee' than Thad Stevens taking over lands."[63] That same month *The Nation,* which had endorsed confiscation two years earlier, no longer considered it necessary. "Now, we totally deny the assumption that the distribution of other people's land to the negroes is necessary to complete the work of emancipation." Success will be determined now by how the landowner received the property, the magazine's editor insisted. "If he has inherited it from an honest father, as most of our farmers have, or has bought it with the proceeds of honest industry, it is pretty sure to prove a blessing. If he has got it by gambling, swindling, or plunder, it will prove a curse. . . . A large fortune acquired by cheating, gambling, or robbery, is almost sure . . . to kill the soul of him who make it—to render all labor irksome to him, all gains slowly acquired seem not worth having, and patience and scrupulousness seem marks of imbecility."[64]

The Nation further criticized confiscation as undermining the sanctity of basic property rights. "A division of rich men's lands amongst the landless," the editor wrote, "would give a shock to our whole social and political system from which it would hardly recover without the loss of liberty." A program "in which provision is made for the violation of the greater number of the principles of good government and for the opening of a deeper sink of corruption has never been submitted to a legislative body."[65] The editorial concluded, "There is nothing to our minds better settled than that there is to be no confiscation, and why Mr. Stevens keeps talking about it unless it be by way of playing bugaboo for recalcitrant Southern politicians we cannot imagine." Confiscation "could only breed heart burning and hatred which centuries of good government could not wipe out."[66] Perhaps not surprisingly, none of Stevens's "usual allies" supported his proposed bill, the vote on which was postponed until December 1867 but "which never saw the light of day again."[67]

Despite the lack of support for his land-confiscation project, Stevens refused to let the idea die. In "Damages to Loyal Men" he noted that confiscation had been ignored by "a treacherous Executive and by a sluggish Congress" and promised to devote the rest of his life to that cause. For those, most notably President Johnson, who challenged the constitutionality of confiscation, Stevens explained, "The power to dispose of the property of a conquered people is vested in the sovereign law-making of the nation, which in this Republic is Congress." Central to his plan was the argument that the ten rebel states yet to be readmitted to the Union (Tennessee regained statehood on July 24, 1866) had "forfeited all their rights under the Constitution." He asked: "Were ever such great malefactors so gently dealt with?"[68]

In May 1867 Stevens wrote David McConaughy, his former law student and a Republican supporter in Gettysburg, venting his unresolved anger at Confederate depredations in six Pennsylvania counties during the war. "Nothing but the proceeds of the confiscation of a small portion of the property of the wealthy rebels can be applied to pay the damages inflicted by these marauders, unless it be paid out of the Treasury of the United States." He justified confiscating rebel property on three grounds:

punishment, remuneration, and justice.[69] And just weeks before his death in August 1868, when making the case for Johnson's impeachment, Stevens again raised the question of confiscation, charging that the president had wrongfully restored land appropriated under the two confiscation acts, property that could have been used to help defray the national debt. In this, his final speech before Congress, Stevens characterized Sherman's reserving land for the freedpeople "as some slight recompense for their lives of toil."[70]

Although confiscation as a means of compensating the freedpeople remained alive until mid-1867, ideological, political, and practical weaknesses led to its demise. Moderates opposed expropriating private estates, even of rebels, because it contradicted basic tenets of Republican free-labor ideology and middle-class understandings of property rights. Once the freedpeople received equality of opportunity, the prevailing notion went, they should rise or fall on their own merits; special treatment and paternalism would vitiate blacks' self-reliance.[71] In 1864 the abolitionist-reformer Lydia Maria Child, while sympathetic to Representative Julian's goal of uplifting the freedpeople, nonetheless objected to his proposed method of doing so. In her opinion people were "generally injured by having property *given* to them. They don't prize it so highly, keep it so carefully, or improve it so diligently, as they do when they take some pains to obtain it." Receiving gifts, she emphasized, could serve to undermine "the strength and dignity of [the freedman's] character. Whosoever would be a *man* must *earn*."[72]

Northern capitalists, eager to invest in the South's cotton trade, also opposed the creation of a large black yeoman class that might impede postwar economic growth. They favored a landless-black labor pool over the uncertainties of a radical new experiment in confiscation, land redistribution, and black landholding. Conservatives, North and South, used confiscation as a negative force against Republicans. They maintained that it would discourage investors from sending money to a land where "hot-eyed agrarians toppled the pillars of property." According to historian Mark Wahlgren Summers, "responsible Republican" leaders generally opposed confiscation, although some radicals favored redistributing land in hopes of reducing the power of the southern Democratic elite and rendering the freedpeople some degree of economic independence. Not surprisingly, land confiscation never gained influence on the local level. Elite white southerners opposed it, and, as a result, "some of its original friends ate their words or issued clarifications to explain their meanings away."[73]

Republicans feared that a class of propertied blacks would alienate ex-Whigs in developing a white-dominated southern party. In July 1867 the *New York Times* mocked Stevens's "rude agrarianism" and "punitive plan" of confiscation and land redistribution.[74] "The same fears aroused by confiscation," writes Eric Foner, including "privilege, corruption, black domination, [and] dramatic social upheaval by government fiat . . . would shortly come to be associated with Reconstruction itself." Republican defeats in northern state elections in 1867 sealed confiscation's fate.[75] "Although many freedmen continued to believe and hope that the federal government would honor its commitment to confiscation, by the end of 1867 Republicans had abandoned the issue forever."[76] Trefousse believes that Stevens's land-reform project always was destined to fail. "The loss of some $4 billion in slave property constituted the largest amount ever expropriated in an English-speaking country, and there was no chance that any more would be extracted." Stevens simply stood "too far ahead of his colleagues" and, for that matter, the nation.[77]

Upon emancipation, however, African Americans grasped W. E. B. Du Bois's contention "that beneath all theoretical freedom and political right must lie the economic foundation." Their "land hunger" constituted the "absolutely fundamental and essential thing to any real emancipation of the slaves."[78] More recently, Foner correctly observes that congressional plans to confiscate land owned by former rebels and to divide it among the freedmen signified "an act of federal intervention comparable in scope only to emancipation itself."[79] The unwillingness of the Radicals to pass land reform, even measures less drastic than what Stevens proposed, left southern economic power in the hands of roughly the same number of men as before the Civil War. Although denied "forty acres and a mule," the freedpeople nonetheless skirmished daily with landlords over crops, livestock, and hunting, fishing, and grazing rights—in short, what Steven Hahn terms the "details of life and labour."[80]

True mobilization of rural black workers demanding land had more potential for real change than Stevens's mathematical projections of the benefits of confiscation. In 1865 Georges Clemenceau, then the twenty-four-year-old New York correspondent of Paris's *Le Temps,* came to know Stevens and observed the southern scene astutely, writing, "There cannot be real emancipation for men who do not possess at least a small portion of the soil." Clemenceau credited Stevens with having "all the wrath of a Robespierre" in his determination to refashion the South.[81]

Even before Appomattox, for example, Sergeant Prince Rivers of the 1st South Carolina Volunteers, an all-black Union regiment, described how the newly freed slaves adamantly preferred owning land to renting it. "Every colored man will be a slave, & feel himself a slave until he can *raise him own bale of cotton* and *put him own mark upon it* and *say Dis is mine!*"[82] And in 1866, at a mass meeting of freedpeople in Virginia, ex-slave Bayley Wyat captured the meaning of land and homesteads to his brethren, framing it within the labor theory of value. "We has a right to the land where we are located," he proclaimed. "Our wives, our children, our husbands, has been sold over and over again to purchase the lands we now locates upon; for that reason we have a divine right to the land." The former bondsman continued: "the United States, by deir officers, told us if we would leave the rebs and come to de Yankees and hep de Government, we should have de land where dey put us as long as we live; and dey told us dat we should be see'd after and cared for by de Government, and placed in a position to become men among men." But that was not to be; in 1866 Freedmen's Bureau officials ordered the Virginia freedmen to vacate the land so that their original owners could reclaim it. To this Wyat retorted: "Dey told us dese lands was 'fiscated from the Rebs, who was fightin' de United States to keep us in slavery and to destroy the Government. De Yankee officer say to us: 'Now, dear friends, colored men, come and go with us; we will gain de victory, and by de proclamation of our President you have your freedom, and you shall have the 'fiscated lands.'"[83]

Speaking in June of that year on the concessions that he and other Radicals had made in fashioning the Fourteenth Amendment, Stevens regretted the measure's limited racial reforms. He had long envisioned that, when given the chance, "the intelligent, pure and just men of this Republic, true to their professions and their consciences, would have so remodeled all our institutions as to have freed them from every vestige of

Lancaster's Negro Civic Congress at Thaddeus Stevens's grave, Shreiner's Cemetery, Lancaster, Pennsylvania, ca. 1920. Courtesy LancasterHistory.org, Lancaster PA.

human oppression, of inequality of rights, of the recognized degradation of the poor, and the superior caste of the rich, that no distinction would be tolerated and in this purified Republic but what arose from merit and conduct. This bright dream has vanished," Stevens lamented, quoting Shakespeare's *The Tempest*, "'like the baseless fabric of a vision.'"[84]

As Stevens predicted, the ex-slaves and their descendants paid dearly for the government's failure to confiscate the former slaveholders' estates. "While African Americans were the only freed slaves [in world history] to be granted political rights so soon after emancipation, those rights were limited for a people without capital or job prospects. Land would have served as the primary source of reparations."[85] Following emancipation, as southern planters transitioned from what historian Gavin Wright terms "laborlords to landlords," the freedpeople found their path to landownership blocked by shortages of credit and capital, discriminatory lending by whites, the stagnant cotton market, and racial violence. By 1880, black-owned farms amounted to less than 10 percent of the South's cotton-growing acreage, an astounding figure given that blacks accounted for almost 50 percent of the South's agricultural population. By the end of the century, most black farmers remained landless tenants, trapped in an economic serfdom.[86]

Assessing the status of the southern rural black proletariat in 1903, Du Bois defined the failure of the US government to confiscate land belonging to the defeated Confederates both as a broken promise and a missed opportunity. "It had long been the more or less definitely expressed theory of the North that all the chief problems of Emancipation might be settled by establishing the slaves on the forfeited lands of their masters,—a sort of poetic justice, said some." But no, Du Bois lamented, "the vision of 'forty acres and a mule'—the righteous and reasonable ambition to become a landholder," became little more than a pipe dream, one that old Thad Stevens took to his grave.[87]

NOTES

The following individuals assisted me with the researching and writing of this essay: Marjorie Bardeen, Amanda Binder, Patrick Clarke, David P. Gilmartin, J. Vincent Lowery, John R. McKivigan, T. Michael Parrish, Ritika Prasad, and Andrew Zimmerman.

1. Fawn M. Brodie, *Thaddeus Stevens: Scourge of the South* (1959; repr., New York: W. W. Norton, 1966), 95, 383n2 (emphasis added). Harris characterized Stevens as "the leading revolutionist of the American Congress . . . who towered as the unconcealed contemner of law and the Federal Constitution." Harris, *A Review of the Political Conflict in America, from the Commencement of the Anti-slavery Agitation to the Close of Southern Reconstruction; Comprising also a Resume of the Career of Thaddeus Stevens: Being a Survey of the Struggle of Parties which Destroyed the Republic and Virtually Monarchized Its Government* (New York: T. H. Pollock, 1876), iii.

2. Walter Lynwood Fleming to J. G. de Roulhac Hamilton, October 22, 1903, J. G. de Roulhac Hamilton Papers, Southern Historical Collection, University of North Carolina, Chapel Hill.

3. See Donald K. Pickens, "The Republican Synthesis and Thaddeus Stevens," *Civil War History* 31 (March 1985): 57–73.

4. Harold M. Hyman, review of *The Selected Papers of Thaddeus Stevens*, vol. 1, *January 1814–March 1865*, vol. 2, *April 1865–August 1868*, ed. Beverly Wilson Palmer and Holly Byers Ochoa, *Journal of Southern History* 65 (February 1999): 163.

5. Charles A. Jellison, *Fessenden of Maine: Civil War Senator* (Syracuse, NY: Syracuse University Press, 1962), 235.

6. Beecher quoted in Richard N. Current, *Old Thad Stevens: A Story of Ambition* (Madison: University of Wisconsin Press, 1942), iii, 278.

7. *New York Times,* August 13, 1868; and *New York Herald,* August 12, 1868, both quoted in A. J. Langguth, *After Lincoln: How the North Won the Civil War and Lost the Peace* (New York: Simon and Schuster, 2014), 234.

8. Eric Foner, "Thaddeus Stevens and the Imperfect Republic," *Pennsylvania History* 60 (April 1993): 152. Richard N. Current asserts that Stevens purposely espoused extreme policies, including land confiscation and distribution, to "stand out as the Radical of Radicals." He doubts "whether he [Stevens] himself took the whole of it [the land-confiscation proposals] seriously" and instead proposed such hyperbolic policies for "political expediency." See Current, "Love, Hate, and Thaddeus Stevens," *Pennsylvania History* 14 (October 1947): 269, 270.

9. Charles H. Glatfelter, "Thaddeus Stevens in the Cause of Education: The Gettysburg Years," *Pennsylvania History* 60 (April 1993): 163–75; David G. Smith, *On the Edge of Freedom: The Fugitive Slave Issue in South Central Pennsylvania, 1820–1870* (New York: Fordham University Press, 2013), 67.

10. "Struggles and Progress: An Interview with Eric Foner," *Jacobin* 18 (Summer 2015): 21.

11. T. Stevens, "The Slave Question," February 20, 1850, App. to Cong. Globe, 31st Cong., 1st Sess., 141–42, 143 (1850); Fergus M. Bordewich, "Digging into a Historic Rivalry," *Smithsonian* 34 (February 2004): 96–107; Daniel W. Crofts, *Lincoln & the Politics of Slavery: The Other Thirteenth Amendment and the Struggle to Save the Union* (Chapel Hill: University of North Carolina Press, 2016), 185.

12. Hans L. Trefousse, *Thaddeus Stevens: Nineteenth-Century Egalitarian* (Chapel Hill: University of North Carolina Press, 1997), 137; Thaddeus Stevens to Simon Stevens, September 5, 1862, in T. Richard Witmer, "Some Hitherto Unpublished Correspondence of Thaddeus Stevens," *Papers Read before the Lancaster County Historical Society* 35, no. 3 (1931): 65.

13. Thomas Bahde, *The Life and Death of Gus Reed: A Story of Race and Justice in Illinois during the Civil War and Reconstruction* (Athens: Ohio University Press, 2014), 6.

14. Trefousse, *Thaddeus Stevens,* 195.

15. Doolittle quoted in Jellison, *Fessenden of Maine,* 202.

16. David B. Davis, review of *Thaddeus Stevens: Scourge of the South,* by Fawn M. Brodie, *Pennsylvania History* 27 (July 1960): 333.

17. Leonard L. Richards, *Who Freed the Slaves?: The Fight over the Thirteenth Amendment* (Chicago: University of Chicago Press, 2015), 5–6.

18. Ralph Korngold, *Thaddeus Stevens: A Being Darkly Wise and Rudely Great* (New York: Harcourt, Brace, 1955), 280.

19. "Struggles and Progress," 16–17.

20. Eric Foner, *Reconstruction: America's Unfinished Revolution, 1863–1877* (New York: Harper and Row, 1988), 102–10; Carol Faulkner, *Women's Radical Reconstruction: The Freedmen's Aid Movement* (Philadelphia: University of Pennsylvania Press, 2004), 113; Alfred L. Brophy, *Reparations Pro & Con* (New York: Oxford University Press, 2006), 26. On the merits of providing homesteads versus enfranchising the freedmen, see Brooks D. Simpson, "Land and the Ballot: Securing the Fruits of Emancipation?" *Pennsylvania History* 60 (April 1993): 176–88.

21. Eric Foner, "Thaddeus Stevens, Confiscation, and Reconstruction," in *The Hofstadter Aegis: A Memorial,* ed. Stanley Elkins and Eric McKitrick (New York: Alfred A. Knopf, 1974), 162, 163n14; James Albert Woodburn, *The Life of Thaddeus Stevens: A Study in American Political History, Especially in the Period of the Civil War and Reconstruction* (Indianapolis: Bobbs-Merrill, 1913), 350, 521.

22. Woodburn, *Life of Thaddeus Stevens,* 525.

23. James Albert Woodburn, "The Attitude of Thaddeus Stevens toward the Conduct of the Civil War," *American Historical Review* 12 (April 1907): 570; Louis P. Masur, *Lincoln's Last Speech: Wartime Reconstruction & the Crisis of Reunion* (New York: Oxford University Press, 2015), 28, 95, 96.

24. Mark Wahlgren Summers, *The Ordeal of the Reunion: A New History of Reconstruction* (Chapel Hill: University of North Carolina Press, 2014), 17, 85.

25. Stevens, "Speech on Emancipation and Confiscation, August 2, 1861, in Congress," in *The Selected Papers of Thaddeus Stevens,* ed. Beverly Wilson Palmer and Holly Byers Ochoa, 2 vols. (Pittsburgh: University of Pittsburgh Press, 1997), 1:224.

26. Stevens, "Attack on General Hunter, July 5, 1862, in Congress," in Palmer and Ochoa, *Selected Papers of Thaddeus Stevens,* 1:317.

27. Lovejoy quoted in Edward Magdol, *Owen Lovejoy: Abolitionist in Congress* (New Brunswick, NJ: Rutgers University Press, 1967), 379–80.

28. Stevens, "Speech on Conquered Provinces, April 4, 1863, to Union League of Lancaster," in Palmer and Ochoa, *Selected Papers of Thaddeus Stevens,* 1:385, 386.

29. James M. McPherson, *The Struggle for Equality: Abolitionists and the Negro in the Civil War and Reconstruction* (1964; repr. with new preface, Princeton, NJ: Princeton University Press, 2014), 259.

30. Brodie, *Thaddeus Stevens,* 167. On the "revolutionary" nature of the programs, including land confiscation, advocated by Stevens and other "advanced" radicals, see Margaret Shortreed, "The Antislavery Radicals: From Crusade to Revolution, 1840–1868," *Past and Present* 16 (November 1959): 74–85.

31. Woodburn, "Attitude of Thaddeus Stevens toward the Conduct of the Civil War," 570.

32. Stevens, "Damages to Loyal Men, March 19, 1867, in Congress," in Palmer and Ochoa, *Selected Papers of Thaddeus Stevens,* 2:287.

33. Stevens, "The Government of the Rebellious States," May 2, 1864, in Palmer and Ochoa, *Selected Papers of Thaddeus Stevens,* 1:464–65, 473n2.

34. Special Field Order No. 15, January 16, 1865, US War Department, *The War of the Rebellion: A Compilation of the Official Records of the Union and Confederate Armies,* 128 vols. (Washington, DC: Government Printing Office, 1880–1901), ser. 1, 47(2):60–62.

35. By early May 1866, Johnson had pardoned 7,197 individuals whose estates valued more than $20,000 each. See Jonathan D. Dorris, *Pardon and Amnesty under Lincoln and Johnson* (Chapel Hill: University of North Carolina Press, 1953), 319.

36. Kenneth M. Stampp, *The Era of Reconstruction, 1865–1877* (New York: Vintage Books, 1965), 124–25.

37. See William S. McFeely, *Yankee Stepfather: General O. O. Howard and the Freedmen* (1968; repr., New York: W. W. Norton, 1970), 104.

38. Foner, *Reconstruction*, 158; Claude F. Oubre, *Forty Acres and A Mule: The Freedmen's Bureau and Black Land Ownership* (Baton Rouge: Louisiana State University Press, 1978), 31.

39. Stampp, *Era of Reconstruction*, 124; Silvana R. Siddali, *From Property to Person: Slavery and the Confiscation Acts, 1861–1862* (Baton Rouge: Louisiana State University Press, 2005), 248–49; Foner, *Reconstruction*, 161.

40. Stevens, "Reconstruction, September 6, 1865, in Lancaster," in Palmer and Ochoa, *Selected Papers of Thaddeus Stevens*, 2:19. Stevens most likely presented this oration on September 7, not September 6. It appears in full in *New York Herald*, December 13, 1865.

41. Woodburn, *Life of Thaddeus Stevens*, 422–23, 523, 524, 525; Stevens, "Reconstruction, September 6, 1865," 16 (emphasis in original).

42. Stevens, "Reconstruction, September 6, 1865," 18–19.

43. Stevens, "Reconstruction, September 6, 1865," 23, 24 (emphasis in original).

44. *New York Tribune*, September 12, 1865, in Korngold, *Thaddeus Stevens*, 283, 285; Benjamin B. Kendrick, *The Journal of the Joint Committee of Fifteen on Reconstruction* (1914; repr., New York: Negro Universities Press, 1969).

45. Stevens, "Reconstruction, December 18, 1865, in Congress," in Palmer and Ochoa, *Selected Papers of Thaddeus Stevens*, 2:52, 54, 52.

46. Stevens, "Remarks on the Freedmen's Bureau Bill, February 5, 1866, in Congress," in Palmer and Ochoa, *Selected Papers of Thaddeus Stevens*, 2:81, 83, 84. As early as October 1865, Stevens queried Charles Sumner, "Where can I find *in English* a correct history of the emancipation of the Russian serfs, and the terms of their liberation?" See Eric Foner, *Nothing but Freedom: Emancipation and its Legacy* (Baton Rouge: Louisiana State University Press, 1983), 8 (emphasis in original).

47. Stevens, "Remarks on the Freedmen's Bureau Bill," 84.

48. Korngold, *Thaddeus Stevens*, 285. Johnson vetoed the Freedmen's Bureau continuation bill, but Congress overrode it on July 16, 1866. The new law specified that land held by blacks under Sherman's possessory titles could be returned to their white owners. The bureau, however, permitted holders of valid Sherman titles on such lands to lease twenty-acre plots elsewhere, with six-year options to purchase the land. A month earlier Congress, with almost unanimous Republican support, passed Representative George W. Julian's Southern Homestead Act, enabling freedmen and white unionists to buy eighty acres of land for five dollars in Alabama, Arkansas, Florida, Louisiana, and Mississippi. In essence, this legislation opened public land in the South and guaranteed freedmen and white unionists preference in buying it. See George R. Bentley, *A History of the Freedmen's Bureau* (Philadelphia: University of Pennsylvania, for the American Historical Association, 1955), 133–34; Patrick W. Riddleberger, "George W. Julian: Abolitionist Land Reformer," *Agricultural History* 29 (July 1955): 109–10; and Riddleberger, *George Washington Julian: Radical Republican* (Indianapolis: Indiana Historical Bureau, 1966), 168, 189. Eric Foner interprets the Southern Homestead Act as evidence of the Republicans' commitment to offering blacks the same land policy it accorded whites in the 1862 Homestead Act, but

"they simply refused to take land from the planters to make farmers of blacks." See Foner, "Thaddeus Stevens, Confiscation, and Reconstruction," 170. The Southern Homestead Act failed because of the inferior quality of the land offered and because blacks possessed so little capital. By 1869, only 4,000 black families sought to buy land under the act, and many later lost their property. See Christie Farnham Pope, "Southern Homesteads for Negroes," *Agricultural History* 44 (April 1970): 201–12.

49. See, for example, Rhonda V. Magee, "The Master's Tools, from the Bottom Up: Responses to African-American Reparations Theory in Mainstream and Outsider Remedies Discourse," *Virginia Law Review* 79 (May 1993): 887. Because Stevens was too ill to read the speech himself, Edward McPherson, his friend and the Clerk of the House of Representatives, read it for him. Stevens and fellow Radicals applauded McPherson for refusing to seat former rebels in the Thirty-Ninth Congress.

50. Korngold, *Thaddeus Stevens*, 289; Bradley R. Hoch, *Thaddeus Stevens in Gettysburg: The Making of an Abolitionist* (Gettysburg, PA: Adams County Historical Society, 2005), 258; W. R. Brock, *An American Crisis: Congress and Reconstruction, 1865–1867* (1963; repr., New York: Harper and Row, 1966), 28.

51. Edward J. Blum, "Exodus, Reparations, and a Speech We Should Remember," December 9, 2014, *Christian Century*, http://www.christiancentury.org/blogs/archive/2014-12/exodus-reparations-and-speech-we-should-remember, accessed May 30, 2015; Dorris, *Pardon and Amnesty under Lincoln and Johnson*, 332–33; Trefousse, *Thaddeus Stevens*, 211.

52. Stevens, "Damages to Loyal Men, March 19, 1867, in Congress," in Palmer and Ochoa, *Selected Papers of Thaddeus Stevens* 2:284, 285.

53. Stevens, "Damages to Loyal Men," 276–77, 283, 288; Foner, "Thaddeus Stevens, Confiscation, and Reconstruction," 177. In his speech Stevens proposed that the government allot $100 to build a dwelling, but section five of the bill specifies $50. See Palmer and Ochoa, *Selected Papers of Thaddeus Stevens*, 2:296n12.

54. Stevens, "Damages to Loyal Men," 279, 280.

55. Stevens, "Damages to Loyal Men," 283, 284.

56. Stevens, "Damages to Loyal Men," 280.

57. Stevens, "Damages to Loyal Men," 281.

58. Stevens, "Damages to Loyal Men," 281.

59. Stevens, "Damages to Loyal Men," 284. Scholars disagree on the benefits the serfs derived from emancipation. Steven L. Hoch maintains that, "unlike slaves in the American South, serfs in Russia got a whole lot more than freedom." Hoch, "Did Russia's Emancipated Serfs Really Pay Too Much for Too Little Land?: Statistical Anomalies and Long-Tailed Distributions," *Slavic Review* 63 (Summer 2004): 274. In contrast, Peter Kolchin argues that "well-informed" contemporaries would have found American emancipation more favorable to the ex-slaves than Russian emancipation was for its former serfs. Russia's "convoluted emancipation legislation provided peasants a tortuous road to freedom. . . . [T]ransition to the new order was gradual, the former serfholders received generous compensation, and the freed peasants were saddled with a myriad of regulations and obligations." Clearly, Stevens was not "well-informed" because Russia's "peasants were

not *given* land but forced to buy it, on unfavorable terms," at inflated prices for almost a half century. See Kolchin, "Comparative Perspectives on Emancipation in the U.S. South: Reconstruction, Radicalism, and Russia," *Journal of the Civil War Era* 2 (June 2012): 209–11 (emphasis in original); and Kolchin, "The Tragic Era?: Interpreting Southern Reconstruction in Comparative Perspective," in *The Meaning of Freedom: Economics, Politics, and Culture after Slavery*, ed. Frank McGlynn and Seymour Drescher (Pittsburgh: University of Pittsburgh Press, 1992), 294–95.

60. Stevens, "Damages to Loyal Men," 284–85.

61. Korngold, *Thaddeus Stevens*, 281, 285; Stevens, "Damages to Loyal Men," 277.

62. Stampp, *Era of Reconstruction*, 128; "Mr. Thaddeus Stevens and Confiscation," *Harper's Weekly*, May 18, 1867, 306.

63. Perry quoted in Thomas Wagstaff, "Call Your Old Master—'Master': Southern Political Leaders and Negro Labor during Presidential Reconstruction," *Labor History* 10 (Summer 1969): 341.

64. Stampp, *Era of Reconstruction*, 130.

65. Stampp, *Era of Reconstruction*, 130.

66. "The Week," *Nation* 4 (May 2, 1867): 345; Woodburn, *Life of Thaddeus Stevens*, 530.

67. Summers, *Ordeal of the Reunion*, 109.

68. Stevens, "Damages to Loyal Men," 276, 281, 282, 288, 289–90, 291.

69. Thaddeus Stevens to [David] McConaughy, May [28], 1867, in Palmer and Ochoa, *Selected Papers of Thaddeus Stevens*, 2:308.

70. Stevens, "Speech on the Impeachment of the President, July 7, 1868, in Congress," in Palmer and Ochoa, *Selected Papers of Thaddeus Stevens*, 2:454.

71. McPherson, *Struggle for Equality*, 251, 254, 412; Stampp, *Era of Reconstruction*, 129–30; Foner, "Thaddeus Stevens, Confiscation, and Reconstruction," 159, 160, 170, 174.

72. Child quoted in Riddleberger, *George Washington Julian*, 192 (emphasis in original). Significantly, five years later Child reversed course and chided Congress for failing to provide the former slaves "small homesteads of their own, at modest prices. . . . If it had been made easy for the freedmen to become owners of land, how much their industry would have been stimulated and the wealth of the nation increased! Nothing improves the characters of human beings like having a home of their own; and a country has no element of prosperity so certain as that of laborers who own the soil they cultivate." L. Maria Child, "Homesteads," *National Anti-Slavery Standard* 29 (March 20, 1869): 2.

73. Summers, *Ordeal of the Reunion*, 127–28. See also Wagstaff, "Call Your Old Master—'Master,'" 344.

74. "How Pardons Might Be Purchased—Agrarianism in a New Dress," *New York Times*, July 9, 1867, 4.

75. Foner, "Thaddeus Stevens, Confiscation, and Reconstruction," 176–77, 183; Michael Les Benedict, "The Rout of Radicalism: Republicans and the Elections of 1867," *Civil War History* 18 (December 1972): 334–44.

76. John Syrett, *The Civil War Confiscation Acts: Failing to Reconstruct the South* (New York: Fordham University Press, 2005), 153.

77. Trefousse, *Thaddeus Stevens*, 214, 223.

78. W. E. Burghardt Du Bois, *Black Reconstruction: An Essay towards a History of the Part Which Black Folk Played in the Attempt to Reconstruct Democracy in America, 1860–1880* (1935; repr., New York: Atheneum, 1973), 197, 601.

79. Foner, *Reconstruction*, 68.

80. Steven Hahn, "'Extravagant Expectations' of Freedom: Rumour, Political Struggle, and the Christmas Insurrection Scare of 1865 in the American South," *Past and Present* 157 (November 1997): 157.

81. Georges Clemenceau, *American Reconstruction, 1865–1870, and the Impeachment of Andrew Johnson*, ed. Fernand Baldensperger (New York: L. MacVeagh, Dial Press, 1928), 40, 165.

82. Thomas Wentworth Higginson, War Journal, November 21, 1863, in *The Complete Civil War Journal and Selected Letters of Thomas Wentworth Higginson*, ed. Christopher Looby (Chicago: University of Chicago Press, 2000), 174–75. Rivers later served as a delegate to the 1868 South Carolina Constitutional Convention.

83. Bayley Wyat, *A Freedman's Speech* (Philadelphia: Friends' Association of Philadelphia and Its Vicinity, for the Relief of Colored Freedmen, [1866]), 2, Rare Book/Special Collections Reading Room, Library of Congress, Washington, DC.

84. Thaddeus Stevens, "Speech on the Fourteenth Amendment, June 13, 1866, in Congress," in Palmer and Ochoa, *Selected Papers of Thaddeus Stevens*, 2:156.

85. Keri Leigh Merritt, "Land and the Roots of African-American Poverty," March 11, 2016, *Aeon*, https://aeon.co/opinions/land-and-the-roots-of-african-american-poverty, accessed March 11, 2016.

86. Gavin Wright, *Old South, New South: Revolutions in the Southern Economy since the Civil War* (New York: Basic Books, 1986), 49, 106; Wright, *Slavery and American Economic Development* (Baton Rouge: Louisiana State University Press, 2006), 125–26; Roger L. Ransom, "Reconstructing Reconstruction: Options and Limitations to Federal Policies on Land Distribution in 1866–67," *Civil War History* 51 (December 2005): 374.

87. W. E. Burghardt Du Bois, *The Souls of Black Folk: Essays and Sketches* (1903; repr., New York: Vintage Books, 1990), 23, 28–29. On the limitations on genuine racial reform during Reconstruction, see Brooks D. Simpson, "Mission Impossible: Reconstruction Policy Reconsidered," *Journal of the Civil War Era* 6 (March 2016): 85–102.

"EASTERN AND WESTERN EMPIRE"

Thaddeus Stevens and the Greater Reconstruction

MICHAEL GREEN

Thaddeus Stevens figures prominently in any discussion of Reconstruction, but for an unusual amalgam of reasons. If Reconstruction continued at least until 1877—and its issues resonate enough to suggest a later end date, if ever—he died nearly a decade before the period ended. While a foreign observer called him "the Robespierre, Danton, and Marat of America, all rolled into one," suggesting a degree of revolutionary leadership, and a *New York Times* obituary branded him as the "Evil Genius of the Republican Party," he told an interviewer, "My life-long regret is that I have lived so long and so uselessly." As he discovered, in explanation for his willingness to accept a less sweeping Fourteenth Amendment than he wanted, "I live among men and not among angels; among men as intelligent, as determined, and as independent as myself, who, not agreeing with me, do not choose to yield their opinions to mine. Mutual concession, therefore, is our only resort, or mutual hostilities."[1]

Stevens's reputation has ebbed and flowed as Radicals have fallen and risen in historical writing. In the wake of the "Dunning School" of early twentieth-century scholars who viewed Reconstruction and African American rights as a horror inflicted upon the South, Richard Current ascribes Stevens's actions to overweening ambition, while T. Harry Williams sees him as one of the "master politicians . . . , caustic, terrifying," and sharing a characteristic with fellow "Jacobins": "They loved the Negro less for himself than as an instrument with which they might fasten Republican political and economic control upon the South." In a 1960 book that did much to hasten the movement away from the older interpretation of Reconstruction, Eric McKitrick characterizes Stevens's congressional career as showing "the effectiveness of the parliamentary tactician, not that of the party strategist," with Reconstruction demonstrating that his "energy was that of a man absolutely convinced, and in a sense rightly, that he and history were for the moment in perfect step." With the civil rights movement of the 1950s and 1960s and the reactions to it casting Radicals in a different light, Hans Trefousse's synthesis refers to them as "Lincoln's vanguard for racial justice." Trefousse agrees with David Donald's description of "Stevens radicals" as the group "prepared to yield on lesser issues in order to secure vital legislation, while the ultras were unwilling to compromise and favored the most extreme measures of reconstruction." Stevens's political career included considerable maneuvering between parties and factions; whether or not that continued to be the case during Reconstruction, historians have maneuvered him through a variety of interpretations. As Eric Foner has observed, his "unusual complexity of motivations and unique blend of idealism with political opportunism made him almost impossible to categorize."[2]

A well-known psychobiography of Stevens labels him as the "scourge of the South," and his most recent and best scholarly biography calls him a "nineteenth-century egalitarian" to describe his career and ideology. Indeed, Stevens remains best known historically for his Radical Republicanism and in popular culture for apparently cohabitating with a mulatto woman, both of which represent, obviously in different forms, a view of equality that distinguished him from many Americans of his time. As a Radical Republican and believer in equality, Stevens fought not only for a Reconstruction that would benefit the freedpeople but also for remaking southern society through land confiscation and redistribution. Thus, he envisioned a far-reaching expansion of the federal government's scope and power. All of this would seem to suggest that he and his ideology seem to fit the traditional mold for the Radical viewpoint during the Civil War and Reconstruction and little else.[3]

Thaddeus Stevens. Courtesy Library of
Congress, Washington, DC.

But Stevens also might well be cast in a less traditional mold that reflects
the latest turn in historical writing on the post–Civil War era. Arguing in
favor of a "greater Reconstruction" that encompasses not only the North
and the South but also the West, Elliott West has written that "to understand the transformation of the nation in the mid-nineteenth century, we
should place at the center of our attention not one but two equally consequential episodes. One, the Civil War, has always been the presumptive
transformative event. The other, the expansion to the Pacific, has yet to
receive its proper recognition as a force that fundamentally reshaped the
United States. The trick is how to fit the two events together into a single
narrative." Suggesting a solution to that puzzle, Heather Cox Richardson has pointed out: "In spring 1865, Americans everywhere had to ask
themselves how the different sections of the country could reconstruct
themselves into a nation that offered individuals economic opportunity
and political freedom at the same time that it protected private property."
The answer, she argues, lay in understanding that the postwar era represented "the heyday of westward expansion, miners, the American cowboy,
Plains Indians, and gunfighters. . . . The history of the West was part and
parcel of the story of the reconstruction years and must be put back into
it. Postwar 'reconstruction' was the literal reconstruction of the North,

American Progress. John Gast, 1872. This work is widely recognized as
the classic exposition of Manifest Destiny and westward growth.
Courtesy Prints and Photographs Division, Library of Congress, Washington, DC.

South, and West into a nation in the aftermath of the Civil War. That
rebuilding stretched from the end of the Civil War until the start of the
twentieth century." Approaching American history—and especially this
period—in such a manner, Steven Hahn has suggested, enhances the possibility of examining "the unfolding of U.S. history as much from West
to East and South to North as from East to West and North to South,
interrogating centers and peripheries as well as nations and regions."[4]

Unquestionably, Stevens helped shape Radical Reconstruction, but
his influence on reconstructing the United States into a unitary power of
North, South, and West may seem less evident. In fact, he envisioned an
imperial, industrial future for the United States that extended the country's population and power from ocean to ocean and beyond but with the
kind of egalitarian, democratic society for which he so long and ardently
fought. Examining Stevens's words and deeds with the "greater Reconstruction" in mind might provide a different context in which to view
him, Reconstruction, and the nation-state being recreated in the process.

Stevens's claim of uselessness and historians describing him as more tactician than leader reflected his disappointment at failing to convince his colleagues that Reconstruction should be far more radical than it was. He believed that the Confederate states, having rebelled against the Union, sacrificed their constitutional rights and became conquered provinces, as one historian has put it, "at the mercy of Congress no less than lands conquered from Mexico." For Stevens, the key to that reorganization entailed remaking southern society by confiscating the land holdings of secessionist planters and awarding them to the emancipated slaves, who also would gain the right to vote. As much as Stevens revered the Declaration of Independence, he also subscribed in part to Thomas Jefferson's belief in the need for independent yeomen, as the former slaves would be when they owned land. They would form the backbone of the Republican Party in the South, and the former rebels would lack the power to rise against or control the government. As he told the *Chicago Tribune*, "I said forty acres of land and a hut are of more importance than the immediate right to vote—both are their due."[5]

Stevens worked with and against two presidents on Reconstruction, with far different outcomes. Although Abraham Lincoln's moderation often irked him, another Pennsylvania politician who knew both men concluded that they "worked substantially on the same lines, earnestly striving to attain the same ends, but Stevens was always in advance of public sentiment, while Lincoln ever halted until assured that the considerate judgment of the nation would sustain him." Stevens praised the president's support for the Thirteenth Amendment but had no inclination to welcome a reconstructed Louisiana—a pet project of Lincoln's— back into Congress when doing so would contradict his legal theory of conquered provinces and his Whiggish belief that Congress, not the president, must control Reconstruction.[6]

While Lincoln's moderation disappointed Stevens, Andrew Johnson's obstructionism and racism enraged him. Six weeks after becoming president, Johnson issued a proclamation pardoning almost every Confederate except high officers and the wealthy, reflecting his loathing for the southern aristocrats who had disdained him. Although similarly disposed toward the planter class, though for different reasons, Stevens despaired of Johnson and his exercise of power—not only the pardon plan but also his call for North Carolina to reconstitute itself under white leadership, which Stevens declared "sickens me." He lamented, "I see our worthy President fancies himself a sovereign power." Still hoping to persuade Johnson to back away and defer to Congress, Stevens told him in July: "I am sure you will pardon me for speaking to you with a candor to which men in high places are seldom accustomed. Among all the leading Union men of the North with whom I have had intercourse I do not find one who approves of your policy." With Congress meeting in December 1865, Stevens spent the next several months trying to whip up opposition to Johnson's attempt to reconstruct the Union before the session.[7]

Stevens fired his first and most public salvo at Johnson in a speech at Lancaster on September 6. "Four years of bloody and expensive war, waged against the United States by eleven states, under a government called the 'Confederate States of America,' to which they acknowledged allegiance, have overthrown all governments within those States which could be acknowledged as legitimate by the Union," he declared, adding that it was "the duty of the Government to inflict condign punishment on the rebel belligerents, and so weaken their hands that they can never again endanger the Union; and so reform their municipal institutions as to make them republican in spirit as well as in name." As a congressman, Stevens had a command of parliamentary procedure and, as a lawyer, a fondness for precedents and loopholes, and he took advantage of those talents. He cited the court-martial in Washington, DC, of the Andersonville prison camp's commandant. If the southern states never left the Union or claimed independence, then he should be tried in Georgia, where he committed the crimes of which he stood accused, and since he never had been part of the Union army during the war, he could hardly be subject to a military trial. Stevens also appealed to financial logic: seizing the estate of every rebel worth $10,000 or with at least two hundred acres would enable the United States to pay off the national debt. Turning to the Constitution's guarantee of a republican form of government, he asked "how can republican institutions, free schools, free churches, free social intercourse, exist in a mingled community of nabobs and serfs; of the owners of twenty thousand acre manors with lordly palaces, and the occupants of narrow huts inhabited by 'low white trash'? If the South is ever to be made a safe republic, let her lands be cultivated by the toil of the owners or the free labor of intelligent citizens."[8]

Stevens's approach never wavered from these core beliefs. In his first congressional speech on Reconstruction during the Thirty-Ninth Congress that December, he repeated his longstanding commitment to equality of opportunity: "This is not a 'white man's Government,' in the exclusive sense in which it is used. To say so is political blasphemy, for it violates the fundamental principles of our gospel of liberty. This is man's Government; the Government of all men alike; not that all men will have equal power and sway within it. Accidental circumstances, natural and acquired endowment and ability, will vary their fortunes." More than a year later, in January 1867, he declared, "Unless the rebel states, before admission, should be made republican in spirit, and placed under the guardianship of loyal men, all our blood and treasure will have been spent in vain." Black suffrage would be crucial to achieving that goal because the freedpeople "form the great mass of the loyal men" in the South. "Possibly with their aid loyal governments may be established in most of those States. Without it all are sure to be ruled by traitors; and loyal men, black and white, will be oppressed, exiled, or murdered." He also proclaimed his desire to "insure the ascendency of the Union party," the coalition of Republicans and War Democrats formed during the Civil War, "for I believe, on my conscience, that on the continued ascendency of that party depends the safety of this great nation." He resolutely supported the Freedmen's Bureau to ease the transition from slavery, the Civil Rights Act of 1866, and the Fourteenth Amendment.[9]

But his resolution and Republican inclinations proved less connected than Stevens hoped. Conservative and some moderate Republicans, including onetime Lincoln cabinet members William Henry Seward and Gideon Welles, stood by Johnson even after riots in Memphis and New Orleans in 1866 demonstrated the dangers still facing the freedpeople. Then Johnson campaigned for his supporters in late summer with his "Swing 'Round the Circle," which struck even some of his backers as unwise and undignified. The president did nothing to reassure them by exchanging insults with hecklers and announcing: "I have been called Judas Iscariot. . . . If I have played the Judas, who has been my Christ that

I have played the Judas with? Was it Thad Stevens?" Even the *New York Times*'s Henry J. Raymond, a Seward ally and Johnson loyalist, lamented, "The President of the United States cannot enter upon an exchange of epithets with the brawling of a mob, without seriously compromising his official character and hazarding interests too momentous to be thus lightly imperiled." But little else changed. Four days later Raymond's *Times* said of Stevens's call for confiscation, black suffrage, and military rule in the South: "It remains for the people to decide whether they are ready thus to sacrifice all hopes and all thoughts of Union and peace, and to plunge the country for ages to come into an anarchy tenfold worse than that which renders free government hopeless in the States of South America. . . . If such a policy as Mr. Stevens foreshadows is carried out, or seriously entered upon, nothing on earth is more certain than the utter overthrow and ruin of this Republic."[10]

While Stevens had long since lost all hope that the president would accept congressional policy on Reconstruction, Congress finally adopted an offshoot of his earlier proposal when it passed the Military Reconstruction Act of 1867, dividing the ex-Confederate states (except Tennessee) into five military districts. "For two years they have been in a state of anarchy; for two years the loyal people of those ten States have endured all the horrors of the worst anarchy of any country. Persecution, exile, murder have been the order of the day within all these Territories so far as loyal men were concerned, whether white or black, and more especially if they happened to be black," he declared. But while Stevens welcomed efforts to protect African Americans, he resented the compromises that went with them and understood their danger. He complained about giving the power over military reconstruction to the president instead of General of the Army Ulysses Grant. "No one doubts the constitutional authority of Congress to detail for particular service, or to authorize others to detail for particular service particular officers of the Army," he said. "But our friends who love this bill love it now because the President is to execute it, as he has executed every law for the last two years, by the murder of Union men, and by despising Congress and flinging into our teeth all that we seek to have done."[11]

The standoff continued, with Johnson battling congressional Republicans and Stevens attacking the president's Reconstruction policies. When

Johnson tried to remove Secretary of War Edwin Stanton after passage of the Tenure of Office Act, which prohibited such an action without congressional approval, the House voted to impeach the president. Stevens encouraged his colleagues, warning, "If you don't kill the beast, it will kill you." He served as one of the seven House managers prosecuting Johnson's impeachment in the Senate, but Stevens's declining health kept him from participating more actively. The Senate voted 35–19 to convict, one short of the required two-thirds majority to remove Johnson from office. Stevens declared, "The country is going to the devil." He continued to fight for universal suffrage and land redistribution until his death on August 12, 1868, shortly after Grant's nomination for president.[12]

Throughout his life, Stevens had fought for equality, but, like any politician who encounters any electoral or legislative success, he was capable of thinking about more than one issue at a time. As the owner of the Caledonia Iron Works, he believed strongly in industrialization and that the federal government should encourage it, a Whig position that he and other members of that party carried into the Republican organization. Stevens envisioned industrial growth spreading from the Northeast not only into the South but also into the West. In this way he reflected—and as a significant figure affected—the Republican effort to remake the Old South and to create the New West. Before the war, this meant keeping the West free of slavery, fighting the South's demands that it spread and Senator Stephen A. Douglas's willingness for the citizens of western territories to vote on it. During and after the war, Stevens continued to pursue policies that promoted the West's growth while also expressing sympathy for those who would suffer or be displaced in the process, thus revealing the contradictions that pursuing such programs could and often did create.[13]

Stevens had an imperial vision for the United States and his party. Not only did the founding fathers want slavery to end, he said, but they also foresaw "the erection of a vast empire over the whole continent." Since the Fourteenth Amendment left him "no doubt of our full power to regulate the elective franchise . . . in every State of the Union," his record suggests a willingness to use federal power for additional causes. While less systematic in his thinking than Secretary of State Seward, Stevens shared Seward's desire for "the continual development of our country." Calling for the Pacific Railroad Act's passage, Stevens declared: "This is not a western measure, and ought not to be defended as such. The western soil is but a platform on which to lay the rails to transport the wealth of the further Indies to Philadelphia, New York, Boston, and Portland, scattering its benefits on its way on St. Louis, Chicago, Cincinnati, Buffalo, and Albany. Then our Atlantic sea-ports will be but a resting-place between China, Japan, and Europe." Despite the secretary's internationalist outlook, Stevens distrusted his fellow ex-Whig, and excoriated him for standing by Johnson. But he backed Seward's failed attempt to purchase Samaná Bay in the Dominican Republic and his more successful quest to buy Alaska from Russia. Stevens presented a paean to Alaska, but "the mere material advantages furnished are not all the chief benefits of this purchase. The vastness of the nation is very often the strength of the nation." Thus, Stevens also foresaw other additions to the United States, predicting that Cuba "will have become saturated and ripe with the bursting principles of freedom, and, together with St. Domingo, Hayti, Jamaica, and their cognate races, will be ready to leap to arms and defend their appropriate dominions, if such aid be needed in the cause of freedom, and if they shall not have been added to our dominion by our enterprising Foreign Secretary," whose president Stevens was at that moment trying to convict of high crimes and misdemeanors—still another reminder that while a Radical and an egalitarian, he also was a practical politician.[14]

Stevens's economic views fit with Republican policies designed to favor industrial development—even one of his less sympathetic early biographers called him a "champion" of northern industrialists. But he tended to vex the potential beneficiaries, businessmen, who saw him as interested only in the cause of African American freedom. Contrary to his radical image, Stevens criticized progressive income taxes as "a strange way to punish men because they are rich" and advocated a flat tax. An avowed protectionist, Stevens supported the Morrill Tariff, among other programs designed to promote American industry. Consequently, his protectionism sometimes conflicted with what westerners thought best for their region. When his colleague James Wilson of Iowa argued that a reduced tariff would help western farmers, Stevens attacked what he considered the illogic "that the raw material of the West shall be shipped in bulk to feed the workshops of Europe, and that we shall take their manufactures in return for it instead of building up a home market in the United States to consume this raw material, thus saving the heavy expense of transportation."

Yet Stevens's vision for the West resembled what he foresaw for the rest of the country: not a bucolic collection of cowboys and Indians, as many later came to see the West, but as what many living there wanted it to be, an industrial and agricultural empire. "I had hoped that the great West, with its great interests, its flourishing cities, its noble soil, had reached a time when we were to see all through the valley of the Mississippi great manufacturing cities," Stevens said, rather than "adhere to the old notion, and insist upon sending the products of the West, its sheep, bullocks, corn, beef, and everything of that kind to England for the purpose of purchasing those articles they need." Later he observed: "If we were to continue adequate protection a few years longer our markets would be enlarged. With the vast water power of the West we would have manufactures established there to consume the products of the country."[15]

Nonetheless, Stevens's monetary views troubled many Republican fiscal experts and the industrialists they sought to win over. He supported paying off war bonds with greenbacks, demonstrating a more inflationary view of currency than most Republicans. It also meshed with his broad views of government power. Late in 1867 Stevens wrote to a banker that "the government has the constitutional power to make money of whatever material it chooses, whether metal or paper, leather, tin or greenbacks, and to regulate its value, and therefore legal tenders are, to all intents and purposes, the lawful money of the country—money in which all debts, public and private, may be legally and justly paid. Money is just what the law makes it." He believed that the road to specie payments required reducing the debt; only then would he contract the currency. Since Stevens believed that his proposals for confiscating rebel landholdings could reduce the debt, the strands of his ideology formed a more coherent whole than his critics—or perhaps even he—realized.[16]

Yet those critics may have seen how contradictory his fiscal views could be when applied to the West. The *Chicago Tribune* lamented his "antipathy against precious metals." Objecting to Stevens's comment that "the government has, at different times, reduced the price of silver, and that, when so reduced, it was made to pass to every creditor as well as debtor at the original price," the *Tribune* replied that this action was no "arbitrary attempt of the government to make a smaller coin pass for the same value as a larger one, but to find out by actual experiment . . . the relative values of silver and gold." Since states like California and Nevada had grown because of and around mining booms—and others would follow suit—Stevens may not have had the West's best interests at heart in advocating the continued use of paper instead of specie. Nor did his party agree with him: the similar monetary views of Senator Benjamin Wade of Ohio, the president pro tempore and thus next in the line of presidential succession, were among the reasons the Senate voted to acquit Johnson. But Stevens also quoted "one of the soundest and most intelligent Democrats I have ever seen in Congress," John Law of Indiana, as saying, "You may rely on it, the 'Great West,' irrespective of parties, are solidly against paying gold on the principal of these bonds, and it will be with great reluctance and misgiving that they will pay the interest in gold, and I will further say that the party, whatever it may be, which indorses such a policy in the Presidential election next fall, will be so far beaten that their own dogs will not know them when they come from the polls." Nonetheless, the "Great West" stood solidly behind Grant and the Republican Party in the next election.[17]

Stevens's advocacy of land confiscation also had western connections. A correspondent for the *Chicago Tribune,* defending Stevens, noted the millions of acres of federally owned land in western states and territories. Also, the United States had gone to war with Mexico, "at the cost of thousands of lives and millions of treasure," with the goal of not only expanding slavery but also "to perfect our title" to Texas, which fifteen years later joined the rebellion. The *Tribune* writer suggested taking "the public lands of this most treacherous and ungrateful of States. It will then have choice lands in abundance in the Southwest, wherewith to reward its loyal poor, whether white or black, with free homesteads." While Stevens appears not to have gone along with this proposal, he did back a freedmen's homestead bill "for the Slaves liberated by the operations of the war and the Constitutional Amendment," similar to the one he and his party had pushed through Congress in 1862, and correctly predicted the measure would fail because, like the wartime legislation, it required the would-be landowner to have capital, which the freedpeople lacked.[18]

Soon after Grant took office as president, the driving of the golden spike celebrated the linking of the Union and Central Pacific Railroads, making it possible to cross the continent by rail—and forever changing western lands. Historian David Potter refers to the Kansas-Nebraska Act and the ensuing controversy surrounding it as "a railroad promotion and its sequel," and the Civil War reinvigorated Republican efforts to complete what northerners and southerners had sought during the 1850s: a rail line to the Pacific. The many motivations for building it included fears that California might choose to go off on its own or fall prey to the imperial ambitions of the Confederacy. Stevens chaired the House committee on the railroad and strongly supported it. Nor would he suffer personally from its construction. Historian William Deverell has described the owners of the Pacific Railroad's western branch, the Central Pacific, as building "an iron empire"—and Stevens owned an iron works. He also owned stock in railroad companies involved in or affected by the construction. But he left no doubt about his real aim in promoting the railroads: "We must either agree to surrender our Pacific possessions to a separate empire or unite them to the Atlantic by a permanent highway of this kind. The Romans consolidated their power by building solid roads from the capital to their provinces."[19]

While Stevens helped shape the transcontinental railroad, the project also provided a testing ground for some of his ideas and insight into where the West might fit into his concept of Reconstruction. "I do not know that I share in the doubt as to the constitutionality of the United States incorporating companies to make railroads through the States," he said, but his awareness of those doubts prompted him to support limiting the Union Pacific, which would be both private and public, to areas within territories. The Central Pacific, heading east through the states of California and Nevada, would be privately owned but would receive ample federal legislative and financial support that gave Stevens few, if any, qualms. He also insisted on requiring all of the iron in the transcontinental railroad to be American made, not to line his pockets but because after the Union defeated the Confederacy and the seceded states returned to Congress, their representatives would engage in "the same arrogant, insolent dictation which we have cringed to for twenty years, forbidding the constitution of any road that does not run along our southern border"; he wanted the railroad completed quickly and to the full benefit of the United States.[20]

Stevens supported and protected the railroad—indeed, the rail industry—for the rest of his life. "I hope every facility will be given by the Government for the building of this road," he told his colleagues, predicting: "After this road is built, I have no doubt the receipts from the business of the Government will be very large between its eastern and western empire." Thomas Scott of the Pennsylvania Railroad had asked the congressman, as Stevens's biographer put it, to "look out for the interests of the Union Pacific. He did so and more," helping that company extend its construction deadline and backing similar financial and land grants to aid the Northern Pacific Railroad. Stevens backed funding to maintain the army as a larger force in peacetime than it had been before—mainly for Reconstruction duty in the South, to be sure. But as western historian Robert Utley has pointed out: "Congress debated long hours over the size and shape of the postwar Regular Army. Radicals bent on harsh treatment of the conquered South demanded a large army to further their plans for Reconstruction. So did western representatives attuned to the needs of the frontier." Accordingly, President Johnson signed legislation increasing the size of the cavalry and the infantry, whose presence would ease the railroad's construction and whose mobility increased as railroads spread throughout the West.[21]

For all of his concerns about the West, Stevens also revealed an attitude and ignorance about the region that proved all too common. Railroad builders received large subsidies and land grants, later making sure that Congress let them keep it all with as few taxes and regulations as possible. Whether or not Stevens foresaw that problem, he clearly lost no sleep over what the railroads received. When his colleague Elihu Washburne of Illinois complained, Stevens mocked his concerns about "political economy, frugality, and especially morality," then warmed to the issue of land grants. "We agreed, also, to double the amount of lands. What lands? Why, the sections on each side of the road! The gentleman lives in the West, and knows all about this matter," Stevens said. "He knows that after we get beyond the one hundredth degree of longitude the land is hardly worth holding." Stevens described the area to the Rockies as "merely of nominal value," the land in the Rockies as "not very valuable," "the plains" west of the Rockies as "a barren valley that bears nothing but sage of the bitterest kind, and that never can be made fertile for any use whatever," and after the Sierra Nevada, "you find no land worth anything until you get into California, and there the lands have all been taken up long ago." Future generations of westerners complained that easterners saw their region as a colony and never understood the space or difficulties it entailed. No western congressmen or territorial delegates disagreed with Stevens's interpretation of western geography, which fit that later paradigm.[22]

The railroad expansion that Stevens encouraged for the sake of American industry and growth reshaped the country in the late nineteenth century. Political scandals roiled federal, state, and local government thanks, in part, to bribery and less criminal forms of influence by railroad companies; given that Stevens benefited personally from railroad legislation over the years, those consequences may have been less unintended for him than other Republicans of his time, especially if, as Eric McKitrick notes, "his conception of politics was that of a low business, full of fools and gamesters." But growth—in population, industry, and agriculture—also created significant problems for Native peoples. Senator Lot Morrill of Maine stated in 1867: "As population has approached the Indian we have removed him beyond population. But population now encounters him on both sides of the continent, and there is no place on the continent to which he can be removed beyond the progress of population." Supporting the transcontinental railroad's completion and deeming it "our duty . . . to make the progress of construction of the great Pacific railways . . . as safe as possible," General William Tecumseh Sherman reported to the House soon after the Civil War, "The poor Indian now finds himself hemmed in."[23]

Although he demonstrated none of the interest in Native American rights that he showed for the plight of African Americans, Stevens made clear that he grasped the difficulties faced by Native peoples. In 1860 he told the House: "I wish the Indians had newspapers of their own. If they had, you would have horrible pictures of the cold-blooded murders of inoffensive Indians. You would have more terrible pictures than we have now revealed to us, and, I have no doubt, we would have the real reasons for these Indian troubles." But what he wanted to accomplish for people of color and for all people as well as the United States could be contradictory. Heather Richardson has written, "After the Civil War, the West seemed to be a region of inexhaustible resources, where labor could easily profit from nature as soon as resistant Native Americans could be overcome." Stevens hoped to develop the West and protect Native Americans. He proved unable to do both.[24]

Undoubtedly out of egalitarianism, and possibly contrariness, Stevens defended Native Americans when others criticized them. After John Hubbard of Iowa called for them to be subject to state laws rather than federal treaties and tribal laws, Stevens made his sympathies clear: "If an Indian goes out of his tribal domains and commits a crime, does the gentleman say that he is not to be tried by the laws of the place where the crime was committed? Does the gentleman want him away from his own reservation, and let white men go in there and try him?" Stevens knew what their fate would be. When North Dakota territorial delegate Walter Burleigh complained about it being "next to impossible to punish an Indian" for a crime, Stevens reminded his colleagues of the different legal status of Native peoples, replying, "Were not these Indians out in a war of nation against nation?" When Burleigh said, "We regard all Indians as hostile who come down and ravage our frontiers," Stevens shot back, "Does the gentleman refer to the terrible slaughter of Indians by the white chief Chivington?" To this reminder of Colonel John Chivington's attack on the Cheyenne and Arapahoe at Sand Creek in 1864, Burleigh said, "I do not refer to anything of the kind." But Stevens later charged that his colleagues "now try to evade" the bargain they had made to assist Native Americans after limiting or taking their land holdings.[25]

Indeed, Stevens looked west and toward Native Americans when justifying taking rebel lands. In March 1867, arguing for confiscation of plantation-sized landholdings in the former Confederacy "both as a punishment for their crimes and to pay the loyal men who have been robbed by the rebels, and to increase the pensions of our wounded soldiers," he ticked off a list of crimes, including shooting or re-enslaving black soldiers, targeting northern cities, conducting germ warfare (sending "infected materials into our most populous towns to destroy noncombatants"), and having "consummated their barbarism by the assassination of the mildest of rulers and the best of men." Citing the Swiss philosopher and legal theorist Emer de Vattel's *The Law of Nations* (1758) and the need to "subdue a fierce and savage people," Stevens said of southerners: "If this is not a 'fierce and savage enemy' whom we have a right to reduce to absolute submission and dependence, point me out one to which the language of Vattel will apply. You would do great injustice to those mild savages who owed us no allegiance by pointing to those who perpetrated the massacre of Wyoming; or to the Comanches or the wild Indians of the West, or the fierce tribes of the Oronoco—and yet you seize their lands and expel them from their native country." Whether Stevens stopped to ponder that one of the reasons for seizing their lands was to make way for the railroads he saw as crucial to industrial development is unclear, though, given his mordant sense of humor, he seems likely to have appreciated the irony.[26]

When Stevens defended Native Americans, he also may have been playing a longer game. When a colleague tried to block the Choctaw and Chickasaw from receiving money promised in a treaty from before the war, in which they sided with the South, Stevens noted, "These Indians went into the rebellion probably for the same reason which influenced most of the southern people—because they were slave-holders." But their postwar behavior distinguished them. "The moment they returned to their allegiance they abolished slavery, even before it was abolished elsewhere," Stevens pointed out, implicitly comparing them with other rebels who refused to accept the reality of emancipation.[27]

Stevens brought to discussions of Native Americans a sense of fairness that his colleagues often lacked. As chairman of the Ways and Means and then Appropriations Committees, he often discussed funding the Bureau of Indian Affairs and annuities promised to Native peoples under treaties. When James Wilson of Iowa proposed to reduce funds for those in Washington Territory, Stevens replied, "the way I understand this matter is this: the Government undertook to make treaties with these Indians, and, in pursuance of them, took possession of their lands. The Government afterward failed to ratify most of the treaties, and kept the lands; and now it is proposed to keep the money." He said that if Natives "are in hostility against us, strike out the appropriation entirely and give them nothing. But the Department removed these Indians and promised to support them until they could support themselves. They are, therefore entitled to this money."[28]

As it turned out, the House voted to reduce the funding, belying again that Stevens dictated whatever Congress did. Further belying that idea were his comments in response to Wilson's claims that Native peoples had engaged in criminal and barbaric actions against whites. "If we had an Indian orator here to tell us the story of his tribe, he would be as eloquent in the recital of their wrongs as the gentleman from Iowa is in his recital of the wrongs of the whites. So far as my experience and investigations have done, they have taught me that, in nine cases out of ten, Indian wars have been produced by the provocations of the whites. The war may afterwards have been carried on barbarously," Stevens admitted, but he repeated that "in nine cases out of ten, the breach of faith has come from the white man; and if the Indian had a historian he would put the pale face to the blush."[29]

What Stevens might have done or tried to do if he had lived to see Grant's "peace policy" toward Native Americans and the next steps in Reconstruction obviously can only be conjectured. Historian Rodman Paul has noted: "When the Civil War was over and slavery ended, reformers whose energies had been absorbed in the antislavery movement channeled them now into the battle for Indian rights. . . . To them the objective was to assimilate the Indian into American life by teaching some of the arts of white civilization. . . . Essential elements leading toward salvation were conversion to Christianity, education, manual arts, and individual ownership of land that was to be worked by the Indian as a farmer, regardless of how unfamiliar with agriculture the Indian might be." Stevens's onetime colleague on the House Ways and Means Committee, John Sherman, pushed through a bill to demonetize silver and supported other legislation to retire greenbacks, contrary to what Stevens wanted in the war's immediate aftermath. But Stevens had said that "this word 'compromise,' when applied to human rights, and constitutional rights, I abhor." Legislation on fiscal and industrial issues were a different matter, but he also demonstrated throughout his life a belief in reform, whatever the era or subject.[30]

During the debate over the Thirteenth Amendment, the House applauded when Stevens said, "I will be satisfied if my epitaph shall be written thus: 'Here lies one who never rose to any eminence, and who only courted the low ambition to have it said that he had striven to ameliorate the condition of the poor, the lowly, the downtrodden of every race and language and color." But in pursuing some of the policies designed to accomplish those goals, perhaps most notably in industrializing the West, with its consequences for Native peoples, Stevens showed how inherent contradictions can interfere with doing the right thing. As Hans Trefousse has observed, "That the United States was, at the same time, developing into one of the world's industrial giants did not make the staggering task of reconstruction easier." Nor did it always promote the egalitarianism that was the main hallmark of the life of Thaddeus Stevens. That he was among those promoting that development underscores the complexity of the issues of the time and those who fought over them.[31]

NOTES

1. The first two quotations are in Eric Foner, "Thaddeus Stevens, Confiscation, and Reconstruction," in *The Hofstadter Aegis: A Memorial,* ed. Stanley Elkins and Eric McKitrick (New York: Alfred A. Knopf, 1974), 154–83, republished in Foner, *Politics and Ideology in the Age of the Civil War* (New York: Oxford University Press, 1980), 128–49. For Stevens's comments about men not being angels, see Cong. Globe, 39th Cong., 1st Sess., 3148 (1866). See also *New York Times,* August 13, 1868. The modern classic work on Reconstruction is Eric Foner, *Reconstruction: America's Unfinished Revolution, 1863–1877* (New York: Harper and Row, 1988). See also Mark Wahlgren Summers, *The Ordeal of the Reunion: A New History of Reconstruction* (Chapel Hill: University of North Carolina Press, 2014), and Heather Cox Richardson, *The Death of Reconstruction: Race, Labor, and Politics in the Post–Civil War North, 1865–1901* (Cambridge, MA: Harvard University Press, 2001).

2. Richard N. Current, *Old Thad Stevens: A Story of Ambition* (Madison: University of Wisconsin Press, 1942); T. Harry Williams, *Lincoln and the Radicals* (Madison: University of Wisconsin Press, 1941), 6; Eric L. McKitrick, *Andrew Johnson and Reconstruction* (Chicago: University of Chicago Press, 1960), 267–68; Hans L. Trefousse, *The Radical Republicans: Lincoln's Vanguard of Racial Justice* (New York: Alfred A. Knopf, 1969), 329, 338; David Donald, *The Politics of Reconstruction* (Baton Rouge: Louisiana State University Press, 1965), 59–64; Foner, *Politics and Ideology,* 128. On the era's historiography, see John David Smith and J. Vincent Lowery, eds., *The Dunning School: Historians, Race, and the Meaning of Reconstruction* (Lexington: University Press of Kentucky, 2013).

3. The psychobiography is Fawn M. Brodie, *Thaddeus Stevens: Scourge of the South* (New York: W. W. Norton, 1959). The scholarly biography is Hans L. Trefousse, *Thaddeus Stevens: Nineteenth-Century Egalitarian* (Chapel Hill: University of North Carolina Press, 1997). Obvious references in popular culture include D. W. Griffith's *Birth of a Nation* (1915), based on Thomas Dixon's novel *The Clansman* (1905), and *Lincoln*, the 2012 film directed by Steven Spielberg. See also Jack Brubaker, "Regarding Lydia Smith, Details Remain Unclear," November 15, 2012, chap. 7 of "Revisiting the Life and Legacy of Thaddeus Stevens," Lancaster Online, https://lancasteronline.com/news/regarding-lydia-smith-details-remain-unclear/article_f3dafc03-226a-51ac-a688-5f159692e2cd.html.

4. Elliott West, "Reconstruction in the West," in "Forum: The Future of Reconstruction Studies," *Journal of the Civil War Era* 7 (March 2017): 14 (available online at http://journalofthecivilwarera.org/forum-the-future-of-reconstruction-studies/reconstruction-in-the-west/); West, "Reconstructing Race," *Western Historical Quarterly* 33 (Spring 2003): 6–26; Heather Cox Richardson, *West from Appomattox: The Reconstruction of America after the Civil War* (New Haven, CT: Yale University Press, 2007), 1, 4; Steven Hahn, "The Widest Implications of Disorienting the Civil War Era," in Adam Arenson and Andrew R. Graybill, eds., *Civil War Wests: Testing the Limits of the United States* (Berkeley: University of California Press, 2015), 265–74; Steven Hahn, *A Nation without Borders: The United States and Its World in an Age of Civil Wars, 1830–1910* (New York: Viking/Random House, 2016). See also Virginia Scharff, ed., *Empire and Liberty: The Civil War and the West* (Berkeley: University of California Press, 2015); and Michael Green, "Abraham Lincoln, Nevada, and the Law of Unintended Consequences," *Nevada Historical Society Quarterly* 52 (Summer 2009): 85–108.

5. Walter A. McDougall, *Throes of Democracy: The American Civil War Era, 1829–1877* (New York: HarperCollins, 2008), 502; *Chicago Tribune*, May 16, 1866.

6. Alexander McClure, *Abraham Lincoln and the Men of War-Times* (Philadelphia: Times Publishing, 1892), 257; Trefousse, *Thaddeus Stevens*, 150–60. On the whiggish approach to the presidency, see David Herbert Donald, "A Whig in the White House," in *Lincoln Reconsidered: Essays on the Civil War Era*, 3rd ed. (New York: Vintage Books, 2001), 133–47; Stephen B. Oates, "Abraham Lincoln: Republican in the White House," in *Abraham Lincoln and the American Political Tradition*, ed. John L. Thomas (Amherst: University of Massachusetts Press, 1986), 98–110.

7. Stevens to William D. Kelley, Caledonia, May 30, 1865, in *The Selected Papers of Thaddeus Stevens*, vol. 2, *April 1865–August 1868*, ed. Beverly Wilson Palmer and Holly Byers Ochoa (Pittsburgh: University of Pittsburgh Press, 1998), 6–7; Stevens to Andrew Johnson, Philadelphia, July 6, 1865, ibid., 7.

8. *Lancaster Evening Express*, September 8, 1865, in Palmer and Ochoa, *Selected Papers of Thaddeus Stevens*, 12–27.

9. Cong. Globe, 39th Cong., 1st Sess., 72–75 (1866); 39th Cong., 2nd Sess. 251–52 (1867, pt. 1).

10. *New York Herald*, September 10, 1866; *New York Times*, September 7, 11, 1866.

11. *New York Times*, January 7, 1867; Cong. Globe, 39th Cong., 2nd Sess., 1076, 1317 (1867, pt. 2).

12. Trefousse, *Thaddeus Stevens*, 224–35. See also Cong. Globe, 40th Cong., 2nd Sess., 1399–1400 (1868, pt. 2).

13. Daniel Walker Howe, *The Political Culture of the American Whigs* (Chicago: University of Chicago Press, 1979); Michael F. Holt, *The Rise and Fall of the American Whig Party: Jacksonian Politics and the Onset of Civil War* (New York: Oxford University Press, 1999).

14. Cong. Globe, 37th Cong., 2nd Sess., 1949–50 (1862); ibid., 40th Cong., 2nd Sess., 3660–61 (pt. 4), 1966–68 (1868, pt. 2), 4136 (pt. 5); Stevens to William H. Seward, Washington, April 11, 1867, in Palmer and Ochoa, *Selected Papers of Thaddeus Stevens*, 303; Seward to Stevens, Washington, April 11, 1867, ibid., 304. The interpretation of Seward as an imperial architect owes a great deal to Walter LaFeber, *The New Empire: An Interpretation of American Expansion, 1860–1898* (Ithaca, NY: Cornell University Press, 1963, 1998).

15. Christopher Shepard, "Make No Distinctions between Rich and Poor: Thaddeus Stevens and Class Equality," *Pennsylvania History* 80 (Winter 2013): 46–47; Current, *Old Thad Stevens*, 197, 320; Cong. Globe, 39th Cong., 1st Sess., 3497 (1866); ibid., 39th Cong., 2nd Sess., 1608–9 (1867, pt. 3). See Foner, *Politics and Ideology*, 137–38; Eugene P. Moehring, *Urbanism and Empire in the Far West: 1840–1890* (Reno: University of Nevada Press, 2004).

16. *Chicago Tribune*, November 11, 1867. See also *New York Tribune*, November 26, 1867, 4; and Irwin Unger, *The Greenback Era: A Social and Political History of American Finance, 1865–1879* (Princeton, NJ: Princeton University Press, 1964).

17. *Chicago Tribune*, November 10, 27, 1867, August 4, 1868.

18. *Chicago Tribune*, November 27, 1866; Cong. Globe, 40th Cong., 1st Sess., 203–8 (1867).

19. David M. Potter, *The Impending Crisis, 1848–1861*, completed and ed. Don E. Fehrenbacher (New York: Harper and Row, 1976), 145–76; Kevin Waite, "Jefferson Davis and Proslavery Visions of Empire in the Far West," *Journal of the Civil War Era* 6 (December 2016): 536–64; William Deverell, *Railroad Crossing: Californians and the Railroad, 1850–1910* (Berkeley: University of California Press, 1994), 27; Cong. Globe, 37th Cong., 2nd Sess., 1949–50 (1862); Heather Cox Richardson, *The Greatest Nation of the Earth: Republican Economic Policies during the Civil War* (Cambridge, MA: Harvard University Press, 1997), 170–208; Michael S. Green, *Freedom, Union, and Power: Lincoln and His Party during the Civil War* (New York: Fordham University Press, 2004), 300–330; Richard J. Orsi, *Sunset Limited: The Southern Pacific Railroad and the Development of the American West* (Berkeley: University of California Press, 2005).

20. Richardson, *Greatest Nation*, 182, 198–200; Cong. Globe, 37th Cong., 2nd Sess., 1949–50 (1862).

21. Cong. Globe, 38th Cong., 1st Sess., 3022 (1864); Trefousse, *Thaddeus Stevens*, 143–44, 194; Robert M. Utley, *Frontier Regulars: The United States Army and the Indian, 1866–1891* (New York: Macmillan, 1973), 10–14, 47, 93–94, 121–23.

22. Cong. Globe, 38th Cong., 1st Sess., 3154–56 (1864). The "colony" interpretation is expressed in Bernard DeVoto, "The West: A Plundered Province," *Harper's Magazine*, August 1934, 355–64. See also William G. Robbins, *Colony & Empire: The Capitalist Transformation of the American West* (Lawrence: University Press of Kansas, 1994).

23. Richard White, *Railroaded: The Transcontinentals and the Making of Modern America* (New York: W. W. Norton, 2011); McKitrick, *Johnson and Reconstruction,* 264; Cong. Globe, 40th Cong., 1st Sess., 672 (1867); Utley, *Frontier Regulars,* 93–94; *Letter of the Secretary of War, Transmissing Information Respecting the Protection of the Routes across the Continent to the Pacific from Molestation by Hostile Indians,* 39th Cong., 2nd Sess., H. Exec. Doc. 23, 10. See also Current, *Old Thad Stevens,* 312–13.

24. Cong. Globe, 36th Cong., 1st Sess., 1805–7 (1860); Richardson, *West from Appomattox,* 37.

25. Cong. Globe, 39th Cong., 1st Sess., 1684 (1866). On Sand Creek, see Ari Kelman, *A Misplaced Massacre: Struggling over the Memory of Sand Creek* (Cambridge, MA: Harvard University Press, 2013).

26. Cong. Globe, 40th Cong., 1st Sess., 204–5 (1867). For this point, see esp. Carole Emberton, "Axes of Empire: Race, Region, and the 'Greater Reconstruction' of Federal Authority after Emancipation," in *Rethinking American Emancipation: Legacies of Slavery and the Quest for Black Freedom,* ed. William A. Link and James J. Broomall (New York: Cambridge University Press, 2016), 119–45.

27. Cong. Globe, 39th Cong., 2nd Sess., 1750 (1867, pt. 3). See also Mary Jane Warde, *When the Wolf Came: The Civil War and the Indian Territory* (Fayetteville: University of Arkansas Press, 2013); Lawrence M. Hauptman, *Between Two Fires: American Indians in the Civil War* (New York: Free Press, 1995).

28. Cong. Globe, 38th Cong., 2nd Sess., 1040 (1865); 38th Cong., 1st Sess., 2342 (1864).

29. Cong. Globe, 38th Cong., 1st Sess., 2342 (1864).

30. Rodman W. Paul, *The Far West and the Great Plains in Transition, 1859–1900* (New York: Harper and Row, 1988), 134–35.

31. Cong. Globe, 38th Cong., 2nd Sess., 266 (1865); Trefousse, *Radical Republicans,* 337.

A CONVERSATION WITH
BRUCE LEVINE AND JAMES OAKES

Moderated by Randall M. Miller

This "conversation" with Bruce Levine and James Oakes, held on September 18, 2015, was the keynote for the conference. It ranged widely but principally focused on the personalities and political ideas, issues, and interests of mid-nineteenth-century America that defined and then disrupted the party systems and tore apart the Union. Levine and Oakes also discussed the ways that James Buchanan, and to a lesser extent Thaddeus Stevens, shaped the politics of the era and the centrality of the slavery question in determining political categories and partisan loyalties.[1]

RANDALL M. MILLER: Welcome. Let me introduce this evening very quickly and then turn it over to our very distinguished guests. Politics is about power—getting power and using power. In America politics largely, but not wholly, has played out through the formation and reconfiguration of party systems, realignments and dealignments, and all those things political scientists like to write about. But in our democratically implied politics, it has also been a product of personality and principles, and also place, recalling Tip O'Neill's oft-quoted maxim that all politics is local. We will be grappling with all of these elements tonight, and tomorrow, as the scholars, and we hope you all too, will ponder, discuss, and debate the characters, the dynamics, and the directions of the politics of the mid-nineteenth century. This was a politics that mixed principles with personalities and with place in what proved to be a very combustible brew that eventually exploded into the Civil War, but it also led to a rethinking of what the nation ought [to] be and even what it might do. The convulsions of the mid-nineteenth century both reflected and affected questions about who belongs in the power struggles that would define that nation and who decides what democracy really meant or might mean. These are questions that echo even today.

Historians and others have been trying to understand American politics since the beginning of the republic. The methodologies have changed over time; so too have the focus and the emphasis, and even the definitions of politics have become more expansive and inclusive. Students of politics now recognize that political interest, identity, and activity extended beyond party systems. Indeed, the people acting outside traditional party frameworks have intruded into, disrupted, and redirected party politics and led us into seeing new people—women, blacks, and others—gaining places in the public square. All this and more will be the interest of our scholars tonight and tomorrow, and we hope it will be one that interests and engages you as well.

To set the stage, we have asked two of America's most eminent historians to have a conversation about the lay of the political landscape of America in what we might fairly now call the Civil War era. They have written much important work on the subject—in fact, essential work about politics. And they are going to ask us to think in new ways, as their work has done, about the politics of that turbulent time. Let me introduce them to you and turn over the stage to them because that is why you are here, for a friendly conversation.

As both panelists are astute political historians who have studied the middle period of the nineteenth century, we will begin by asking them to comment briefly on what they consider to be the principal features and dynamics of politics during the mid-nineteenth century—what drove it and what undid it—because it was also a time not only of people continuing or to trying to keep [the] party systems but also the party systems coming apart and even giving rise to a new party, that we call the Grand Old Party, even though it is the second-oldest one we still have.

So, if you would, just comment on what you see to be the central features of mid-nineteenth-century politics and especially anything you think we need to know to understand the dynamics and directions of those politics.

BRUCE LEVINE: I think the central fact is the one already alluded to: the breakup of what historians call the Second Party System—the dominance of political life in the United States by two parties, the Democratic Party and the Whig Party. Mainstream Whig and Democratic leaders knew very well that if slavery should come to occupy center place in American politics, both parties would likely split, since both were national parties. So they made tremendous and protracted efforts to keep that issue muffled. But the slavery issue simply proved too powerful to be suppressed. Instead, it played a central role, first, in the destruction of the Whig Party, and then, in the splitting of the Democratic Party. And in the midst of these processes there emerges, as Randall said, this brand new party (the Republican Party), which on its first outing in 1856 does tremendously well in the free states and on its second outing, as you well know, gets the majority of votes in the free states, which is enough to put its candidate in the White House. I think this is testimony, among other things, to the limits of what party leaders can do. More specifically, it testifies to the intrinsic power of this slavery question—that it simply cannot be eternally suppressed because it and its implications resonate so strongly in the minds and hearts of the voters so that those who work so hard to kill it are themselves destroyed.

JAMES OAKES: I think the $64,000 question then would be, Why *couldn't* the slavery issue be suppressed? What was there about the North or the South that made this question of slavery so politically explosive? Part of the answer goes back to one of the anomalies of US history: Most New World slave societies were colonies of one European nation or another, and emancipation in many of those colonies was imposed by the imperial center back in Europe. In the Spanish American colonies, abolition was the byproduct of imperial crises that spun out of control and became revolutions. The anomaly that emerged out of the American Revolution was that a slave society was no longer a colonial society. Instead, a free-labor society and slave society were fused together within a single polity that, as a result of the Revolution, moved in two very different directions. First, a "North" had come into existence as slavery was abolished in a series of states, and second, slavery in the plantation colonies got an unanticipated boost by the emergence of "King Cotton," making the South much stronger for much longer than anyone would have imagined in 1776. The irony is that the cotton economy came into existence to meet the exploding demand of consumers and textile man-ufacturers in the North. The South's dependence on the developing capi-talist economies was both the source of its strength and its fatal weakness. So out of the Revolution comes this fundamental difference—ultimately a fundamental antagonism—between the slave and free states.

The suppression of the slavery issue in the Second Party System, the "shutdown" as it were, emerged in the wake of the Missouri crisis. Lead-ing American politicians came to the conclusion that the slavery issue was so divisive, so explosive, that it could very easily tear the Union apart. Antislavery politics had to be suppressed for the sake of the Union. That is the point at which I would pick up on Bruce's observation: What the collapse of that Second Party System shows is that the shutdown did not work in the long run. Why it did not work is, as I said, the $64,000 question.

LEVINE: Just to throw in two more cents: you can see this very deliberate intention to build and use the two parties of the Second Party System precisely to preserve the unity of the country in the famous letter that Martin Van Buren wrote to a Richmond newspaper publisher during the Era of Good Feelings, saying that this Missouri crisis occurred ex-actly because we did not have strong nationwide parties dedicated to suppressing this issue.

OAKES: National parties with northern and southern wings.

LEVINE: That is right. Van Buren said that when we had national parties, northern members of these parties knew it was necessary for them to help their southern colleagues suppress this kind of issue for fear of the destruction of the party on which they both depended for success. There-fore we need to put parties like those that once existed back together

South Carolina's "Ultimatum." Currier and Ives, 1860. Courtesy Eberly Family
Special Collections Library, Penn State University, State College.

again, and what we especially need to do is unite the common folk of the
North with the southern elite. And that is not a bad description, at least
in rough terms, of what the Democratic Party tried to be and succeeded
in being to a large extent and for a long time.

OAKES: One of the ways to understand James Buchanan—whose most
significant career was in the 1850s—is as a leader of the Democratic Party
that had traditionally suppressed the slavery issue at a moment when
the issue could no longer be contained. The northern wing of the Democratic Party was collapsing because of the slavery issue, and Buchanan
was engaged in a desperate effort to keep that issue out of politics. Faced
with an essentially intractable choice between the two wings of his party,
Buchanan chose to go pro-southern, thinking that was the only way to
hold the national party together, rather than save his northern base and
ally with Stephen Douglas to form a de facto northern Democratic Party.
After all, the national party could not exist without the southern wing.
The point is that the whole system was on the verge of collapse no matter

which path Buchanan chose. It is easy to conclude that he made the disastrously wrong choice, but the fact was that either one of the choices he had was going to lead to a crack up.

MILLER: My understanding of Buchanan's role, since you brought that up, was [that] he was central in the 1850s because of what he did and what he represented. Are you suggesting that he was part of the Democratic Party's effort to continue to suppress the slavery issue because invariably it was not just divisive but it was destructive?

OAKES: Yes.

MILLER: But there are those who will also argue that he was so bound over to the southern interest that he was willing, if necessary, to play to that interest even against those Democrats who were becoming increasingly wary of the costs of bowing before the so-called slave power. Perhaps you want to comment on not just the personal or political dilemma of Buchanan, but the dilemma people like Buchanan faced, at that critical moment, with a newly emerged political party—and nobody knew that that Republican Party would be the successful party.

OAKES: That is right, nobody knew.

MILLER: But as Bruce has pointed out, they did remarkably well electorally in 1856 and continued to do well so that clearly the Buchanan Democrats knew what they were up against. Could both of you comment on Buchanan's role in these developments and what he represented within the northern Democratic Party.

OAKES: Just to elaborate on what I said before, by the late 1840s, Buchanan could see that an explosion was coming from David Wilmot and other Pennsylvania Democrats, who broke with the proslavery consensus in the party and provoked the beginning of this disruption whose end result was the Civil War. Buchanan, again like all those Democrats, had a decision to make: Am I going to side with the southern wing, or am I going save the northern Democracy by pulling away from our dependency on the southerners? He makes this conscious decision, very early on, that he was going to go the pro-southern way. His position in 1850 endeared him to the Nashville Convention, which was a kind of protosecessionist convention that ultimately fell apart, but Buchanan was the person, the northern Democrat, the southerners already trusted the most. And he stayed that way all through the 1850s. So Buchanan's great nemesis in the 1850s was not, ironically, Thaddeus Stevens; it was Stephen Douglas. Douglas became, in spite of himself, the leader of the movement to pull the northern Democrats, northern Democracy, away from its excessive dependence, its destructive dependence, on the southern wing. Buchanan was the person who said no, we cannot go that way, we have to stay with the southern wing, and as a result you got a brutal—I mean really vicious—internal division, internal war, inside the northern wing of the Democratic Party led by Buchanan on one side and Stephen Douglas on the other side. And in the background as the northern Democrats and southern Democrats split apart, which they finally did in 1860, along came this other party, the overtly antislavery Republican Party, which ultimately sent Thaddeus Stevens to represent almost exactly the same area in Congress that Buchanan came from. As Bruce said in his opening remarks, a cavernous gap opened once the Second Party System collapsed.

LEVINE: I want to follow up on Jim's remark about the role of Stephen Douglas. One of the most interesting aspects of all this is the conduct of Stephen Douglas—who I think could also have been called, for a considerable period of time, a northern man with southern principles (or "doughface," as they were more commonly known). Like Martin Van Buren (who was arguably the architect of the Democratic Party), Douglas found himself bending and being forced to bend to the pressures he felt from the population of the North. I am emphasizing this because it was very common, especially in an earlier generation of historians, to explain everything that happened by focusing on a rather thin stratum of politicians and then judging the degree to which they did or did not succeed in holding the Union together. This previous generation of historians eventually judged that these people let it fall apart because there was something about their intrinsic qualities that was wrong—they were careerists, or they were weak, or they got carried away. But you have to start recognizing that the population at large was very much involved in this story.

One of the great pleasures of being a historian, as has been said before, is that we get to read other people's mail. Among other things we now get to read is a bunch of letters circulating in the 1840s among northern Democratic politicians saying we are going to get killed at the polls if we keep kowtowing to the southern members of our party in the defense of slavery and that we are already suffering for the role we played in bringing in Texas and in initiating a war with Mexico. We have to find a way to prove to antislavery northern Democratic voters that we are not simply putty in the hands of the South. That is where the Wilmot Proviso comes from. When David Wilmot of Pennsylvania gets up and proposes a resolution that would bar slavery from any lands taken from Mexico, that was an attempt to prove his bona fides to the northern Democratic rank and file even though it meant taking on southern Democrats. And the proviso gets overwhelming support at all levels of northern political society. Wilmot was acting for the Van Buren faction of the northern Democrats, and Van Buren winds up in 1848 as the presidential candidate of the newly formed Free-Soil Party—the last person in the world you would have anticipated playing that role ten years earlier. And the same kind of thing happens to Stephen Douglas later on over Kansas, when, once again, we read a plethora of letters from his allies saying, if we are perceived in the North as turning Kansas over to the South, we are finished as a political party in the North, and if the South wants to destroy the northern wing of the Democratic Party, they should just keep pushing us to play this ignominious proslavery role; we need to draw the line and say "no more." And I think Douglas's fight against Buchanan is partly the expression of that pressure from below.

OAKES: We do not have public opinion polls, and there are very few places we can point to where the electorate expresses its views on slavery directly. There were no referenda on slavery except in particular places like Kansas. But one way to gauge the significance of northern public opinion and the strength of northern antislavery sentiment is to look at the votes in the House of Representatives. There were about 140 northern representatives in the House in 1850 and only about 35 voted for the Fugitive Slave Act. A majority of northern congressmen had voted against admitting Missouri as a slave state; a majority of them voted for the Wilmot Proviso; a majority of northern congressmen voted against the annexation of Texas, against the Kansas-Nebraska Act, [and] against the Lecompton Constitution. Whig representatives cast most of those anti-slavery votes. But more and more Democrats in the North were feeling this pressure from voters, in part because the southern Democrats were pushing harder and harder, making increasingly aggressive demands on northern Democrats to demonstrate their commitment to slavery. Those southern demands were aggravating northern voters and making the situation impossible for people like David Wilmot, Martin Van Buren, and Stephen Douglas. Under that pressure, each decided in the end to break with the South. Buchanan made a different decision; he wanted to hold the Democratic Party together by purging it of those dissident factions. But as I said at the beginning, one way or another, it is hard to see how that party could have held together given those pressures.

MILLER: It almost seems that when you talk about destruction of the Second Party System and the rise of the Republican Party and the dissensions in the Democratic Party, that it seemed to be nonnegotiable almost because of the slavery question, that there is a kind of inevitability that the whole system had to come apart and in so doing, as some people argue, that the failure of the Democratic Party in 1860 meant the end of the last national institution that could even hope to bind the sections together. But one can almost read that once the slavery issue was in, and there is no way of getting it out, that secession is almost inevitable, especially given the ramped-up politics of the southerners, who were demanding that either northerners submit to their interests or they would leave the Union. Would you argue something along those lines?

OAKES: I do not argue inevitability.

MILLER: Not even if the Democrats—

OAKES: Irreconcilable but not inevitable, I would say. Then it comes down to a set of events and circumstances that could have played out in different ways, I suppose, but the conflict was fundamental even if the war was not inevitable. Douglas, for example, could not take an overtly pro-slavery position that would mollify southerners because it would alienate northerners, so he tried desperately to unite northern and southern voters through his increasingly demagogic racism, but that failed miserably because it was an evasion of the fundamental issue of slavery.

LEVINE: I agree with that. You have got the classic case of an irresistible force meeting an immovable object. People ask, as Randall Miller did, whether or not this collision is inevitable, I think that certainly the answer is no. If an irresistible force ceases to be irresistible, then it need not collide, and if the immovable object moves, the problem goes away too. So to make this a little bit more concrete, if one side or the other had been prepared to capitulate, which is how these things often resolve themselves, then no, there would not have been secession and war. But what you had, instead, was a situation in which, at least by 1860, not only was the South unwilling to yield but at last the North was unwilling to yield too. My boy Thaddeus Stevens had been waiting, and waiting, and waiting for the North to get up on its hind legs and finally say, "No." He said he did not fault the southern members of Congress for what they were doing; they were just standing up for their interests. I wish (Stevens said) the people that I live among would do the same thing. By 1860, they were prepared to do the same thing.

OAKES: At a certain point, there was no way to avoid the war, but the conflict was irreconcilable long before the war became inevitable. Instead, there were important changes that took place, altering the balance of power between the North and the South. For example, the northern economy began to grow much more rapidly, as did the northern population, and those things made the North economically more powerful than the South and the northern majority an increasing political threat. Now, we cannot say that the transformation of northern society was *inevitable,* or that it made the war inevitable. But we can say that it was a crucial precondition for the situation that developed in 1860.

You also needed an abolitionist movement to cut through that suppression in the 1830s and force Americans to come to the realization that slavery was a problem that had to be addressed and at the same time made a number of practical political proposals by which slavery could be dealt with. This "second wave" of abolitionists is crucial to understanding what the Republican Party in the 1850s, including Abraham Lincoln, meant when they vowed to put slavery "on a course of ultimate extinction." This was a genuinely radical proposal, no matter how moderately it was framed. It meant that Lincoln and the Republicans were committed to the destruction of southern slave society—slowly, rapidly, however. When you talk about putting the largest and wealthiest slave society on Earth on a course to "extinction," as far as I am concerned, you are talking radical social and political transformation. Once you grasp that, there is no need to describe the South's behavior as inexplicable or "hysterical." The triumph of antislavery politics was an existential threat to slavery. The slaveholders knew this. They understood the terms of the debate. And once somebody committed to that project was elected president, it made sense to secede from the Union, even if secession turned out [to be] a spectacular miscalculation. It made sense by 1861 for southern leaders to decide that *we gotta get out of here. We gotta get out of here.*

MILLER: Related to what you are talking about as to irreconcilability and the crisis of the late 1850s, as you were suggesting, not only were they at loggerheads, it seems that there was no backing down. I am just curious of the extent to which it all added to this element we might call the rubric of personality. The rhetoric in itself has gotten so amped up in terms of threats and counterthreats, but also not just threats to the other party but threats given to the politicians themselves, that if they do not do what is necessary—that is, if the Republicans do not stand up for their principles, if the Democrats do not stand up for their principles, North or South, or whatever it is—we are going to punish you at the polls and perhaps in other ways. This could also relate to the extent to which manhood figured in the posturing and the rhetoric, and even the politics of the time, once it becomes almost an all-or-nothing thing. And that, I think, comes back to the personality of people like Buchanan, people like Douglas, people like Thaddeus Stevens, whoever, so perhaps you want to say something about that combination, or you do not want to talk about it at all.

LEVINE: Undoubtedly, personality issues feature in these things. But I think that is a secondary factor. By 1860, people with certain kinds of personalities have been selected out by this historical process, so it was not a coincidence that they were the ones who found themselves in the positions to make the major decisions at that point. When the Crittenden Compromise was proposed, which would have extended the Missouri Compromise line all the way across the country and allowed slavery south of it anywhere in existing territories *or any territory acquired in the future* (like Cuba and possibly other parts of Mexico and Central America), Lincoln basically said that if we give in, the party is dead; that is the end of the Republican Party. We have taken all this time, put all this effort, into building this kind of party up to where it was able now to win a presidential election. If we capitulate now on this question, not only will the South do this to us over and over and over again in the future, but there will be no "us" because this party will implode, because the rank and file will not tolerate that capitulation. And reading the letters that Republican congressmen were getting from their constituents bears that out—that the Republican base, the Republican voters were pushing their representatives not to cave in. Now here "manliness" undoubtedly does figure in, but I cannot help remembering an entry in the diary of Mary Chesnut, one of the prominent plantation mistresses of the day, saying during the secession crisis that she had had enough of the talking—she wanted war. I do not think she was demonstrating her manliness at the time; she was demonstrating a sentiment that pretty well cut across gender lines by 1860.

OAKES: We know that over the course of the 1850s, as the slavery issue in Congress was becoming increasingly divisive, there were more and more physical fights breaking out on the floor of Congress—knife wielding, pistol waving, challenges to duels. The most famous case was when [Massachusetts senator] Charles Sumner was beaten by [South Carolina representative] Preston Brooks, but that was only one of many such incidents. What was going on? Was this an outbreak of masculine hubris? For years and years and years southern politicians would threaten opponents if they tried to bring up any antislavery issues, but as long as most of the opposition to slavery was limited to the Whigs, antislavery people would back down. Remember that as a party the Whigs, like the Democrats, were officially committed to suppressing the slavery issue in national politics—despite the fact that most northern Whigs were antislavery. After the Whig Party collapsed in the 1850s, it was replaced in Congress by an increasing number of Republicans whose party was openly and unashamedly antislavery, and *those* people, people like [Ohio senator] Ben Wade, responded very differently to southern bullying. When he was threatened, he would not back down. He would stare down his opponents, as if to say: *bring it on.* The southern militants were not used to that. So it did become this kind of macho thing, and the manifestation of it was more and more physical violence on the floor of Congress.

There were other aspects of the sectional controversy that sometimes reflected the broader cultural assumptions about masculinity. Matt Pinsker has a great story about the way Lincoln would belittle the manhood of a fellow Republican—[Massachusetts congressman] Anson Burlingame, I think it was—even though Lincoln was hardly the most macho of politicians. But he *was* the one who held the line in the secession winter and said we will not go there, this is where we stop. Was it in Albany, on his way to Washington, where Lincoln says it is time "to put the foot down," while literally raising his foot and stomping the floor? The point was clear: We are not to go any further. So there is that sort of thing. That said, I think we can go only so far with the issue of manhood. Lincoln was not Ben Wade, and he was not the kind of person who went out of his way to pick fights. He tended to avoid them.

MILLER: We are in Lancaster County, Pennsylvania, close to Maryland. Pennsylvania, Maryland, and Virginia were border states, as was Illinois. One of the questions that often arises is whether people in the border states were more amenable to working out compromises (because of their cross-familial, cross-commercial, and other connections across a border that separated the slave states from free states), or whether that border had the opposite effect. Were the border states the tinderbox for conflict because they had already been at each other over all kinds of border questions, including those relating to slavery? With people running away to liberty going from Virginia to Pennsylvania, it would beg the question of what Pennsylvanians are going to do about it. And then the other question would be what were Virginians doing that caused enslaved people to flee. Do border-state dynamics mean anything? Does the border mean anything in terms of people's identity? And, of course, Lancaster County had these two border-state politicians who tracked off in different directions, which complicates our story.

OAKES: Yes and no. By 1860, the Democratic Party that Buchanan represented was dead in most of the North. The fact that he kept it alive in Pennsylvania is a testimony to the kind of power Buchanan was able to exercise in the state, but his northern Democratic Party really was dying in the 1850s and is pretty much finished by 1860. I do think there is something to the fact that the border is the area where you see a lot of this fighting—the border war, as Stanley Harrold calls it.[2] And certainly if one looks at the difference between the electoral results in 1856 and 1860, it was the border North that flipped between those two elections and therefore definitively turned the tide of American politics.

So, yes, the border North is significant, but so is the border South, if only because the *goal* of the antislavery movement was always to get the border South states to abolish slavery on their own, thereby isolating and weakening slavery in the Deep South. We think of New Jersey's abolition of slavery in 1804 as the end of "the first wave" of state abolitions, but antislavery northerners looked at New Jersey and asked, "*Why did it stop?*" It was not supposed to have stopped. Let us restart it, beginning with the border states. So the border South is also crucial to the understanding of the antislavery project for many of the reasons secession did not succeed in those states. The slaveholders were not as powerful in the border South, and the states had stronger ties to the North. Their economies were the most diversified of the slave states. So the assumption among the antislavery people was that those places were most likely to abolish slavery, especially when the federal government shifted to an antislavery bias. The border states were not going to get their escaped slaves back so easily. It would no longer be safe for masters to travel in the North with their slaves. The drain of slaves from the upper to the lower South would accelerate as border-state masters migrated to the cotton belt to protect their assets, but they would be locked out of the western territories. If the opponents of slavery managed to take control of the federal government, the first slave states to feel the pressure of federal hostility would be the border states.

LEVINE: Yes, once again I substantially agree with Jim. I think there is no question but that the border states play a different role than does the Deep South or the far North. It is not an accident that secession begins farther south or that the most steadfast support for the Republican Party is found farther north, including in the upper Midwest, across the northern tier of the midwestern states, whereas the lower halves of Illinois, Indiana, Ohio tend to be far slower to move that way, partly because much of the southern portions of these states had been settled by migrants out of the South, migrants who may not have liked slavery much but who still felt a residual loyalty to their friends, family, culture, and so on, and were not interested in seeing those people and things threatened. So, as Jim was saying, in 1856 there is a tier of free states who go for Buchanan.

And then the question is going to be how is the Republican Party going to get them, because they are going to need those states, including Pennsylvania, if they are going to win in 1860. And a number of people in the Republican Party are fighting in the name of a desired victory to lure these less strongly antislavery voters into their ranks and urging the Republican Party to tone down its antislavery politics, believing that that is the way we are going to win these people over, by being less aggressive in our opposition to the expansion of slavery. Lincoln and others say no, we are not going to do that, and they carry the day at the party's 1860 convention. And then, even though they did not bend to those moderating pressures, they do win those states of the lower North during the election. So while the border states of the North may not have been as firm in their antislavery convictions and fervor as New England or the upper Midwest, still the South was pushing them by 1860 harder than they were willing to tolerate. *Dred Scott*, the beating of Sumner, a whole series of questions of conscience—the attempt to steal Kansas for the South—had finally pushed even those states too far, thereby overcoming this political difference within the North.

Concerning differences between the upper and lower South: It is often said if only Lincoln had not issued a call to arms after [the attack on Fort Sumter], the upper South never would have joined the Confederacy, and the war could have been avoided, because the initial Confederacy (of the lower South) would have died. But that argument ignores the fact that the upper South, while it did not immediately secede, had said, essentially, we'll stay if Lincoln basically backs down, abandons the Republican Party's platform of 1860, and agrees to allow slavery to expand into all or some of the federal territory. When they eventually discovered that Lincoln was going to stick to his guns, I think those people were probably going to leave.

MILLER: Both of you have suggested that there was something at least of an antislavery sentiment that had grown up across the North that, by the late 1850s, included the border areas of Pennsylvania, even perhaps the middle parts of Illinois. Is that a fair representation?

LEVINE: Yes.

MILLER: And most people who rallied to the colors after the Confederacy fired on Fort Sumter insisted that they were fighting for the Union and they were not fighting against slavery. They might be anti-southern but they were not antislavery, if antislavery meant that war would mean the end of slavery as an institution. Now we know if they went in that direction, the question would be, if they had so much antislavery sentiment supposedly by 1860 that they could not tolerate a slave power, how do you explain this emphasis upon Union, initially accompanied in many cases by a public denial that they were not really fighting in order to end slavery?

OAKES: I would dispute the second part of the question, but—

MILLER: We are hoping you will dispute something; that is the whole idea.

OAKES: It is an important question. Some of the reason has to do with the makeup of the army, which was disproportionately Democratic and was primarily fighting to save the Union. I think it is not correct to say that Union soldiers were fighting only for the Union and not to end slavery. Rather, from the very beginning there was a substantial dispute within the army about this, and I think it is better to think of it as an internal conflict within the army. The army was forced over time, over the course of the first year, to come into line with policy coming out of Washington. After June or July of 1861, many if not most of the complaints about what the army was doing about slavery involved individual soldiers or officers who *failed* to comply with the policies of admitting blacks into the Union army camps and not sending them back. By late 1861, hardly anybody in Washington was complaining that soldiers were *allowing* slaves to come into their lines, and what complaints there were came almost exclusively from the loyal slave states, where it was much harder for the federal government to justify emancipation. By August of 1861, the official policy of the Union was to emancipate slaves escaping into Union lines from disloyal states or disloyal masters. So I think it is not entirely correct to say that the Union army was [predominantly] pro-Union and not antislavery.

The second thing I would say is I think it is a false dichotomy to say that they were fighting either for the Union or against slavery. One of the things that happened in the middle of the 1830s—and one sees it in the reasoning behind Van Buren's shift and John Quincy Adams's apparent reversal—is that antislavery nationalism or antislavery unionism began to emerge in response to repeated and increasingly aggressive threats of secession coming from the South. By the 1850s, there was a fairly widespread view in the North that being for the Union and being antislavery were essentially the same thing. To put it more simply, proslavery sentiment was increasingly associated with *disunion,* while antislavery northerners were increasingly committed to the perpetuity of the Union. So to say that soldiers were fighting for the Union rather than against slavery misreads the nature of unionism, at least within the Republican Party.

Finally, I think we need to remember that as far as nearly all Americans were concerned—and I think most historians today would agree—the Constitution did not allow Congress to "interfere" with slavery in the states where it existed. This is known among historians as the "Federal Consensus." It followed that, as far as most antislavery politicians were concerned, the Union could not, constitutionally, prosecute a war *for the purpose* of destroying slavery. Yet they "all knew," as Lincoln later said, that the war was caused by slavery, and they believed they had every right to use all the means at the government's disposal to undermine slavery as a means of suppressing the rebellion. If that meant emancipating slaves, they were going to do it. And there is an awful lot of that sort of sentiment during the secession crisis.

The Republican insistence that the war was being fought for the restoration of the Union merely highlights a legal limitation on how the war could formally be defined. From beginning to end, it was *always* [a] war for the restitution of the Union—but that does not mean it was not also an antislavery war. Once again, it was not an either/or proposition. You can see this in the diplomatic correspondence Massachusetts statesman Edward Everett was writing to leaders in England right from the start of the war, saying: "You don't understand. Under the Constitution we can only prosecute this war for the purpose of restoring the Union, but make no mistake," Everett went on (I am paraphrasing here), "this war was caused by slavery and everybody knows the war is about slavery."

Before the war, Thaddeus Stevens was clear about the constitutional limits on federal authority. We have no power under the Constitution to attack slavery in the states where it already exists, he said in 1850. Instead, we are going to attack it this other way. We are going to surround slavery with a cordon of freedom, block it in the territories, and abolish it in Washington DC, suppress it on the high seas, and frustrate your attempts to enforce the fugitive slave laws in the northern states. Lincoln said the same thing in his inaugural address: We have no intention of interfering with slavery in the states where it is legal. He said what Stevens had said, what William Lloyd Garrison, Joshua Giddings, Salmon Chase, Charles Sumner, and Ben Wade said—and their radical antislavery credentials are impeccable. So it is a mistake, I think, to read Lincoln's inaugural remarks as evidence that he did not believe in the war caused by slavery or that slavery was not going to be touched by this war. A few paragraphs after stating that he would not "interfere" with slavery in the states where it existed, he announced that if the slave states seceded, the North would stop returning their fugitive slaves. He had said the same thing in 1859. So there was a difference between promising that the federal government would not *abolish* slavery in a state and promising not to touch it.

LEVINE: I want to emphasize the number of northern soldiers who are not Republicans—the Constitutional Unionists and two wings of the

Democratic Party. In the free states, they get about 45 percent of the vote. Now I think even the northern Democrats disliked slavery, but they were especially anxious to exclude it from where they lived, not (as were the Republicans) aiming to strangle it where it already existed. So if we just assume that non-Republicans made up at least that sizeable a portion of the Union army, that is a big bloc of people who do not want to embark upon an antislavery war in the South. And the interesting story that occurs is how many of those northern soldiers change their minds over the course of the war. And I think those include people whose letters we are acquainted with, who at the beginning of the war are saying "I'll be damned if I am going to fight to free these people." But some of them are saying about a year later "I'm not sure that is right anymore. Now I think the emancipation proclamation is necessary; there is no other way to win this war." And some of them go further still and say "the more I see of slavery now that I'm actually here in the South, the more I realize what a horrifying institution it is, and from now on I am effectively an abolitionist."

MILLER: By the end of the war, most northerners were willing to crush slavery because of the war and the continued maintenance of the war. But it is not the same as being for blacks as being against slavery.

OAKES: Right.

MILLER: Is it not just the matter of crushing the Confederacy and slavery, but also what are we going to build from this war? And these are questions of race and a host of other things. Did the prospect of Reconstruction affect the way people thought about reconstructing American politics? Part of Reconstruction would of necessity be the introduction of at least one new element into politics, the enfranchisement of black men. But was there talk during the Civil War about "reconstruction" in terms of potentially being a revolution? Was Reconstruction also a political revolution?

LEVINE: That is a great question, and it has many, many dimensions. To answer it, first of all, the enfranchisement of black males was an enormous change. Just conceptually, it was an enormous change because in 1857 the Supreme Court said in the *Dred Scott* case that African Americans were not even citizens; in fact, they have no rights at all that white men are bound to respect.[3] Ten years later, or at least a little bit more than that, we were talking about not only acknowledging some sort of citizenship status but enfranchisement as well. So that development, in of itself, was huge.

But, by the way in passing, I think it is unquestionably a revolution. You cannot take the social structure of half of the society and completely change it. You cannot take almost the entire labor force, the people who are really producing the wealth, move them from slavery to freedom, even if they never get any further than that in terms of citizenship or enfranchisement, and not call that a revolution. If that was not a revolution, I do not know what is. And both Thaddeus Stevens and Lincoln said as much.

The other side of Reconstruction is the transfer of political power at the national level out of the hands of the South and its apologists and allies. From Washington through Buchanan with very few exceptions, the federal government, all three branches, had been controlled by southerners and doughfaces. It will be fifty years after the war ends before a man born in the South will sit in the White House again, and the same kind of trend applies to the Speaker of the House, the cabinet, president pro tempore of the Senate, [and] the composition of the Supreme Court. The South, the southern leadership, is pushed into a corner for quite a while in terms of national political power, and I think that is quite clearly a political revolution.

OAKES: And one more thing, of course, is the constitutional structure of the federal government. For the first time, the federal government was asserting its primacy on questions of who is a citizen and who gets to enforce the privileges of citizenship, ultimately enforcing things like black voting in the South. So there was an enormous decrease of southern power and an increase in the power the federal government *claimed it had* to go into states and enforce civil rights. Of course, claiming the power to do something does not mean you have the "bureaucratic capacity" to actually do it. Ultimately, the federal government could not and would not remain in the South to enforce civic equality and voting rights. Still, the

The Last Speech on Impeachment—Thaddeus Stevens Closing the Debate in the House. From *Harper's Weekly,* March 21, 1868, 180.

Civil War and the Reconstruction amendments radically transformed the structure of the American government, at least at the constitutional level.

MILLER: Eric Foner calls Reconstruction the "unfinished revolution," and there was at least one member of Congress who hoped that it would be a revolution that would be not only more radical but [also] more durable than it turned out to be in the short term: Thaddeus Stevens.[4] So, was the "revolution" a failure if one looks at it from the perspective of a Thaddeus Stevens? Or was that revolution, as you suggested, part of a longer process of extending freedom? And was Reconstruction, to ask one of the classic questions, a failure (which I am asking by looking through the experience of Thaddeus Stevens, and what he hoped to achieve)? What was it?

LEVINE: Compared to what Thaddeus Stevens hoped to achieve, it fell far short, and he said shortly before his death that one of the great sorrows of this life was to have fought so hard and lived so long only to see once again the forces of white-supremacist resistance advancing again in the South. He said, basically, it has all been for naught. Well, it had not all been for naught. I do not think that what took place was a counterrevolution, because I think of a counterrevolution as something in which all the gains of the revolution are lost. And, as I said a moment ago, all the gains of the revolution were not lost. Even in the 1870s and 1880s, slavery did not come back, and as bad as life in the post-Reconstruction South was for African Americans, it was not slavery. And there were not too many African Americans calling for the return of slavery in the 1880s. They still saw emancipation as an improvement.

That kind of dynamic, where some of the gains of the revolution at its high point are later lost, it is pretty common in world history. It happened in the French Revolution; it happened in the English Revolution, it happens all the time. At a certain point the forces for revolution run out of steam, it runs out of support, it has exhausted its resources and its energy, and its opponents start to push back, but I think it is a real counterrevolution only if everything in the old regime is restored. And that was not true in France; the peasants had title to the land (and were relieved of feudal burdens) after the French Revolution despite the return of the monarchy. And despite what happened to African Americans under Redemption, they were not driven down to the level at which they had been kept before 1860. Not only socially and politically, but their economic living standards rose, precisely because it was not possible to exploit them to the same degree in legal freedom as was possible in the state of slavery.

OAKES: I agree, and I think it is important to understand that the subtitle of Eric Foner's book is an *unfinished* revolution, not a *failed* revolution. There were specific failures, but I do not think he views Reconstruction as a failed revolution. All revolutions, as Bruce has said, are unfinished. I do not like to say Reconstruction failed; I prefer to say that it was overthrown. You can say that the Republicans should have enforced the civil rights acts and amendments more aggressively or for a longer period of time, but once they lost control of Congress in the 1874 elections, there was not much more they could do. The eminent historian John

Hope Franklin wrote a pioneering book on Reconstruction back in the early 1960s, and at one point he said, almost in passing, that one way or another, at some point the federal government was going to have to return power to the state governments, and when that happened white majorities were going to take control and do what they could to undo whatever they could of Reconstruction. I am not so sure it was quite that inevitable. One reason populism was so brutally repressed was because, even in the 1890s, it represented a real possibility that poor whites and poor blacks could unite around issues of economic justice and democracy. In the end the disfranchisers did succeed in "undoing" an awful lot of Reconstruction, but they could not undo all of it.

LEVINE: Jim and I were at a conference about a year ago where Jim invited the audience to join us to participate in a thought experiment. I am going to do the same thing because I like the idea a lot. Try to imagine the civil rights movement of the 1960s if the African American population is still enslaved. In fact, try to imagine almost all the improvements that took place after the Civil War if slavery had remained in place. I think it simply underlines the fact that change, especially in so-called race relations, has been accomplished by building on the achievements of an earlier period. If slavery had not been eliminated, then we could not have had migration to the extent that it occurred by black people out of the South and out of the countryside into the towns and cities, a migration that made much of the civil rights movement later on possible. So, again, it was the successful destruction of slavery that opened the door to further successes later on. A complete counterrevolution would not have allowed that. We would still have been stuck with slavery very likely until well into the nineteenth century and conceivably even into the beginning of the twentieth. That in turn would have changed everything else.

MILLER: We could go on and on with the gentlemen-scholars' insights, but I would like to shift and invite people from the audience to ask questions.

Because of the need for this to be recorded, I am going to paraphrase the question and get the panel's response. The gentleman asked about an essay yesterday by Sean Wilentz, who argued that slavery was not in the

Constitution per se, and suggesting that one could argue for an antislavery basis for the Constitution, as the antislavery people maintained, and the questioner was asking for a comment.[5]

OAKES: I have read the long forty-to-fifty-page version of Wilentz's arguments at least a half-dozen times, and it is much more nuanced than what appeared in the [*New York*] *Times* yesterday. One needs to understand the very specific nature of what he was saying. Wilentz is saying there was a crucial question on the table in the decades of struggle over slavery between the Revolution and the Civil War: Was there or was there not a constitutional right of property in slaves? Chief Justice Roger Taney declared in his *Dred Scott* decision that there *was* a right to slave property "expressly" stated in the Constitution. Sean is saying that that issue came up in the Constitutional Convention in 1787 and that the southern delegates repeatedly tried to get an explicit recognition of a constitutional right into the Constitution and were repeatedly rebuffed. Previous arguments about what the Constitution has to do with slavery focus on what was *in* the Constitution, on the compromises we can all see in the text. In the longer essay Sean fully acknowledges all the compromises that are in there, the compromises we can all see. But he is also saying that there is something important that is *not* there, deliberately not there—the right of property in slaves that Taney later *put* there, but which the founders emphatically did not. There was simply no way the majority of delegates at the Philadelphia convention were going to insert a property right in slaves into the Constitution. The result was, in Sean's words, a "paradoxical" Constitution, one that recognized and protected slavery in the states where it existed but did not sanction slavery in national law. I am sympathetic to Sean's argument. At the very least it is interesting, and I am persuaded that it is broadly correct.

MILLER: One of the most important things I would argue—and I am not alone in this—is that it is not so much about what is in the Constitution (although there are important elements there that support slavery interests), it is what is not in the Constitution—nothing explicit prohibiting slavery. Thus the Constitution left slavery as a local institution, which is why people like Lincoln can say that there is nothing the federal government can do directly against slavery where it already existed in law. And that was always the problem. That is why slavery had its flashpoints in those places where the federal government might act, and southerners and even northerners wanted them to do something about it. Thus, the conflict occurred in the western territories, where Congress had authority, and the District of Columbia, where Congress had authority. But the key thing was that it was a local institution; so the Constitution protected slavery by keeping the federal government from acting directly on it.

OAKES: There is too much anachronism in the way historians treat the subject of slavery and the Constitution. Most discussions assume that in 1787 the founders built an enormously powerful central government that could easily have abolished slavery everywhere, had the men in Philadelphia not caved in to the threats from Georgia and South Carolina. I myself have indulged in this anachronism in the past. But although the Constitution invested the central government with more specific powers than it had under the Articles of Confederation, it left virtually all control over "domestic" institutions to the states. So part of the anachronism has to do with underestimating how much power was left to the states, in all realms of government, including slavery.

But the anachronism goes much deeper. In the years just before 1776, one of the colonists' objections to English rule was how England repeatedly vetoed the attempts by individual colonies to suppress the slave trade. By 1787 *every single state* except Georgia had suppressed the slave trade. At the same time, individual states began abolishing slavery one by one. The men who came into the Constitutional Convention in Philadelphia had fought a revolution in the name of allowing *states* to control slavery and abolish it if they wanted to. They went into the Constitutional Convention with that assumption, and they came out of the Constitutional Convention with that assumption. The question, then, is whether the Constitution, by leaving slavery to the states, was not only recognizing it in the states where it existed but was also protecting emancipation in the states where slavery was being abolished? Everybody agreed that Congress could not abolish slavery in a state. But there is solid evidence that the Federal Consensus was also understood to protect state abolition from federal interference.

This point suggests that we should avoid reading backward from the fact that seventy-five years later the federal government marched armies into the South emancipating slaves as it went. We assume that the federal government should have been empowered to abolish slavery in 1787 and that the Constitution "failed" to allow the government to do so. But for the leaders of the Revolution, the central government—in London—had *prevented* individual colonies from regulating slavery. From that perspective, independence lifted that central-government restraint, allowed the states to begin attacking slavery, and the Constitution preserved the right of states to ban the slave trade and even abolish slavery altogether. Cotton changed all that; it breathed new life into slavery in the southern states and brought abolition in the slave states to an end. Ultimately, the Constitution had to be rewritten to abolish slavery nationwide.

MILLER: And which is how it ends with the Thirteenth Amendment.

OAKES: Yes, but the amendment bypassed the Federal Consensus. At no point in the Civil War did Congress abolish slavery in a state, nor did the Thirteenth Amendment empower Congress to abolish slavery in a state. Under the various pressures created by the war, six slave states abolished slavery and three new free states came into the Union, so that by 1865, there were enough free states to ratify an amendment that abolished slavery everywhere in the United States. It was not the rejection of the Federal Consensus that made abolition possible, it was nationwide abolition that rendered the Federal Consensus moot.

MILLER: [*Paraphrased question*] We hear negatives about Buchanan. What in your estimation did he do in his four years as president that might have been worthwhile?

OAKES: He so weakened the Democratic Party and made possible the victory of the Republican Party in 1860 [*laughter*].

LEVINE: I cannot top that, but he tried to reinforce Fort Sumter by sending a ship there. Of course, the *Star of the West* turned around when fired upon. That was too bad. It would have been better if a whole armada had been sent, but at least the actual attempt was creditable.

MILLER: Evidently, too, he brought a lot of good dancing into the White House. [*Paraphrased question*] You have both argued that the Second Party System supported efforts to suppress slavery, largely because slavery debates proved so disruptive. Were there elements in the parties who wanted to suppress debates on slavery in the short term while also addressing slavery's future over the long term?

OAKES: There was one group of people, a substantial group, who might have felt uncomfortable with the situation, and that was the northern Whigs. They pretty consistently voted against slavery when the issue arose, but still, the position of their party was that slavery was something that ought to be kept out of national politics. So there was a lot of squirming among those people. It is not a surprise that, by most estimates, about two-thirds of the Republicans were people who came out of the Whig Party after it fell apart. It fell apart before the Democrats because the Whigs were less able to contain slavery within their party.

LEVINE: I think it is useful to recall that many of the people who tried to suppress debates regarding slavery believed that, at various points, they had succeeded. After 1820, good, we have this compromise [the Missouri Compromise]. Now this question is in abeyance and we do not have to deal with it again. After 1850, notoriously, leaders of the Whigs and Democrats were again all patting each other on the back for finally having once and for all resolved the slavery question. If you mean, was there a significant body of people who were willing temporarily to suppress the slavery question but also hoped in the end to see slavery itself go away, sure. There were certainly people who were predicting that slavery would eventually die a natural death. These same people also hoped that the country's population growth would drive down the price of free labor, compared to the cost of slavery, and that this dynamic would ultimately end slavery. And Stephen Douglas promised northerners that popular sovereignty would keep slavery successfully out of the territories. But more important than these dreams was the false hope that Americans could keep together, eternally if need be, a society half slave and half free. To assert otherwise, these Americans believed, was just unacceptable and effectively treason. We were founded as a society that mixed two different social systems, and anybody who thought that we should end slavery was in the wrong.

MILLER: [*Paraphrased question*] Did the *Dred Scott* decision put Buchanan in a bind—that there was nothing he could do?

OAKES: I think that Buchanan's reaction is a perfect example of what Bruce was just talking about. He really did believe that a broad Supreme Court decision in the *Dred Scott* case would definitively, finally, and forever shut this issue down and keep it out of politics. And it seems to be one of the reasons that he schemed with the members of the court in the aftermath of the 1856 election. He wanted the court to issue a broader, rather than a narrower, decision and expected that *Dred Scott* would end the sectional debates regarding slavery in the territories.

MILLER: An audience member just commented about Buchanan's success in suppressing the African slave trade (or at least step up that process) and also to suppress filibustering in the West Indies.

OAKES: I would say that if you are looking for something good, Buchanan gave the Africa Squadron more resources to suppress the slave trade, so that it was much more effective in 1858–59 than it had been ever since the trade had been outlawed as piracy forty years earlier. Curiously, one of the consequences of his doing so was to revive the fortunes of the American Colonization Society, which depended on the receipts it received for each slave it brought back to Africa who was caught on a ship. Conversely, one of the inadvertent consequences of the treaty that Lincoln signed with Great Britain a couple of years later to suppress the African slave trade was that [Secretary of the Navy] Gideon Welles could just pull all those American ships back from the African coast to use in a naval blockade. He could do this because England was finally able to suppress the slave trade so effectively. But pulling American ships also pulled all the receipts from the American Colonization Society. I do not exactly know the Buchanan administration's motives for taking these actions, but there is no question that a dramatic increase in the suppression of the slave trade occurred right at the very end of the 1850s.

LEVINE: I would just add to that simultaneously, or even as he helped suppress the filibustering, he was one of the most determined politicians to acquire Cuba, effectively as a slave state, with money if possible but by force if necessary because he was one of the signers of the Ostend Manifesto, at the instigation, of course, of the Pierce administration in 1854. And it is pretty clear that as president he still wished to pursue the same course. So while he may have been trying to shut down private attempts to filibustering, he was still in favor of federal attempts to acquire Cuba.

MILLER: [*Paraphrased question*] What was the motivation of people like Buchanan, or earlier presidents like Van Buren, of holding the Democratic Party together—of holding the nation together—by not letting slavery disrupt it? And was their concern protecting slavery or was it a respect for the Constitution?

OAKES: Well this is a bit like the issue of Union and antislavery, which is to say it is a somewhat artificial distinction. This was a period in which constitutional politics prevailed. Every position a politician took, on anything—on internal improvements, on foreign affairs, on slavery—had to be justified in terms of the Constitution. Obviously, Buchanan takes the position that the Constitution recognized slavery as a fundamental right of property, but he also went around giving speeches that were hideously racist and notoriously proslavery. Which is following which? Do his constitutional politics follow from his proslavery principles or does the proslavery stance follow his constitutional politics? It is a silly and an artificial distinction, and I do not know what motivated people internally; I can only go by the way they present their arguments.

LEVINE: I think in the case of Buchanan, you have someone, as far as I can tell, whose sympathies were with the southern elite. These are the people he gravitated toward socially, people with whom he felt most comfortable and whom he put in his cabinet, and who became his circle of friends and confidants. I think he had a great deal of sympathy for, and a high level of tolerance of, southern slaveholders, even if he had no desire to spread slavery through the United States. And I think that issue is really the key to all of these so-called doughfaces. Even if they did not have the same kind of personal affinities as Buchanan, I think Buchanan is at the far end of this doughface spectrum. Others are characterized by what Lincoln accused Stephen Douglas of believing, which is, you do not care about slavery, you do not feel any hostility to slavery, you find it morally indifferent, you find it perfectly tolerable, and you do not consider doing anything about it. Doughfaces believed that anybody who threatened to upset the Union or break up the era's crucial political parties in the name of attacking slavery was in the wrong.

MILLER: [*Paraphrased question*] Assuming that abolitionism was the main driver that led to the Civil War, were there any minor drivers that hitched themselves to abolition for whatever reason, and if so, what were they and what effect did they have?

LEVINE: There are questions of tariffs, there are questions of internal improvements, and there are all of these economic issues that do tend to break down on North-South lines because of the difference in the forms of society and labor systems in the North and South. It is also a genuine cultural issue. Cultural differences arise between the North and the South based on being different kinds of societies—producing a national-identity feeling on each side. "I subscribe to all the values of this society—subscribe to all these religious, familial, and other kinds of notions that in fact grew up on the soil of our society—and I really do not like those people who dislike our values and kind of society." And all of that made it easier for a war to occur. If free-labor and slave-labor relations, instead of being grouped into two separate geographical places, had been evenly distributed throughout the United States, it seems unlikely, to me at least, that this would have devolved as quickly as it did because I doubt if you would have had the same degree of cultural hostility growing up within the same region.

OAKES: I think that is right, and this is a point that Eric Foner made in his first book a very long time ago.[6] The critique of slavery was also a defense of northern free-labor society and all the things that went with that society: schools, transportation improvements, economic development, and cities. Republicans looked to the South, noted the relative absence of those things, and concluded that the region was not simply backward but that this institution of slavery held back the South. By the 1850s, even northern Democrats favored some tariffs and other government projects for economic development. So I think that those other issues were there, but they were bundled up in the larger defense of a free-labor society that supported issues like the Homestead Act [1862], public schools, a sound banking system, and interstate transportation projects.

MILLER: [*Paraphrased question*] What difference does Stephen Douglas's candidacy make in 1860?

OAKES: Douglas's candidacy reinforces a point I made earlier about constitutional politics, but which may need some clarification. I do not want to be understood as saying that the Constitution just does not matter; I want to say that every position Stephen Douglas took on any issue was likely to be framed in constitutional terms. Nobody could take any position if they could not get right with the Constitution. Douglas's conception of the Constitution came bundled in a constellation of views about local government and federalism that were different from the positions adopted by Lincoln and the Republicans. Among northern Democrats, hostility to federal activism was relatively muted compared to the views northern Democrats held in the 1830s when Andrew Jackson was president, but that hostility to federal activism was still there; it was simply transferred to the slavery issue. Before the war most northern Democrats supported popular sovereignty on the grounds that the federal government should leave decisions about slavery to the inhabitants of the territories. During the war, Democrats voted against every single piece of antislavery legislation passed by Congress, denounced the Emancipation Proclamation as an illegitimate usurpation of executive power over a local institution, and even denounced the Thirteenth Amendment as "unconstitutional." And after the war they kept it up, denouncing all the federal efforts to protect the rights of freed people in the southern states, again on the grounds of limited federal authority. That is why I think, as I mentioned earlier, that one of the best dates to end Reconstruction is 1875, when the Republicans lost control of Congress because they did not have a response to the depression that was as popular as the Democratic Party's, with its traditional suspicion of banks and capitalists.

LEVINE: Stephen Douglas's campaign in 1860 was to avoid the Civil War and to prevent what he regarded as the extremists from winning the election. He determined that despite the split in the Democratic Party, the victory of northern Democrats, or the victory of northern Democrats plus the Constitutional Unionists, the two-middle-of-the-road parties, would hold back further deepening of the sectional division. That is what he was campaigning to do, and he predicted that they were going to succeed in that. Of course, they were miserable failures because, again, the historical process was too strong for either of the two middle-of-the-road parties to prevail, and the election results just rolled over them. So the "difference" Douglas's campaign makes is that it serves as an aid to historians: it shows us the power of the sectional-political polarization at work.

OAKES: Douglas genuinely believed that a house divided against itself *could* stand. On standard Jacksonian principles, if slavery were left entirely to the people of the states and territories, if the federal government stayed completely out of it, the divided house could stand indefinitely. The nation had existed for seventy-five years half slave and half free; there was no logical reason why it could not continue to do so—if it were not for these fanatics in the North pushing the slavery issue and these fire-eaters in the South calling for disunion. For all his deviousness and scurrility and deceitfulness, Douglas articulated a genuine position, and he really did believe in 1860 that he was the only person who could hold both the North and the South together in the Union.

MILLER: One almost hates to close on Stephen A. Douglas. We have time for one more question. [*Paraphrased*] There is one good thing that Buchanan did not do and that was to hand Lincoln a war. Could 1856 have made a difference in terms of the direction of the dynamics of the next four years if [John C.] Frémont, for example, had won?

OAKES: One of the things that happened because of Buchanan's victory was his relentless, systematic use of bribery and patronage to wipe out the northern Stephen Douglas Democrats—to force them out of office and thereby hold the line in a situation where the party was falling apart. If Douglas had had all that money and power at his disposal, maybe he could have bought off enough southern Democrats and enough northern Democrats to hold things in place a little longer. I do not know.

LEVINE: I do not know, either. But it was the *actual* dynamic that engages me. Every time something was done to prevent the crisis from escalating, it wound up escalating the crisis—no matter what the compromise, no matter what the measure taken, no matter what repressive actions taken, it only served, as Frederick Douglass said more than once, to raise the temperature even further. And so people have also asked, what if Henry Clay had been elected president in 1844 and prevented the Mexican War, preventing the South from acquiring those territories, could not that have avoided the issues that led to the Civil War? I wonder whether, if that had happened, the southern elite would not have felt tremendously frustrated, being denied one of its cherished goals. How would that, then, have led to national reconciliation? Every time we deny one or the other side something that it needs or feels that it needs in an attempt to avoid more conflict, it only seems to spur the conflict on further.

MILLER: Even though we are closing down this discussion tonight, we are not closing it down. The questions that were raised, and the comments, are uniformly pertinent and provocative and powerful and should keep us thinking about this issue. Let us again thank Bruce Levine and James Oakes [*hearty applause*]. And thank you all for coming [*applause*].

NOTES

1. The conversation presented here was videorecorded by the Pennsylvania Cable Network (PCN) at the conference and later transcribed by Robert E. Coley, archivist emeritus, Millersville University, using the videotape from PCN. Randall Miller reviewed the tape

and the transcript and sent the latter to Levine and Oakes for their review and approval. They in turn made corrections and clarified some statements. The text of this chapter includes Miller's corrections and theirs as well as minor editing for grammar in several instances. It is complete, except for the "housekeeping" instructions and introductions of the speakers at the conference.

2. Stanley Harrold, *Border War: Fighting over Slavery before the Civil War* (Chapel Hill: University of North Carolina Press, 2010).

3. *Dred Scott v. Sandford*, 60 US 404, 407 (1857).

4. Eric Foner, *Reconstruction: America's Unfinished Revolution, 1863–1877* (New York: Harper and Row, 1988).

5. Sean Wilentz, "Lincoln and Douglass Had It Right," *New York Times,* September 16, 2015.

6. Eric Foner, *Free Soil, Free Labor, Free Men: The Ideology of the Republican Party Before the Civil War* (New York: Oxford University Press, 1970).

CONTRIBUTORS

Thomas J. Balcerski is an assistant professor of history at Eastern Connecticut State University. He is the author of *Bosom Friends: The Intimate World of James Buchanan and William Rufus King* (New York: Oxford University Press, 2019), which explores the personal and political relationship of two leading Democrats of the 1840s and 1850s.

Michael J. Birkner is professor of history at Gettysburg College, where he has taught since 1989, chairing the department from 1993 to 2003. He is the author or editor of fourteen books and many articles on nineteenth- and twentieth-century American political history. Recent books include *Eisenhower's Gettysburg Farm,* coauthored with Carol Hegeman (Arcadia Press, 2017); *Encounters with Eisenhower* (Gettysburg College, 2015), co-edited with Devin McKinney; and *James Buchanan and the Coming of the Civil War* (University Press of Florida, 2013), coedited with John W. Quist.

Joan E. Cashin is a professor of history at Ohio State University. She received her doctorate at Harvard University and is the author or editor of seven books, most recently *War Stuff: The Struggle for Human and Environmental Resources in the American Civil War* (Cambridge University Press, 2018).

Douglas R. Egerton is a professor of history at Le Moyne College. His publications include *Year of Meteors: Stephen Douglas, Abraham Lincoln, and the Election That Brought on the Civil War* (Bloomsbury Press, 2010) and *Thunder at the Gates: The Black Civil War Regiments That Redeemed America* (Basic Books, 2016).

Michael Green is an associate professor of history at the University of Nevada, Las Vegas and the author of several books about the Civil War, including *Lincoln and Native Americans* (Concise Library series, Southern Illinois University Press, forthcoming).

Amy S. Greenberg is George Winfree Professor of American History and Women's Studies at Penn State University. She is the author of five books about nineteenth-century America, including *A Wicked War: Polk, Clay, Lincoln and the 1846 U.S. Invasion of Mexico* (Knopf, 2012) and *Lady First: The World of First Lady Sarah Polk* (Knopf, 2019).

Bruce Levine is the J. G. Randall Distinguished Professor Emeritus at the University of Illinois. The author of four books on the Civil War, including *The Fall of the House of Dixie* (Random House, 2005), he is now writing a study of Thaddeus Stevens as a revolutionary to be published by Simon & Schuster.

William P. MacKinnon, an independent historian living in Montecito, California, has been publishing about the American West since 1963. He has served as a fellow of the Utah State Historical Society, the president of the Mormon History Association, and the chairman of the Yale Library Associates. MacKinnon is an alumnus of Yale and Harvard Universities and a veteran of the US Air Force and General Motors Corporation.

Randall M. Miller is the William Dirk Warren '50 Sesquicentennial Chair and Professor of History at Saint Joseph's University and the author or editor of many books. His two most recent on the Civil War era are *The Northern Home Front during the Civil War,* coauthored with Paul Cimbala (Praeger, 2017), and *Women and the American Civil War: North–South Counterpoints,* coedited with Judith Giesberg (Kent State University Press, 2018).

James Oakes is Distinguished Professor of history at the City University of New York and the author of several books on slavery and antislavery. He is currently writing a history of the Civil War.

Matthew Pinsker is a professor of history and holds the Pohanka Chair for American Civil War History at Dickinson College, where he also serves as director of the House Divided Project. He writes frequently on Abraham Lincoln and nineteenth-century American politics.

John W. Quist is professor of history at Shippensburg University. He is the author of *Restless Visionaries: The Social Roots of Antebellum Reform in Alabama and Michigan* (Louisiana State University Press, 1998) and coeditor, with Michael J. Birkner, of *James Buchanan and the Coming of the Civil War* (University Press of Florida, 2013).

John David Smith is the Charles H. Stone Distinguished Professor of American History at the University of North Carolina at Charlotte. He is the author or editor of twenty-nine books, including *Dear Delia: The Civil War Letters of Captain Henry F. Young, Seventh Wisconsin Infantry*, coedited with Micheal J. Larson (University of Wisconsin Press, 2019). Smith currently is writing an intellectual and social history of the slave-reparations movement.

Frank Towers teaches at the University of Calgary. He is a specialist on the Civil War era and the author or coeditor of three books and more than twenty essays on the period, including *The Urban South and the Coming of the Civil War* (University of Virginia Press, 2004), *The Old South's Modern Worlds* (Oxford University Press, 2011), and *Confederate Cities* (University of Chicago Press, 2015). He also serves as the associate editor for the journal *Civil War History*.

INDEX

Abolitionism, 186–87, 246–47, 250, 253, 262

African Americans, 255–56, 258–59; land distribution and, 189, 192–93, 196–97, 205–8

Antislavery petitions, 31, 32, 48–49, 51, 53

Appleton, John, 110, 130–31

Army, U.S., 115–16, 120, 133–34, 192–93, 228, 252–53

Atkinson, David R., 65–66, 67

Bachelors, 2, 32, 35–36

Bachelor's mess, 32–41, 43–54

Baker, Jean, 17, 73, 85

Bayard, James A., Jr., 153, 154, 156, 162

Bayard, Thomas, 156

Bedford Springs (Virginia): politicians gathering in, 44, 50

Bell, John C., 38, 142, 178

Benjamin, Judah P., 180–81

Benson, Lee, 148–49

Benton, Thomas Hart, 73

Bigler, William, 110, 126, 153

Black, Jeremiah, 110–11, 118

Blair family, 173, 181

Boarding houses, congressional, 32, 37–39, 42, 54. *See also* Bachelor's mess; F Street mess

Border states, 2, 54, 142–43, 249–52

Breckinridge, John C., 67, 141–48, 163

Brown, Bedford, 34, 38, 39–41, 43, 52

Buchanan, James, 2, 174; bachelorhood and sexuality of, 10, 25–26, 32, 34, 40–41, 54, 109, 174–75; and cabinet of, 83; and Democratic Party, 2, 241–43, 250, 262; as doughface, 33, 49, 54, 255–56; and election of 1856, 69, 70; and friendships, 35, 110–15, 132, 161, 174–79; painting of, 3; and patronage, 126–27, 128, 130–31, 132, 160; presidency of, 17–18, 104, 109–10, 115–16, 133–34, 264–65; and slavery, 32, 48–50, 137–38n7, 142, 264–66; and Stephen Douglas, 63, 71, 85–91, 92–96, 100–101, 113, 152, 241; and U.S. expansion, 6–9, 12–14, 133–34, 265; and voting record of, in Congress, 51–52

Bucks County (Pennsylvania): political identities in, 159, 160, 161–62

Cadwalader, John, 126–27

Calhoun, John (of Illinois and Kansas), 96–100, 102

Calhoun, John C. (of South Carolina), 48–49, 91

Cameron, Simon, 112, 163

275